345.73 Hans, Valerie P.
HAN
        Judging the jury

                                    29199

$17.95

DATE			

© THE BAKER & TAYLOR CO.

Judging the Jury

Judging the Jury

Valerie P. Hans
and
Neil Vidmar

PLENUM PRESS • NEW YORK AND LONDON

Library of Congress Cataloging in Publication Data

Hans, Valerie P.
  Judging the jury.

  Bibliography: p.
  Includes index.
  1. Jury—United States. I. Vidmar, Neil. II. Title.
KF8972.H27 1986   345.73'075   86-446
ISBN 0-306-42255-7   347.30575

Acknowledgment is made of permission to use materials from previously published works:

We quote throughout from Kalven, H., and Zeisel, H. (1966). *The American Jury*. Boston: Little, Brown. Copyright by H. Kalven and H. Zeisel. Reprinted by permission.

Material about the DeLorean trial in Chapter 1 is taken from Brill, S. (1984). Inside the DeLorean jury room. *American Lawyer*, December, pp. 1, 94–105. Reprinted by permission.

Material on the Angela Davis trial jury quoted on pp. 101–102, 110 is from Timothy, M. (1974). *Jury Woman*. San Francisco, Calif.: Volcano Press. Reprinted by permission.

An earlier version of portions of Chapter 10 appeared in Hans, V. P. (1985). The jury's political role: "To see with their own eyes." *Delaware Lawyer, 4,* 20, 22–25. Copyright by the Delaware Bar Association. Reprinted by permission.

Quotations from the Spock jurors on pp. 156–157 are from Mitford, J. (1969). *The Trial of Doctor Spock*. New York: Alfred A. Knopf. Copyright by Alfred A. Knopf. Reprinted by permission.

First Printing—March 1986
Second Printing—November 1987

© 1986 Valerie P. Hans and Neil Vidmar
Plenum Press is a division of
Plenum Publishing Corporation
233 Spring Street, New York, N.Y. 10013

Printed in the United States of America

Foreword

The merits of the jury system have been the subject of dispute for a very long time. When *The American Jury* appeared some 20 years ago, it did not resolve the dispute but it did advance it to new ground. The debate moved from generalities to specific, often testable issues.

The research tradition it initiated has proved to be of help to the courts. There is hardly an opinion involving jury law that does not cite empirical research findings. Perhaps the most far-reaching, if for the time being modest, effect of that tradition has been the growing awareness of the law that social science research can frequently contribute to the resolution of legal and legislative problems.

Judging the Jury has assembled and critically analyzed the old and new knowledge we have of the jury. And although one will not necessarily agree with all of the author's evaluations, by weaving the research findings into the lively narratives of actual jury trials, they have written an attractive and important book.

It is fitting that it was written by an American and a Canadian scholar; the British commonwealth and the United States are the only realms in which the jury forms an important part of the judicial system. And it is fitting that one of the authors is a lawyer and the other a behavioral scientist; the integration of these skills is now finding a home in a great many of law schools.

The jury is undergoing two major changes. One change, the democratic broadening of the reservoir from which jurors are recruited, was highly beneficial. The other change, the manifold reductions of the jury's size has not been helpful.

The states are now allowed to try criminal cases before a six member jury. The civil jury in our federal courts was reduced from 12 to 6 jurors, and in some of our largest states, 5 jurors out of 6 can now find a verdict. Lifting the unanimity requirement has been another form of reducing the jury's size.

The price of these economies is lesser representation of the community, and a greater likelihood of a wrong verdict, because the collective wisdom of the 6 jurors is less than that of 12. When this self-inflicted emasculation

5

becomes too obvious in the trial of large complex civil cases, courts and litigants often try to repair some of the damage by allowing at verdict time the alternate jurors to join the deliberation.

Blaming the jury for occasionally unsatisfactory performance that partly grew out of the very reduction of its size, has become the newest platform for attacking the jury. Efforts are being made to remove complex civil cases from its jurisdiction. Before considering such removal, the courts should first use all their power to make the jury's task in such cases easier. They could instruct the jury not only at the end of the trial but also at its outset, perhaps even every morning, on the issues in the evidence they will hear on that day.

The criminal jury is being diminished by a different threat. Unknown to the general public, some jurisdictions have reduced jury trials to the danger point. In one of our major cities, the share of jury trials of all dispositions after felony arrest has sunk to 2 percent. This is the result of a sentencing policy that discourages jury trial by giving defendants after conviction by a jury on the average more than twice the sentence they had been offered (and refused) for a guilty plea.

Despite the jury's deep roots in the Constitution and in the consciousness of the people, it remains an embattled institution. Any systematic clipping of the jury's wings is dangerous; curtailments that reduce the jury's performance swell the ranks of its critics, and thus start a vicious circle.

For the time being though, the jury, in Harry Kalven's words that "daring effort in human arrangements to work out a solution to the tensions between law and equity and anarchy," is in good health. Its long run future is not certain; many good countries live without the jury. But whatever its future, those who guide it will benefit from the research tradition of which *Judging the Jury* is a welcome part.

University of Chicago   HANS ZEISEL
Law School

Preface

In 1982, Plenum editor Linda Regan approached us to write a book about the jury for a general audience. She pointed out that recent controversial cases such as that of John Hinckley, Jr. had stimulated many questions about the pros and cons of trial by jury, yet no contemporary book about the jury was available for nonspecialists. Both of us had conducted jury research for more than a decade, had written in scholarly journals and given many lectures about the jury, and had served as jury consultants to attorneys and to the government. We liked the idea of presenting a comprehensive view of the jury to the public, and thought that writing such a book would be a fairly straightforward (and quick) task.

It soon became more complicated. As we analyzed what we wanted to say and whom we wanted to address, we realized that a variety of audiences could benefit from a book on the jury. Social scientists have been studying the jury intensively for well over two decades, but their work has usually appeared in professional journals, and has been written for other scientists. We would translate their research studies and make them accessible to the layperson. Lawyers and judges, intimately familiar with the law and jury in the courtroom, could learn about the latest research findings on jury selection, the competence of the jury, and the best ways to minimize prejudice and enhance fact-finding in jury trials. Students in courses on law, the trial process, and criminal justice could also profit from reading about the jury in more depth than is customary in textbook presentation. Finally, we and our colleagues who did scientific research on the jury often focused on specific aspects of jury functioning in laboratory settings. By describing the historical, legal, and political contexts of the jury as it operates in our society, we could broaden our own horizons.

The danger in attempting to serve too many masters, of course, is that none may be served well. However, we found that as we wrote about the jury for these very different audiences, we ourselves developed a richer, multidimensional understanding of the institution of the jury trial. As we combined the vivid accounts of individual jury trials with case law and the systematic research studies of social scientists, we gained insights into the

7

functioning and the purposes of the jury that we had not had before. Our fondest hope is that our book will provide new insights for others as well.

Acknowledgments

We are indebted to a large number of people who graciously reviewed drafts of our manuscript and made valuable suggestions about its content and style. First and foremost is Linda Regan, who was largely responsible for turning our social science jargon into livelier, more readable prose. Colleagues Richard Lempert, Steven Penrod, and Tom Tyler magnanimously agreed to review the entire manuscript in draft form. Their insightful comments on what we had underemphasized, overemphasized, or left out entirely, proved to be particularly valuable. After agreeing to write the Foreward, Hans Zeisel made trenchant observations about the jury and our book that we were happily able to incorporate into the final version. Numerous friends and colleagues read individual chapters and provided extremely useful comments, including William Allen, Margaret Andersen, Catherine Fox Byers, Christopher Boorse, Samuel Gaertner, Craig Haney, Betsy Hans, James Inciardi, Catherine McLaughlin, James Nathan, David Saunders, Dan Slater, Pat Steele, and Robert Takasugi. A number of our students at the University of Delaware and the University of Western Ontario also read many of the chapters and gave their reactions. *Judging the Jury* thus reflects not only our own views but the collective wisdom of these friends, students, and colleagues.

Supportive environments at our respective universities encouraged us in our collaborative scholarship. Valerie Hans is indebted to the University of Delaware for a special Grant-in-Aid to facilitate preparation of the manuscript and a General University Research Grant. Neil Vidmar would like to acknowledge support from the Russell Sage Foundation, Battelle Seattle Research Center, the Social Sciences and Humanities Research Council of Canada, and the Faculty of Social Science and the School of Law at the University of Western Ontario. This financial and institutional support made our task much easier. Finally, we would like to recognize our debt to each other. Either of us probably could have written this book alone, but the experience would not have been nearly as much fun.

VALERIE P. HANS
NEIL VIDMAR

Contents

Part I. Introduction

Chapter 1. Introduction 13

Chapter 2. From Trial by Ordeal to Trial by Jury 21

Chapter 3. The Evolution of the American Jury 31

Part II. Jury Selection

Chapter 4. A Jury of Peers—But from an Unbiased Community 47

Chapter 5. Jury Selection: Eliminating Some of the Peers 63

Chapter 6. The New "Science" of Jury Selection 79

Part III. Jury Decisions

Chapter 7. Inside the Jury Room 97

Chapter 8. Jury Competence: Twelve People of Average Ignorance? 113

Chapter 9. Mr. Prejudice or Miss Sympathy: A Thirteenth Juror? 131

Chapter 10. The War with the Law 149

Chapter 11. Six versus Twelve, All versus Some 165

Part IV. The Jury in the Eye of the Storm

Chapter 12. Mad or Bad? Juries and the Defense of Insanity 179

Chapter 13. Jurors' Views of Rape: Anger and Ambivalence 199

Chapter 14. The Jury and the Executioner 219

Part V. Conclusion

Chapter 15. Today and Tomorrow: A Summary View and Judgment   245

Notes   253

Name Index   273

Subject Index   279

PART I

Introduction

CHAPTER 1

Introduction

In 1982, wealthy, jet-setting carmaker John DeLorean was arrested for conspiracy to smuggle cocaine. Despite the fact that the FBI had videotapes of DeLorean with a suitcase full of drugs, DeLorean was found not guilty by a jury of his peers. Why? DeLorean's trial makes for a vivid and instructive first look at the jury.[1]

Assistant United States Attorney James Walsh, Jr. spearheaded the investigation of DeLorean and prosecuted him on charges of conspiracy to smuggle drugs. According to Walsh, in June of 1982, DeLorean, in a desperate attempt to save his failing car company, had told James Hoffman, a drug dealer and old neighbor of DeLorean, that he wanted to invest two million dollars in a heroin deal. Later, cocaine was substituted for heroin, and still later DeLorean put up stock in his car company rather than money to finance the deal.[2]

Unbeknownst to DeLorean, Hoffman was an undercover government informant. Hoffman had joined the government's fight against drugs after being caught with drugs himself in 1981. Hoffman and other law enforcement officials proceeded to set up a sting operation. Hoffmann arranged for undercover agents to meet with DeLorean about the drug deal; many of these meetings were videotaped. After one particularly vivid episode in which the agents brought DeLorean a suitcase full of cocaine, and DeLorean exclaimed that it was "good as gold," the agents arrested DeLorean on charges of conspiracy to smuggle drugs. The stage seemed to be set for DeLorean's conviction.

Steven Brill, editor of the *American Lawyer*, interviewed some of the participants and 11 of the 12 jurors who served in the DeLorean trial. Brill described the sequence of events in the case and the deliberation process that ultimately led the jurors to acquit DeLorean on all charges. By providing a juror's-eye view of the trial, his account contributes considerable insights into why DeLorean was saved from what appeared to be a sure-fire conviction.

DeLorean hired the law firm of Weitzman and Re to defend him against

13

the government's charges. Howard Weitzman and Donald Re soon discovered that they had problems. A poll they conducted before their client stood trial showed that 92% of the respondents in the Central District of California, the court district in which the offense would be tried, had heard about the DeLorean case. Furthermore, fully 70% of the respondents already believed that DeLorean was guilty![3] That was *before* CBS Television aired videotapes procured by Larry Flynt, the publisher of the magazine *Hustler*. One videotape showed the "good as gold" episode in which DeLorean appeared to be gloating over the suitcase of cocaine before being arrested by the undercover agents. No doubt the videotape further biased an already prejudiced public.

DeLorean's defense team hired a psychologist who helped them develop an extensive questionnaire for prospective jurors in the DeLorean case. The questionnaire was 42 pages long and contained 99 questions about jurors' backgrounds, what they knew about the case, what they'd seen in the media, whether they had ever used drugs, and their attitudes toward law enforcement, politics, and religion. Presiding Judge Robert Takasugi was very concerned about the impact of pretrial publicity on DeLorean's right to a fair trial. He had originally ordered that the Flynt tapes could not be aired, but his order was overturned on constitutional grounds by the Ninth Circuit Court of Appeals. To aid in uncovering biases in jurors, Judge Takasugi allowed the attorneys to study the questionnaire responses and permitted them to question the potential jurors extensively about their answers.[4]

Jury selection took a total of seven weeks. According to Brill, the defense attorneys believed that the jury selection process was probably the most important aspect of the DeLorean trial. The defense strategy was not the usual one, in which the lawyers would seek "typical types to be sympathetic to defendants—liberals, people who themselves have used drugs—who'd hang the jury." Rather, the defense team looked for people who were "thoughtful enough to see this complex case," and who would understand the complicated conspiracy and entrapment issues that the defense planned to raise.[5]

The defense also used the pretrial questioning period to attempt to educate or sway the jurors. As Weitzman stated, "You use that opportunity of questioning jurors to begin your case."[6] Apparently, the attempt was successful. In Brill's posttrial interviews, several jurors said their initial confidence in DeLorean's guilt was eroded by the questioning. Consider one juror's comment: "It dawned on me that there might be a different story from what I'd seen on TV when Weitzman asked me a question about the tapes and if I was prepared to consider that they might not be what they seem to be. From then on, I was skeptical."[6] This was exactly what the defense had hoped would occur.

The jury was finally selected. It contained equal numbers of men and women. Eleven jurors described themselves as political moderates or conservatives. Seven were college graduates, and four had had some prior work in law enforcement.[7] Few observers would have described it as an overly sympathetic jury.

The trial began with prosecutor Walsh laying out the basics of the government's sting operation against DeLorean. But in the opening statement by defense attorney Weitzman, he called the case a "travesty of justice." He belittled the informant Hoffman who was to testify, and he said the videotapes and the sting were "orchestrated" by the government. Brill's interviews with jurors after the trial indicated that although they thought both attorneys were effective, they were unmoved by the opening statements. They were waiting for the evidence itself.[7]

The prosecution witnesses took the stand first. The government lawyers would have been very worried if they had known what was going on in the jurors' minds during the testimony. The lead witness, FBI agent Benedict Tisa, who played the role of a crooked banker, came across as evasive. As one juror quipped, "Ask him what time it was, and he'd start telling you how to make a watch."[8] Another juror said that anyone looking as polished as Tisa should have testified better: "A guy who pays as much attention as he does to the crease in his pants when he sits down could not have been that unprepared and stupid."[8] Tisa stated that he and DeLorean discussed laundering some money and having DeLorean invest two million dollars in a drug deal. DeLorean told Tisa later that he couldn't come up with the money. The next day, Tisa called DeLorean back to say that he could put up collateral instead—stock in a DeLorean car company shell corporation that was later acknowledged to be worthless. That did it for several jurors: "When I heard that they had called DeLorean back after he said he wasn't putting in the money, that was it for me."[8] Tisa's testimony triggered three strong not guilty votes, not a propitious beginning for the government's case.[8]

Then things got worse, as the prime witness, informant James Hoffman, took the stand. As one juror put it, "He never looked anyone in the eye. He was just not believable from the minute he spoke." One juror kept thinking: "If Hoffman can do this to DeLorean, he can do this to any of us."[9] Hoffman maintained that his son and DeLorean's son had played together when the two had been neighbors in 1980. He said that it was the sons' friendship and not an attempt to lure DeLorean into a drug deal that had led Hoffman to call DeLorean two years later, coincidentally around the same time he had become an undercover informant.

The defense lawyers argued that the government had tried to entrap

DeLorean. They claimed that it had become a major priority for the law enforcement officials to "get" DeLorean. Indeed, there were some embarrassing moments for the prosecution team. During the trial it came out that after one apparently successful taping of DeLorean, prosecutor Walsh and FBI agents had toasted the case with three hundred dollars' worth of wine, with Walsh saying: "Gentlemen, I can see this on the cover of *Time* magazine!"[10]

Throughout the trial, another phenomenon was occurring. The jury was developing into an extended family. They took their task extremely seriously.[11] During the five months of jury selection and trial, not one juror was late or absent from court.[12] Jurors discussed everything but the case itself, which the judge had forbidden them to mention until they began deliberations. So some jurors tried to estimate how the other jurors were feeling by making inferences from social and political attitudes. Some of these inferences proved to be wrong. For instance, one woman was politically liberal and thus was widely assumed to be a sure bet for a not guilty vote. She turned out to be the last holdout for conviction.[13]

The beginning of deliberation was a big release for the jurors. Finally they could drop discussion of politics (ten of the twelve voted for Reagan) and get to work. The first item of business was to select a group leader. Vern Lahr, a former highway patrolman, mentioned the issue first and stood capably at the blackboard asking for nominations.[12] Not surprisingly, he was chosen for the job. The position of jury leader often goes to an authoritative male, and Lahr not only had experience in law enforcement but also previous leadership positions to his credit.

The DeLorean jury followed Robert's Rules of Order, at least initially. Lahr suggested an initial vote on the basic charge of conspiracy, to see where everyone stood. But other jurors disagreed. They argued that they should consider the evidence more methodically. Everyone felt that a unanimous vote was essential if it could be accomplished without pressuring anyone unduly; in the jurors' view, the attorneys and the judge "deserved" it.[12] Their delay of an initial vote may have helped them achieve unanimity. Studies of group decision-making show that delaying an initial vote increases the likelihood of consensus, although the discussion takes longer.

The jurors' discussion was thorough and laborious. They reviewed their extensive notes. They requested individual copies of Judge Takasugi's jury instructions about the law. They examined the transcripts of the government tapes. Their first vote, described as "nonbinding," was taken late the second day. On the charge that DeLorean engaged in a conspiracy to smuggle drugs, seven of the jurors voted not guilty, two voted guilty, and three abstained.[14]

Writing about the jury deliberation, Steven Brill stated that "[t]hen the real debate began."[14] However, studies of jury decision-making suggest that the real debate was nearly over. The jury's vote was already unusual. Most juries begin their deliberations with a majority favoring a guilty verdict. And most juries beginning with seven votes to acquit inexorably reach a verdict of not guilty.

However, the jury had to work itself out of a possible deadlock. Several jurors feared they would not be able to agree on a unanimous verdict. With split opinions about DeLorean's guilt on the charge of conspiracy to smuggle drugs, the jurors debated the evidence for and against the conspiracy charge. No closer to unanimity, they retired for the night.

The following day, the grounds of the discussion shifted. One juror introduced a new argument. If they found that the government had *entrapped* DeLorean, then even if DeLorean had been involved in a conspiracy they could find him not guilty. During his final charge to the jury, Judge Takasugi had outlined three conditions for deciding that there had been entrapment: The idea for the crime had to have come from the "creative acts" of the government; government agents had to have induced DeLorean into committing the crime; and DeLorean could not have been "ready and willing" to commit the crime before the government agents induced him to do so.[15] After reviewing the entrapment instructions, the three jurors who had previously abstained from voting on a tentative verdict quickly switched to the not guilty side. One of the jurors who had voted guilty on conspiracy resisted momentarily, saying that she just wasn't sure that DeLorean had been entrapped beyond a reasonable doubt. Another juror reminded her, however, that once DeLorean argued that he had been entrapped by the government, it was then up to the government to prove beyond a reasonable doubt that DeLorean had not been entrapped. She too switched to a vote for not guilty.[16]

Only one juror was still unconvinced. She just didn't buy the entrapment defense. As this juror stated, "People make their own fates. [DeLorean] could have chosen not to be involved."[17] On the fourth day of deliberations, the jury recessed deadlocked.

It was another female juror who finally convinced the holdout to change her vote to not guilty. She argued that the holdout shouldn't render a verdict based on her own moral evaluation of DeLorean. As the holdout later reported: "I began to see that I was taking it on myself to punish [DeLorean] because the government hadn't made its case. Well, it wasn't my fault the government screwed up . . . and I wouldn't be doing anything wrong by voting not guilty."[17]

The announcement of the not guilty verdict caused jubilation for DeLorean and his attorneys. The prosecutor's team was stunned. What had they

done wrong? In a posttrial interview, one juror summed up what the jury had communicated by acquitting DeLorean:

> We weren't trying to make policy or send messages, but there is a message here. . . . It's that our citizens will not let our government go too far. We just looked at the evidence, and I for one saw that the government had gone too far in this case. It was like the book *Nineteen Eighty-Four*. They set one trap after another for DeLorean and then tried to prove a case when they still didn't have the evidence. In this country, the government can go only so far and then its citizens will draw them back into line. And that's what we did—*in this case only*. . . . We were not making any kind of statement about what the government does generally. We were simply telling the government that it went too far on this one. You see we just did our job as jurors, which is one hell of a responsibility.[18]

*   *   *

Was the DeLorean acquittal a fair and competent verdict? Some people would say that the verdict illustrates some of the strengths of our jury system. After all, the community as a whole was strongly prejudiced against DeLorean before the trial began. Yet, pretrial questioning of jurors, careful jury selection, persuasive arguments by the defense, clear judicial instructions, and thoughtful evaluation by the jury ultimately led to an acquittal. In the eyes of some people, including the defense team, DeLorean was persecuted by the government, and the institution of the jury allowed representatives of the public to intervene and acquit him. Supporters, then, would say that the system worked, and worked admirably, in the DeLorean trial.

Yet others might well argue that the entire affair did not constitute a fair administration of justice. They could point to DeLorean's money and fame, which allowed him to obtain an extraordinarily strong defense team, including social scientists who helped pick a favorable jury. Friends and relatives announced to one juror after the trial, "We knew you'd find [him] innocent. . . He's too rich to get caught."[19] Opponents might argue that Weitzman and Re swayed the jury with emotion rather than facts. As one of the prosecutors said after the trial, "[The jurors] were intelligent, but not smart enough to see the truth."[6] Critics might also point out that while the jurors eventually decided on the same verdict, it was for entirely different reasons. Some voted for acquittal because of the conspiracy charge and some because of perceived entrapment; one juror might well have just caved in to group pressure.

What we have learned from our own research and that of other social scientists is that the DeLorean jury is typical of many juries. True, few juries participate in cases which are front-page news every day of the trial. Yet the DeLorean jurors' reactions to evidence, their deliberations, and the way they

reached their verdict appear similar to those of other jurors deciding the vast majority of less celebrated cases. In addition, the varied reactions to the DeLorean verdict, the questions over jury competence, the debate about whether psychologists should be involved in picking the jurors, and the ultimate propriety of the verdict illustrate in a single case many of the arguments involved in the debate over trial by jury.

Many people argue that the jury, although once a vital component of the criminal justice system, is no longer important. They point out that juries decide only about 8% of all criminal cases, with the rest resolved by a judge or through plea-bargaining. Opponents of trial by jury have major questions about the competence and fairness of jurors. One critic has described the jury as, at best, twelve people of average ignorance. The eminent judge Jerome Frank complained that juries apply law that they don't understand to facts that they can't get straight. Judge Frank's view has some prestigious contemporary support. Warren Burger, Chief Justice of the United States Supreme Court, has made it known that although he supports trial by jury in criminal cases, he is favorably disposed to its elimination in civil trials.[20]

Proponents of trial by jury argue that even though the jury decides only a small proportion of cases, it has important effects on the entire criminal justice system. The prosecutor's decision to charge someone with a crime and the defendant's willingness to plea-bargain depend upon their views of how likely they are to win their case before a jury. Studies of jurors themselves have shown that participating on a jury both educates and enhances regard for our system of justice. Verdicts by representative juries, especially in controversial trials, increase the legitimacy of the process in the public's eyes, because jury verdicts are trusted to represent the community more than are verdicts by judges. Proponents of trial by jury maintain that juries are competent and not prejudiced, or at least no more prejudiced than judges. Furthermore, because juries deliberate in secret and need not give reasons for their verdicts as judges must, they retain a flexibility denied to judges: the ability to bend the law to achieve justice in individual cases.

Who is right—those who see the jury as a barbaric relic, a bastion of bias and incompetence, or those who view the jury as a lamp of liberty? For centuries we had to be content with rhetoric on both sides of the debate over the merits of trial by jury. But over the last several decades, researchers have subjected the jury to a more systematic, scientific inquiry. In this book, we will synthesize what has been learned about how the institution of trial by jury operates in our society. This knowledge comes from many different sources. We consulted archives to trace its history and to examine its origins and changes over the centuries in the United States, England, Canada, and

other countries. Court documents provided information about the mechanics of trial by jury, while appellate court opinions indicated problems in developing fair procedures for jury trials. Moreover, we participated in jury selection and conducted our own research studies on jury decision-making, and here incorporate these findings with those of others. Finally, jurors themselves contributed to our knowledge: those who wrote books about their experiences, those who granted interviews, and those who participated in jury research. By integrating these varied source materials, we hope to convey the essence of the contemporary jury.

We will begin by examining the origins of trial by jury in England and describe the ways in which the jury's use changed over the centuries. We give particular attention to how historical events pushed the American jury on a distinctive evolutionary path. We will then explore the key issue of jury selection, including its underlying assumptions, the procedures required by the courts to select unbiased jurors, and the recent trend toward "scientific jury selection." From there we will turn to an in-depth look at jury decisions themselves and how jurors combine their sundry, individual perspectives into a single verdict. In judging the jury, we will address three central criticisms: that the jury is incompetent, that the jury is prejudiced, and that the jury ignores the law. Recent changes in jury size and the requirement for unanimous verdicts are also considered. Then we will focus on the jury in three controversial types of trials: where the defendant raises the insanity defense, where the charge is rape, and where the penalty is death. By judging the jury, we can finally speculate on what the jury's role, if any, in the future might be.

CHAPTER 2

From Trial by Ordeal to Trial by Jury

The year was 1670. The place was the Old Bailey in London, England. The defendants were William Penn, subsequently the founder of the Colony of Pennsylvania, and William Mead. The indictment stated that Penn and Mead along with "divers other persons . . . unlawfully and tumultuously assembled and congregated themselves together in Gracechurch Street, in London." Further, it asserted that Penn, aided and abetted by Mead, preached and spoke to the people assembled in the street "by reason whereof a great concourse and tumult of people a long time did remain and continue, in contempt of the king and his law, and to the great terror and disturbance of many of his liege people and subjects."[1]

The real motive behind the charges, however, was the government's dislike for religious nonconformists. Penn and Mead were both Quakers, a Protestant group that had recently come into existence and whose members espoused unique doctrines as well as unusual modes of dress and demeanor. Viewed as radicals and extremists of the most dangerous kind, their meeting houses were closed by the authorities, and they were forbidden to assemble and preach in the streets. Of course, the Quakers defied these orders and continued to preach.

The trial took place before the Lord Mayor and aldermen. Several witnesses were called to testify that Penn had indeed preached in the streets and that Mead was present at the scene. The recorder summarized the government's case for the jury, who were then instructed to retire to a room upstairs to consider their verdict. After an hour and a half of deliberation, eight of the twelve jurors came down prepared to render a verdict; four dissenters remained upstairs. The dissenters were led down and one of them, Bushell, was singled out by the recorder: "Sir, you are the cause of this disturbance, and manifestly show yourself an abettor of faction; I shall set a mark upon you sir!" Bushell protested. Several of the aldermen also set upon Bushell, calling him an impudent fellow and a troublemaker. The jury, including Bushell, was ordered back upstairs.

21

After considerable time had elapsed, they returned. The room was called to silence and the clerk of the court turned to the foreman of the jury. "Look at the prisoners at the bar. How say you? Is Willian Penn guilty?" The foreman replied, "Guilty of speaking in Gracechurch Street," but said nothing about unlawful assembly. A tumult of questions and threats were then directed at the jurors: "Is that all?" "You had as good say nothing." "Was it not an unlawful assembly?" Some of the jurors appeared to buckle under the intense pressure, but Bushell and his juror allies stood firm.

The jury was instructed that the law of England would not dismiss them until they had rendered a proper verdict. The jury retired again. Shortly it returned with a written verdict finding Penn guilty of speaking or preaching in Gracechurch Street. There still was no mention of an unlawful assembly, and Mead was found not guilty. The court officials were nearly apoplectic. After some considerable discussion, the recorder said to them, "Gentlemen, you shall not be dismissed till we have a verdict that the court will accept: and you shall be locked up, without meat, drink, fire, and tobacco; you shall not think thus to abuse the court; we will have a verdict, by the help of God, or you shall starve for it." The jury was led out, and the court adjourned until the next day. Again the jury returned a verdict of guilty of speaking in Gracechurch Street, and again Bushell and others were set upon by the court. The Mayor even threatened to "cut his nose." Once again, the clerk commanded them to retire and reconsider. The next day they returned with another written verdict, signed by all: Not guilty! The court then polled each juror separately, but the individual jurors stood firm. Finally, the recorder turned to the jury and made the following pronouncement: "I am sorry, gentlemen, you have followed your own judgments and opinions, rather than the good and wholesome advice which was given you; God keep my life out of your hands; but for this the court fines you forty marks a man, and imprisonment till paid."

Even though the Crown at last accepted the verdict of not guilty, Penn was sent to Newgate prison for contempt of court—but he had company, because the twelve jurors were sent to prison with him. Eventually, the jurors were released, and Bushell filed a lawsuit over his imprisonment. He won, and his case is seen as a landmark that helped to abolish the English Court's practice of punishing jurors for bringing in what the Court considered to be a wrongful verdict.

Slightly more than a century before the Penn trial, the jurors in Sir Nicholas Throckmorten's case were not so lucky.[2] Throckmorten was tried in 1554 on charges of high treason, and for conspiring and imagining the death of the Queen, as well as other crimes. The jury found him not guilty,

and as a result eight of the twelve jurors were brought before the Star Chamber where three were fined 2000 pounds each and the other five received fines of 200 pounds each, enormous sums by the standards of the day. In fact, in still earlier days, jurors could be fined, imprisoned, stripped of their lands, and they and their heirs could be labeled "infamous."

These historical cases illustrate rather dramatically that serving on a jury could, on occasion, be a hazardous undertaking. Nevertheless, in spite of the hazards, juries frequently exercised great courage to render justice. Moreover, the cases serve to remind us that our present conception of justice and the role and functions of the jury have sharply changed over the centuries. Indeed, the present-day jury is not the invention of an individual or a single statute passed by a legislative body. Rather, it is the result of literally centuries of slow evolution.

Though some scholars have maintained that the modern jury evolved from early Scandinavian and German tribunals, others have argued, more convincingly, that the similarities are only coincidental. No documents preceding the Norman invasion of England by William the Conqueror in 1066 make mention of juries.

Nevertheless, the roots of the jury may be found in both civil and criminal inquiries conducted under old Anglo-Saxon law. In cases of a property dispute, the contending parties might summon witnesses to testify about the validity of the claims. For example, around 900 A.D., Alfnoth claimed title to some land in Swaffham that was currently in the possession of the monastery of Ramsey.[3] The court hearing the case consisted of some king's officers and a number of prominent men of the county. The two parties and the court agreed that the dispute should be decided by thirty-six persons, eighteen of whom would be friends of one party and eighteen of whom would be friends of the other. These individuals, called *compurgators,* retired to consider the merits of the claim. Their unanimous decision was that the monastery should keep its title to the land and that Alfnoth should forfeit his property to the King for making a false claim.

Depending on the nature of the case, the compurgators had different duties. Sometimes their role was to support the credibility of one of the parties by taking an oath that the party was honest, just as today's character witnesses are allowed to testify in a trial. On other occasions, they might attest by oath that they had witnessed a business or other contractual transaction The number of compurgators required for a trial was usually twelve or some multiple of twelve, such as forty-eight.

In criminal cases, groups of individuals were also summoned to bear witness to facts. About 997 A.D. King Ethelred set forth a law requiring that

prominent persons in various regions of the realm be summoned to court to tell about any crimes in the community. These persons were forced to take an oath that they would accuse no innocent person or conceal a guilty one.[4] These witnesses were similar to compurgators in civil cases because they testified under oath about their knowledge of criminal activity and about the character of accused persons. However, their role in the legal process was more similar to today's grand jury than the petit, or trial, jury. Their testimony only confirmed the validity of an accusation; it was not proof of guilt.

Guilt or innocence in criminal matters was determined by two principal methods, oaths of compurgators or the ordeal. If the accusation did not involve a crime of violence or if there were no immediate witnesses to the act itself, the reeve of the district would select a number of relatives and neighbors of the accused person. From these the defendant would choose twelve to be compurgators to swear an oath about his or her credibility. These compurgators were called the "equals" or "peers" of the accused person. If the accused was generally known to have a bad reputation, the number of peers required was triple, that is, thirty-six. If the required number of compurgators swore to his or her credibility, the accused person was, in effect, found not guilty and freed.[5]

If, however, the accused person could not obtain a sufficient number of compurgators, had been notoriously guilty of perjury previously, had been caught red-handed, was charged with a violent crime, or was not a freeman, the method of ascertaining guilt or innocence was by the ordeal. The ordeal took a number of forms. The ordeal of the hot iron required the accused person to carry a red-hot pound of iron in his or her hand for a certain distance, usually nine feet. An alternative test was the ordeal of hot water. The accused was required to dip one hand in a pitcher of boiling water and pluck out a stone hanging by a string. In both ordeals, the injured hand was bound up in bandages. If after three days the hand had not become infected, the person was judged to be innocent. In another variant called "going to the water," accused persons were bound with a rope and thrown into a body of water; if they sunk to a prescribed depth they were pulled out and declared innocent, but if they floated they were judged guilty. Yet another test was the ordeal of the accused morsel, or *corsnaed*. Defendants were required to swallow a piece of bread after reciting a prayer that were they guilty the bread would surely choke them. While the corsnaed seems a little less painful and risky than the other forms of the ordeal, Godwin, the Earl of Kent, was believed to have choked to death while trying to swallow the bread. All these various ordeals were usually conducted at the height of the Mass and accompanied by prayers and incantation. The assumption underlying the ordeal, of course,

was that God would intervene on the side of the innocent person.[6] Perhaps the Earl of Kent was guilty, but we have no idea how many innocent persons were convicted, or guilty ones escaped punishment, in the ordeals. To the extent that people believed in the power of divine intervention, the ordeal may have served as an effective mechanism to resolve disputes.

Hence, prior to William the Conqueror, the jury as we know it did not exist. However, the practice of compurgation in which twelve or more peers took oaths in the court does have some elements of similarity to today's jury.

For the most part, once King William along with his Norman followers conquered the different regions of England, he did not make any immediate sweeping changes in the legal institutions. Rather, the institutions were used to support the goals of the Crown and were only gradually modified. William did summon local noblemen to an assize court. The nobles were required to state under oath the names of manors in their area, the owners of those manors, the number of hides, ploughs, and people each contained, and their overall worth. These data were collated in the famous *Domesday Book* for taxing purposes. A century later, these assizes were elaborated on and used for the settlement of disputes as well as for taxing purposes.[7]

The Normans probably introduced another form of settling legal disputes, namely trial by battle, which was used primarily in civil cases. The two parties to the dispute would fight on the battlefield and the winner of the battle won the legal case. Often, rather than doing battle themselves, the disputants would hire "champions" to fight for them. In some criminal cases, an accused person could similarly challenge the accuser to battle. The trial by battle ought to be considered an ordeal, since it was believed that God's intervention would determine the outcome of the battle.

Making a "wager of law" through compurgators remained, however, the principal means of settling private and many criminal disputes under the Norman kings.[8] Although like the ordeal it was based upon an oath, its underlying principle seems obviously more in tune with our modern view of the trial. A concerned party was required to find twelve persons to take a solemn oath that in their opinion the concerned party's own oath was trust-worthy. But the difficulties are apparent. What if the adversary also got twelve compurgators to swear that his or her oath was reliable? Sometimes, disputes were resolved on the basis of who got the most compurgators. To make matters worse, bribery and other inducements to compurgators were common. Indeed, one legal historian asserted that "[p]erjury was the dominant crime of the Middle Ages, encouraged by the preposterous rules of compurgation."[9] Making one's wager of law was useful only insofar as the taking of the oath was surrounded by religious mystique. Greed, threats, and loyalties to friends

and relatives often overcame the fear of God's wrath—at least while the case was before the court. Penance to God could come later.

The unreliability of the other forms of the ordeal was also apparent to a growing number of persons more advanced in rational thought. By the beginning of the 13th century the ordeal as a means of trial was in trouble. The Church in Rome had been opposed to it from as early as the late 9th century, and in 1215 Pope Innocent III in the Fourth Lateran Council forbid priests to participate in religious rites surrounding the ordeal, thus removing its religious sanction.

Sometime during the 13th century the jury began to replace the ordeal. Even before 1215 the King's justices would occasionally summon a jury to determine which form of ordeal was to be used or whether some legal action was brought maliciously. After 1215 an accused person was allowed to opt for a trial by jury instead of submitting to the ordeal. The jury, however, was not the same as our present-day jury. The judge or other officer of the King's court would usually choose twelve people who testified about what they knew personally about the facts or the involved parties. Thus, jurors were more akin to witnesses than judges of fact. They were questioned about their knowledge of the case, and often their only role was to provide the court with information on which to base a verdict.

For example, in 1220 Hamo of More complained that Philip le King had stolen his mare. Philip asserted in court that he had honestly obtained the mare from one Edward. Edward was brought to court whereupon Hamo accused him instead of Philip. Edward denied any thievery and asserted that he had obtained the mare from Elias Piggan. Hamo then leveled the charges at Elias. Trial by battle over the matter was considered, but Hamo then offered the King the sum of one mark, a not inconsiderable amount of money, to have a trial instead. At the trial, Hamo testified that the mare was foaled by a horse which he owned. Elias, however, said that he had obtained the mare, along with some pigs, at Cardiff in Wales from a man to whom he had given fencing lessons. At this point, the court called eight men from each of four neighboring towns of Chestnut, Waltham, Wormley, and Enfield. The jurors of Waltham were sworn and testified that the mare belonged to Hamo. Similar testimony was provided by the Enfield jury on a different day. On still another day, the jury of Chestnut said they didn't know if the mare was foaled to Hamo but thought probably not. The jury from Wormley swore that they didn't know much either, though they did testify that Edward gave the mare along with his daughter in marriage to Philip le King. These four juries never met as a single group and in fact produced conflicting evidence. They were never asked to pronounce a verdict of guilty or not guilty—a decision that

was left to the King's court. The court ruled that Hamo and Edward should settle their conflicting claims by compromise. It also ruled that Elias should lose his foot and be admonished that the court was actually lenient in that he deserved a greater punishment.[10]

Eventually the role of the jury began to change. Jurors began to be asked whether the facts warranted a verdict of guilty or not guilty. Rather than taking separate verdicts from different juries, as in Hamo's trial, a petit jury of twelve people was selected. At first, some of these jurors would be witnesses from the "presenting jury" which had given testimony leading to the indictment of the defendant. It was still assumed that at least some of the members of the jury should be familiar with the people and the facts of the case. This practice led to difficulties, however. Such jurors were under considerable pressure to maintain consistency between their accusations in the presenting jury and their verdicts in the petit jury. But it was not until 1352 that the English Parliament passed a statute allowing prospective petit jurors, that is, those who would render the verdict of guilt or innocence, to be excluded on the ground that they had served on the presenting jury.[11]

During this formative period, the legal status of the jury was still in question, which led to an intriguing dilemma—and subsequently to an interesting practice. The ordeal of fire or water was no longer accepted, but on the other hand the newfangled idea of trial by jury had not quite achieved legitimacy. No law had been passed to make jury trial the means of determining guilt. Thus, while the courts would not allow the ordeal, they also would not force an accused person to undergo a jury trial unless he or she agreed to it. With no other options available, in some instances accused murderers who refused to submit to trial by jury were simply banished from the region because legally the court had no other choice. In response to this dilemma, the Statute of Westminster in 1275 provided that accused persons who would not submit to a jury trial were to be subjected to *prison forte et dure*—confinement under harsh conditions—until they relented. For reasons that are unclear to today's historians, the phrase was translated into *peine forte et dure*—punishment strong and hard. As a consequence, accused people who refused to submit to trial were placed between two planks and heavy stones were gradually set on top of the top plank until they relented—or painfully suffocated. As late as 1658, a prisoner was crushed to death in this manner. One might be tempted to ask why anyone would undergo such torture rather than submit to a trial by jury. The answer is obvious if the accused man was pretty sure he would be convicted anyway and if he put his family's welfare before his own. A convicted person's goods and properties were always forfeited to the Crown, but a person crushed to death could not be

found guilty, so that his family could inherit his wealth. It was not until 1772 that *peine forte et dure* was replaced by considering a defendant's refusal to submit to trial as a plea of guilty. In 1827 the rule was changed so that a prisoner who refused trial by jury was considered to have entered a plea of not guilty.[12]

As the Middle Ages drew to a close, there were developments on other fronts. As we have seen, initially some or all of the jurors were chosen from the presenting jury because they were considered to have some knowledge of the case. The legal scholar Bracton described this theory:

> If the jurors are altogether ignorant about the fact and know nothing concerning the truth, let there be associated with them others who do know the truth. But if even thus the truth cannot be known, then it will be requisite to speak from belief and conscience at least.[13]

Some time later, witnesses other than those on the jury were questioned at trials. While this practice was at first a rather informal part of a trial, it gradually became more frequent and more formal. Eventually, the jury's decision became based less and less on its own knowledge than on the evidence presented before it. In short, juries became finders of the facts rather than providers of the facts, just as are today's juries.

A related development was the gradual discontinuance of the practice of punishing jurors for bringing in what the court considered a wrongful verdict. As jurors became increasingly dependent on the evidence produced by others, it became obvious that a "wrong" decision was probably due to an honest error in judging the facts, not dishonesty on the part of jurors. Of course, in political trials such as that of William Penn, the jurors' "responsibilities" were viewed in a more serious manner. It was not until after juror Bushell won his case that jurors became truly immune to legal sanctions concerning their verdicts. At no time, however, was the jury viewed as anything but an instrument of the court and the judge. If a jury did not reach the desired verdict, a new trial in front of a different jury could be ordered. (The notion of double jeopardy as found in the U.S. Bill of Rights developed much later.)

Ideas about jurors being representative of the community also underwent change. Originally, when jurors were considered to be witnesses, it made sense that they should be from the community in which the alleged incident took place. Only community residents would have knowledge bearing on the case. As the jury developed into a body of impartial fact-finders, community residence was no longer so important. However, a new rationale developed. It was argued that the jurors should be from the county in which the incident took place so that the jury could express the opinions of the community about

a fair and proper verdict. This requirement, nevertheless, led to some interesting anomalies of justice. Due to quirks of ancient surveying practices, certain roads, bays, creeks, and harbors did not fall within any county. As late as 1536, crimes committed in those areas could not be tried by jury. Until 1826, pickpockets in stage coaches could only be tried in the county where it was assumed the actual theft took place as the stage rolled through the countryside. In 1856 a law was passed to allow a change of venue to a new county if it was believed the jury would not be impartial.[14] Interestingly, it was usually the Crown that applied for the change when it believed the local jury would not convict; today, most applications for a change of venue are made by the defense.[15]

The notions of a jury of one's peers and of an impartial jury also developed during this period, but as exemplified in William Penn's trial, they were not quite what we consider them today. Jury selection was not done by a random process. To the contrary, the sheriff picked the jurors, and he was inclined to pick jurors who were partial to the Crown's case. Indeed, partiality was sanctioned by the courts. In 1852 Lord Chief Justice Coke asserted that "in respect of his allegiance the sheriff ought to favor the king [in choosing jurors]."[16] The idea that individual jurors could be challenged and excluded on grounds of bias also developed during this period. Shortly, we will delve into this subject as it pertains to the evolution of the American jury.

By the middle of the 18th century, the jury was similar in basic structure and functions to our contemporary jury. However, the process of evolution continues through the present. In the 1960s, England changed its jury selection procedures. Instead of being selected for "intelligence and character," a new jury selection act provided for a more representative sampling of men and women from the population.[17] Changes were also made in the traditional requirement that jurors in criminal trials reach a unanimous verdict. Now, in England, the jury is intially instructed to reach a unanimous verdict. If unanimity is not reached after a few hours, the jury is called back into the courtroom and instructed that a majority vote of ten members will do. Whatever our current view of their merits, it is possible that a century from now, legal historians will give both of these reforms the same revolutionary significance that we now accord to the abolition of the practice of intimidating and punishing jurors.

*   *   *

In the colonies of the British Empire, the English jury system was transported, though it was often modified over time. In Scotland, the origins of

the jury were almost coeval with those in England, but it developed unique characteristics. The Scottish criminal jury consists of fifteen members, not twelve. Moreover, unanimity has never been required, and a defendant can be convicted by a mere majority vote. In addition, the Scottish jury is allowed to choose one of three verdicts: "guilty," "not guilty," and "not proven." The latter verdict means that the prosecution has not produced evidence to convince the jury beyond a reasonable doubt, but the accused person's innocence has not been established either.[18] Canada's jury system has followed the English model pretty closely. Until just recently, if a contentious issue arose where there was no previous Canadian legal precedent, the judges and lawyers were likely to rely on English cases. Australia makes use of the jury as do former British colonies in Africa and Asia.

The jury system, as least as we know it, has not fared so well in most countries in Continental Europe. Introduction of a jury system in France followed the French Revolution of 1789. Beginning in 1808 Napoleon introduced the jury in the countries that he conquered. During the rest of the 1800s, Germany, Switzerland, Spain, Norway, Belgium, Greece, and Portugal, among other countries, adopted forms of the jury. Even Czarist Russia experimented with the jury in 1871. However, many of these countries subsequently abolished juries altogether. In the remaining countries, juries are still sometimes used, but the members are often not representative of the population, and their verdicts can be easily overturned upon judicial review.[19]

These facts about the nonuse or decline of the jury in other countries lead to an interesting reflection to be shared before we proceed to the American jury. Most Americans, Canadians, and Britons do consider the jury system to be synonymous with and essential to democracy. Yet, many countries that have strong commitments to democracy do not have jury systems such as ours. To what extent does the existence of the jury in a society affect the citizens and their relationship to their legal system as well as to the society at large?

The Evolution of the American Jury

The right to a trial by jury is deeply embedded in the American democratic ethos. The Sixth and Seventh Amendments to the U.S. Constitution guarantee the right to a jury for all criminal cases and in all civil suits exceeding twenty dollars. In addition, the constitution of each state guarantees a trial by jury.[1] In contrast, England, Scotland, Wales, and Canada do not have as liberal a standard concerning trial by jury. In those countries, persons accused of nonindictable crimes—less serious crimes for which the prescribed punishment is less than two years in prison—do not have the right to trial by jury. Indeed, Blackstone, the 18th century English scholar of law, was at pains to point out that in English law, trial by jury was a privilege, not a right. These other countries also make less frequent use of the civil jury; indeed, outside North America, the civil jury has all but disappeared. Estimates are that 80% of all jury trials worldwide take place in the United States.

In the United States, prospective jurors may be questioned not only on whether they have any personal interest in a case, but also about their general beliefs and prejudices as well. A judge will excuse anyone whose biased attitudes will interfere with his or her duties as a juror. This pretrial phase called the *voir dire*, which weeds out biased jurors, is typically absent in England and Canada. Except for special circumstances, questioning jurors about their beliefs is forbidden. English and Canadian jurors are more or less randomly selected from the jury pool. At one time, American juries were instructed that after hearing the evidence, they had the right both to decide the facts of the case and to interpret the meaning of the law, regardless of what the judge told them. Though this practice has changed in all but two states, American juries still have more power and discretion than English and Canadian juries. American juries play an important role in deciding whether or not the death penalty should be given to persons convicted of first-degree murder. Additionally, thirteen states give the jury the authority to prescribe the length of sentence for defendants convicted of other serious crimes. When English and Canadian lawyers and judges are asked about the American

judicial system, they express disapproval concerning the powers given to American juries. In their countries, juries are far more subservient to judges. Judges alone pronounce the law and set sentences.

Since the American jury began as a direct transplant from Mother England, why did it change? How did it become so deeply embedded in American democratic ethos? The roots of the separate evolution began in the Colonial period. After the American Revolution, new theories of law as well as social and political forces and pragmatic concerns had a strong impact on the jury's role, sometimes expanding it and other times curtailing it. Even today, the jury is not a static institution but one which continues the process of gradual evolution.

While it is true that many colonists, including the Puritans and, later, people like William Penn, were rebels and dissenters, nevertheless they thought like the English, felt an allegiance to the King, and brought with them English customs, political institutions—and the law. It was natural for the colonists to model their laws on those of the mother country. Thus, early Colonial law was based upon the English common law and British parliamentary statutes.

However, England was a long way off in the days of sailing ships. The King and his legal institutions were distant figures as the colonists had to cope with the special problems of an expanding society with uncertain frontiers. One of these problems was a paucity of judges trained in law. Another was the tendency of the Crown to send over governors and administrators who were greedy and unsympathetic to the needs of the colonists, and who frequently treated the colonists as less than equal. For this reason, American colonists began to develop their own perspectives on law and justice rather than to trust poorly trained judges or authorities whose interests lay elsewhere. Furthermore, the jury of peers in itself became a ready-made vehicle for implementing revolutionary ideas and principles, particularly when the needs of new colonists and the dictates of the Crown were in conflict. Although the historical records of that period are incomplete, there is evidence showing that very early on the jury began to acquire a new political significance.[2] This difference from the English jury was subtle and largely unnoticed until an eloquent Philadelphia lawyer gave voice to "the law of the future" in the trial of John Peter Zenger.

Most American history books hail the trial of Zenger for seditious libel in 1735 as the leading case for freedom of the press and as an example of a victory of the people over an aristocracy.[3] In 1732 William Cosby, the King's appointed governor, arrived in the Colony of New York. Arrogant, quick-tempered, and greedy, he quickly managed to alienate the people of New York. Among other actions, Cosby dismissed a Chief Justice of the Supreme

Court who asserted that a legal suit brought by Cosby was improper. Cosby also used his official powers to support his cronies against another group in a profitable land speculation dispute. The opposition to Cosby organized itself and gained control over the Common Council of New York City.

In 1734 the opposition went so far as to send a representative to England to plead for the Governor's removal. Simultaneously, they launched a newspaper, *The New York Weekly Journal,* as a propaganda voice against the *New York Gazette,* which supported the Governor. Though the *Journal* was published in the small shop of John Peter Zenger, the effective editor and principal gadfly was James Alexander, a lawyer. As the conflict heated up, Alexander used almost every section of the paper, including the advertising section, to criticize and satirize Governor Cosby and his associates. Alexander's role was hard to prove but eventually, charges of seditious libel were laid against the hapless publisher Zenger. He spent eight difficult months in jail awaiting trial while Alexander continued to stir the populace against Cosby.

Alexander and another lawyer, William Smith, prepared to defend Zenger vigorously, as well as make the trial an indictment of Governor Cosby and his administration. Again Governor Cosby and his associates acted with disdain for fairness. On a technicality, the governor had Alexander and Smith disbarred. Zenger was then required to petition for a new counsel. Since there were few lawyers in New York as experienced and skilled as Alexander and Smith, he was forced to accept the services of one John Chambers. Chambers was a competent lawyer but unfortunately was on the side of the governor. In addition to this tactic of depriving Zenger of the counsel of his choice, the clerk of the court produced a list of prospective jurors, many of whom were either favorable to the Governor or actually in his employ. Fulfilling his obligations to his client faithfully, Chambers pleaded not guilty and filed a motion to strike the biased people from the jury list. The motion was successful and of the twelve jurors finally selected, at least six could be identified as favorably disposed toward the political faction opposed to Governor Cosby.

Despite these actions on the part of Chambers, Alexander and Smith were not convinced that he would put forth the best defense. Thus, in a clever maneuver they persuaded Andrew Hamilton of Philadelphia to defend Zenger. Eloquent, experienced, and always prepared, Hamilton was perhaps the best lawyer in the American colonies, When the trial began in August of 1735, Hamilton was sitting among the spectators. The Attorney General read the charges against Zenger, and Chambers made his opening remarks. The legal position of Zenger appeared weak. Then, dramatically, Hamilton rose from his chair and announced that he would assist in Zenger's defense.

The laws of libel in 1735 prescribed a very narrow role for the jury,

specifically to render only a "special" verdict rather than a "general" verdict of guilty or not guilty. In Zenger's trial the jury's only task was to determine whether Zenger had actually published the newspaper. The question of the libelousness of the articles printed in it was to be determined by the judge. The evidence was clear that Zenger had published the *Journal* and the prosecution's case took less than a day to present. The stage was set for Zenger's conviction—except that Hamilton chose to present some novel arguments to the jury. As historian John Fiske stated, Hamilton argued the case around the "law of the future" rather than the law of the day.

Part of Hamilton's presentation to the jury was addressed to the laws of libel. He accepted the English law principle that questions of law were left to the judges while the jury determined only questions of fact, but he asserted that charges of libel involved an intertwining of law and fact: What makes a statement a libel is the factual question of whether it is a falsehood. To require the jury to return a special rather than a general verdict would, therefore, usurp the rights of the jury, since it was supposed to decide factual questions. Second, he suggested that although the laws of England might be good laws for England, they were not necessarily good laws for America where there was greater equality between the people and those who governed them. Finally, Hamilton propounded to the jury a theory about the relationship between law and politics. It was not part of their English heritage, but it was one with which many New Yorkers would be sympathetic. Calling attention to the fact that Zenger was not dissimilar to the jurors themselves, he asserted that citizens had the right to criticize their rulers and that Zenger was on trial because he asserted that right. Central to Hamilton's theory was the notion that the state existed to protect the liberties of its citizens. When the state fails in this regard and the King's authorities use their power to destroy individual citizens, the citizens do not need to obey these authorities:

> When the representatives of a free people are by just representations or remonstrances made sensible of the sufferings of their fellow subjects, by the abuse of power in the hands of the governor, they have declared . . . that they were not obliged by the law to support a governor who goes about to destroy a province or colony.

One of the best safeguards against the King's authorities abusing their power, Hamilton argued, was through public criticism such as that in Zenger's *Journal*.

Chief Justice DeLancey, presiding over Zenger's trial, took strong issue with Hamilton's position and asserted to the jury that they did not have the right to decide the law. Nevertheless, when the jury retired, it took only a few minutes to deliberate and returned a verdict of not guilty.

Hamilton's arguments were not against the King, but rather against those who administered under the King's authority. While the genesis of the case

was the warring of two political factions, Hamilton moved it to the level of political principle. The lasting significance of Zenger's trial resides in Hamilton's articulation of developing American ideas about the relationship between state and citizen—and the place of the jury in this new scheme of thinking. In Hamilton's words:

> Jurymen are to see with their own eyes, to hear with their own ears, and to make use of their own consciences and understandings, in judging of the lives, liberties or estates of their fellow subjects.

Hamilton's arguments about the relationship between the law and the role of the jury predated the Declaration of Independence by four decades and by over five decades the amendments to the U.S. Constitution providing for jury trials. In this sense the Zenger trial truly was about the law "of the future."

In the decades after the Zenger case, political dissent against the distant, unsympathetic, and arbitrary mother country increased. As more and more trials having political significance appeared in colonial courts, the Crown sought every means possible to secure convictions. One of these was the selection of jurors favorable to the Crown. As we noted earlier, English courts had long accepted the notion that in criminal trials, particularly ones involving defendants with divergent political views, it was quite acceptable, even laudable, for the sheriff to choose jurors partial to the Crown. It is true that defendants were allowed a number of peremptory challenges. They also could challenge jurors on the grounds of specific bias, for example, a familial tie or economic relation to one of the parties in the case. However, challenges on the grounds of general bias, such as attitudes or political views, were not allowed.[4] This precedent had been set in 1696 when Peter Cook was tried, convicted, and eventually hanged for conspiring against William and Mary in support of the exiled Catholic King, James II. Cook's trial opened amid widespread prejudice against Catholic supporters. Furthermore, extensive pretrial publicity had connected Cook with several other persons who had already been tried and hanged for treason. As a result, Cook sought to question potential jurors about their political beliefs and biases. The court denied this request on the grounds that such questions would bring discredit to the jurors who, after all, were not on trial. The precedent set in Cook's case was the standard that guided English and early American cases.[5]

In Massachusetts, however, the famous Yankee ingenuity helped to thwart, at least for a time, attempts of the Crown to stack the juries with Tory sympathizers. If the sheriff drew up the jury list for the trial and defendants were not allowed to question prospective jurors about their beliefs, a logical step was to move to an earlier stage in the selection process.[6]

The Massachusetts Jury Selection Law passed by the colonial legislature

in 1760 required that the venire, or panel, from which the sheriff drew his list should be chosen by a town meeting. Before people were placed on the list, they were subjected to questioning which helped to expose their character and biases. With the information acquired from these town meetings, defendants could exercise their peremptory challenges to eliminate those jurors who would be prejudiced against them.

Following complaints by Tory sympathizers that "the examination of jurors is now more in the hands of the people than ever before," the English Parliament was persuaded that the selection of jurors should be regulated by the Crown. Hence, in 1774 a parliamentary act was passed that canceled the Massachusetts Jury Selection Law, removing jury list selection from town meetings and placing it in the hands of the court. After 1774, therefore, the Crown had a more or less free hand to compose the jury list so as to favor the Tory cause. But the Declaration of Independence was only two years away.

Not surprisingly, after the Revolution, the newly independent Americans were very aware of the importance of the jury, particularly after their experience with colonial political oppression. They recognized the jury as an instrument for the protection of individual liberty. Throughout the remainder of the 18th century and for the first half of the 19th century, the jury occupied a position of exalted status in American thinking. Thomas Jefferson wrote:

> Were I called upon to decide, whether the people had best be omitted in the legislative or judiciary department, I would say it is better to leave them out of the legislative. The execution of the laws is more important than the making of them.[7]

But if there was agreement as to the jury's importance, there was clearly disagreement over the degree to which the functions of the jury and procedural safeguards for it should be spelled out.[8] In the first draft of the Constitution, there was no guarantee of jury trial for civil actions. In one of the Federalist papers, Alexander Hamilton went to considerable effort to indicate that the omission was not intended as a diminution of the role of the jury: "The friends and adversaries of the plan of the [Constitutional] Convention, if they agree on nothing else, concur at least in the value they set upon the trial by jury." Ultimately, of course, the right to a jury trial for civil actions was guaranteed by the adoption of the Seventh Amendment, just as the right to a jury trial in criminal matters was ensured by the Sixth Amendment.

A second issue hinged on the role of the jury to decide the law as well as the facts. Although historical records are sketchy at best, there is some evidence that juries in the various colonies had been deciding issues of law well before John Peter Zenger's trial.[9] This practice may have intially de-

veloped because few judges were trained in the law; moreover, the judges held office "not for the purpose of deciding cases, for the jury decided all questions of the law and fact; but merely to preserve order, and see that the parties had a fair chance with the jury." In any event, even before the Revolution, John Adams in 1771 asserted that the jury should ignore the judge's instructions to them if these instructions violated fundamental principles of justice:

> It is not only . . . [the juror's] right, but his duty, in that case, to find the verdict according to his own best understanding, judgment, and conscience, though in direct opposition to the direction of the court.[10]

The final draft of the Constitution was silent about the specific role of the jury. But the writings of Adams, Jefferson, Elbridge Gerry, and other framers of the Constitution made it clear that they believed that the jury could, and should, decide law as well as fact.

A third issue of contention concerned the spelling out of the right to challenge jurors. As we already noted, English law did not allow challenges for general bias. The House of Representatives was, however, very specific on this right in its first draft of the Bill of Rights: "The trial of all crimes . . . shall be by an impartial jury of the freeholders of the vicinage with the requisite of unanimity for conviction, the right of challenge and other accustomed requisites. . . ." The Senate eliminated this clause, largely on the grounds that it was redundant with the guarantee of an "impartial jury."

Emotions ran high. In the Virginia ratification debates, Patrick Henry spoke against the failure of the Constitution to specify the right to challenge with the same passionate eloquence that he had mustered for liberty or death:

> If [the people] dare oppose the hands of tyrannical power, you will see what has happened elsewhere. They may be tried by the most partial powers, by their most implacable enemies, and be sentenced and put to death, with all the forms of a fair trial. . . . I would rather the trial by jury were struck out altogether. There is no right of challenging partial jurors. . . . Yet the right is as valuable as the trial by jury itself.

James Madison took a somewhat different position:

> Where a technical word was used [trial by jury], all the incidents belonging to it necessarily attended it. The right to challenge is incident to the trial by jury, and, therefore, as one is secured, so is the other.

Madison and others who favored the less specific language prevailed. Yet, these debates indicated that, unlike English practice, it was intended that in a pretrial hearing, or *voir dire*, as it was called, defendants should have the right to challenge and reject jurors for their general attitudes as well as

specific interests in the case. In the period immediately following the adoption of the Constitution, court decisions at both the federal and state level were consistent with the sentiments expressed in the Constitutional debates.

Although the U.S. Supreme Court primarily hears appeals from lower courts, it occasionally serves as a trial court as well. In one civil case, *Georgia v. Brailsford* (1794), Chief Justice Jay made his charge to the jury by noting that it was presumed that while juries were to determine the facts, the courts were the best judges of law; nevertheless, it was the jurors' "right to take upon . . . [themselves] to judge of both, and to determine the law as well as the fact in controversy."[10] The right to decide law was also confirmed in criminal cases. For example, in *Commonwealth v. Blanding* (1825), the Massachusetts Supreme Judicial Court approved a charge to a jury stating that they did not have to accept the judge's interpretation of the law "if they knew the law to be otherwise"; and in *Commonwealth v. Knapp* (1830) the jury was instructed that it had the "duty to decide all points of law which are involved in the general question of the guilt or innocence of the prisoner."[11]

The right of the jury to decide law as well as facts and the right of a defendant to question jurors in a *voir dire* were also affirmed in the impeachment trial of Supreme Court Justice Samuel Chase in 1805. An attempt was made to impeach Justice Chase for high crimes and misdemeanors, largely on the grounds of his conduct as a trial judge. The first article of impeachment charged that in the treason trial of one John Fries, he had refused to allow the defendant's lawyer to address the jurors on questions of law and therefore usurped the jury's right to determine their verdict upon questions of law as well as fact. The second article charged that in the seditious libel trial of one James Thomson Callendar, Justice Chase had refused to allow the defendant to challenge a juror who admitted to having a general bias on the question of guilt. Though the impeachment of Justice Chase failed for lack of a two-thirds majority, the trial, carried out by the U.S. Senate, made it clear that Chase's behavior was contrary to prevailing notions of jury functions and jury procedure.

*   *   *

Beginning about 1850, Americans' unfettered enthusiasm for the jury began to wane.[12] Perhaps part of the cause can be attributed to the memory of colonial oppression having faded and American minds being occupied with other problems. Another reason might also be that in older parts of the United States, there were more well-trained judges than in the immediate post-Revolutionary period. They were perceived as more expert than the lay judges

had been. On the American frontier the number of trained judges was few. Mistrust in them continued while faith in the people's jury remained high; hence, juries continued to decide on the law as well as the facts. Back East, however, the judicial system had become developed and entrenched. It began to raise a jaundiced eye toward the jury, especially the extent of the powers that it had been given. Some of this power was consequently curbed, though legislative attempts were made to reassert some of that power.

The jury was restricted on several fronts. The "directed verdict" was one such mechanism. In an 1860 decision, *Commonwealth v. Merrill,* for example, the Massachusetts Supreme Court held that the judge could direct the jury to reach a verdict of not guilty if the judge determined that the evidence set forth by the prosecution was legally insufficient. Also, during this period many of the states adopted the concept of a "special verdict," especially in civil trials. With the special verdict the jury was asked to answer particular questions about factual issues in the case but not allowed to deliver a general verdict on which of the adversaries should prevail. Upon receiving the special jury verdict, the judge applied the law to the factual determination and decided who won and who lost. Thus, the jury was not given the opportunity to comment on the law.

Though Massachusetts did not adopt the special verdict, it did develop the practice of interrogating juries in civil and criminal trials after they had rendered their general verdict. If the judge decided that the jurors' answers to specific factual questions were not logically consistent with the general verdict, he could order a new trial. While not as limiting as the special verdict, jury "interrogatories" at least allowed the judge to take power away from one jury and give it to a new one, as we will see shortly.

Some relatively minor forces arose to counter these restrictions. English common law and American practice had always allowed the judge to comment on the evidence as he addressed the jury. For instance, the judge might comment on the credibility of the witnesses or interpret the meaning of certain evidence. But as the new restrictions on the jury's role were enacted, a number of state legislatures passed laws that forbid the judge to comment on the evidence. By curbing the judge's role, these laws in effect allocated more power to the jury. In many state jurisdictions today the judge is still forbidden to comment on the evidence, though other jurisdictions allow it.

The limit to the notion that the jury should decide the law came with the U.S. Supreme Court decision in the criminal case of *Sparf and Hansen v. United States* in 1896. Justice Harlan, writing for the Court, acknowledged that the practice of instructing juries that they were judges of both the law and the facts had been affirmed time and again by lower courts and by the

Supreme Court itself. Nevertheless, the Court ruled that in federal criminal cases the jury should follow the judge's instructions on the law. Juries still had the *power* to ignore the judge and effectively nullify the law by turning in whatever general verdict they chose, but after *Sparf* they did not have the legal *right* to do so in federal courts, as we will discuss later. Most states eventually followed the *Sparf* ruling.[13]

In the period around 1920 the right of the defendant to question prospective jurors also began to have limitations imposed on it, at least in federal courts.[14] Up until this time the defendant or the attorneys had the right to question jurors about bias. A judicial council formed by Congress in 1922, however, recommended that the presiding judge should conduct the *voir dire* questioning. The council believed that this procedure would promote effective judicial administration, and a new rule to this effect was officially adopted in 1928. Under the rule the opposing counsel could suggest questions that should be asked but the trial judge had the final say as to whether they would be asked. Many judges at both the federal and state level continued to allow the defendant's lawyer to examine the prospective jurors. Yet, legal challenges to the new rule failed in the appeals courts. The end result was that, particularly in the federal courts, the defendant's ability to challenge potential jurors was substantially curtailed. No doubt Patrick Henry would have said, "I told you so!"

At the beginning of this chapter, we mentioned that thirteen states allow juries a significant role in sentencing in noncapital crimes.[15] (Juries also play a crucial role in death penalty sentencing, a topic discussed later.) Some states give sentencing authority to the jury in all serious criminal cases, while others restrict the authority to particular types of cases. In Texas a defendant has the right to be sentenced by the jury rather than the judge. This is a significant departure from the English common law and from most American jurisdictions where traditionally the judge has sentencing authority. Does jury sentencing indicate respect for the jury over the judge? The answer is not at all clear, because the sentencing authority was granted at different times under different conditions in the various states.

In the midst of the turmoil of the Revolution, the first Virginia General Assembly in 1776 passed a statute making it a "misdemeanor" (a crime punishable by a fine not to exceed 20,000 pounds nor imprisonment to exceed five years) for anyone to defend the authority of Great Britain over the new American states.[16] In this special case, the jury was to determine the appropriate degree of punishment within the statutory limit. This grant of sentencing authority was probably not a general mistrust of judges because for all other crimes authority was vested in judges. However, in 1846 jury sentencing

authority was expanded to include all felony cases, with judges allowed to set sentence only for misdemeanors. In 1887 sentencing authority for misdemeanor cases was also given to the jury. In all cases, if the jury declined to fix the sentence, the judge was allowed to do so.

In Texas the authority to prescribe the defendant's sentence was given to the jury in 1846, immediately after Texas had joined the Union. Members of the first legislature that passed the statute may have had the same negative experience with Mexican-appointed judges that the colonists had had with British-appointed judges. Moreover, Texas had few formally trained lawyers. Thus, it was reasonable to place as much faith in juries as in judges.[17]

In Kentucky and Georgia the common law practice of judges assigning punishment was followed until around 1915.[18] At that time the state legislatures passed laws introducing indeterminate sentences whose purpose was to bring about uniformity of punishment for defendants who committed similar offenses. The jury was authorized to fix the convicted person's sentence within the minimum and maximum terms authorized for the crime by the state. However, the judge had the power to overturn the jury sentence if it appeared too harsh.

In brief, there is no single explanation for the practice of jury sentencing in those states that allow it. It developed at different times and under different circumstances.

*   *   *

Historians constantly remind us that their discipline becomes more unreliable as they seek to explain the remote past or the immediate present. The remote past has few records, and these may be unrepresentative, sketchy, and untrustworthy. We are forced to guess about what the records meant. As for the immediate present, the records are all there, but we may be too close in time to draw back and see the larger picture. Again we are forced to guess about the ultimate meaning of the events that are recorded. In looking at the jury's place in the legal system over the past several decades, we are well advised to heed the historians' warning. Yet, we should note a few events during these decades, which will provide us with a sense of closure for our brief survey of ten centuries of legal history. They also set the stage for the major issues which will be the focus of the rest of this book. Let us begin with the Baby Doctor's trial.

By the middle of the 1960s, opposition to the war in Vietnam had grown at a tremendous pace. Prominent Americans from various walks of life spoke against the war. Some took actions intended to publicize their resistance to

military involvement in that country. A focal point of the resistance was the military draft. To publicize their disenchantment with the draft, a number of students on college campuses burned their draft cards in symbolic acts of defiance. Dr. Benjamin Spock, whose books on child rearing had untold influence on several generations of American parents, and earned him the title of "the Baby Doctor," was a member of this peace movement. Along with Yale University chaplain William Sloane Coffin and others, Dr. Spock spoke at several peace rallies in 1967 at which students subsequently burned their draft cards. Federal charges of conspiracy to counsel draft evasion were brought against Dr. Spock and three others.[19]

After the evidence and arguments at Dr. Spock's trial had been presented, the judge charged the all-male[20] jury. The jurors were told that their task was to return a general verdict of guilty or not guilty. But in addition, the jurors were instructed that after their general verdict had been reached, they were to answer a "special interrogatory" of ten questions. These questions were of the following sort: Did the defendants knowingly counsel people to evade the draft? Did they give aid? Did they abet? Did they hinder or interfere with the draft law? The jury returned a verdict of guilty, which Dr. Spock and his codefendants appealed.

The federal appeals court reversed the convictions. It said that requiring the jury to answer the special interrogatory infringed upon the jury's power to render a general verdict. To the Court of Appeals, the question of whether Dr. Spock's actions exceeded the bounds of free speech was one to which community standards and conscience must apply. And in its view, "the jury, as the conscience of the community, must be permitted to look at more than logic," that is, it can apply principles of fairness or morality that are beyond the law.

Aside from the broader moral and political questions raised by the reversal of Dr. Spock's conviction, the decision may also be seen as a restatement of the importance of the criminal jury in American law. Some might even suggest that it is one sign that the erosion of the jury's power to decide law has slowed ever since *Sparf v. United States*. There are some other signs as well. In *Duncan v. Louisiana* (1968), the U.S. Supreme Court stated that one function of the jury is to guard against official departures from the rules, but an equally important function is, on proper occasions, to depart from unjust rules or their unjust application. Also, in its 1976 decision concluding that the death penalty was not *per se* unconstitutional, the Supreme Court placed the jury in a pivotal vote to decide whether a convicted person shall live or die.

But if these are interpreted as signs of the apparent health of the American

jury, there are some equally bleak signs. Two traditional aspects of the jury, the twelve-person jury and the requirement that jurors must reach a unanimous verdict, were evaluated by the Supreme Court in the 1970s and found unnecessary. In *Williams v. Florida* (1970), the Supreme Court concluded that the traditional jury size of twelve is not constitutionally required in state criminal trials. In *Apodaca v. Oregon* (1972) and *Johnson v. Louisiana* (1972), it asserted that the centuries-old unanimity rule is not necessary either. It held that verdicts in state courts based upon a majority of the twelve jurors are not unconstitutional. We will discuss both of these changes in detail later. In civil cases, use of the jury has declined. Moreover, a very recent series of cases suggests the future possibility that jury trials may be eliminated in complex civil cases, even though the Seventh Amendment guarantees the right to a jury.[21] There is also much opinion in favor of eliminating jury sentencing.[15]

Similar conflicting signs may be detected in the way juries are selected. The movement to take control of the *voir dire* process out of the hands of the defendant and place it in the hands of the trial judge, which began in the 1920s, has recently accelerated.[22] On the other hand, the 1970s witnessed great strides on the other side, through court decisions requiring that the jury pool be truly representative of the community. As we will soon discuss, a series of laws and court decisions has forbidden discrimination in jury selection on the basis of race, ethnicity, gender, or other characteristics.

Some historians maintain that the jury's overall role in the administration of justice has declined. In the past, they contend, the main components of the criminal justice system were the defendant, the victim, the judge, and the jury; and the major form of disposition of criminal cases was trial by jury. Today, however, the critical components are the police, the prosecutor, and the judge; and the main way that cases are disposed of is the prosecutor's decision to dismiss charges or to develop a plea bargain with the defendant. The contemporary American jury hears a relatively small proportion—about 8%—of all criminal cases. Nevertheless, juries hear a much larger percentage of contested cases—those in which the defendants maintain their innocence. It may be particularly important to retain the option of trial by jury in these cases.[23]

*   *   *

Thus, the jury is in a process of continual evolution. Sometimes the process goes forward; sometimes it is halted; sometimes it goes backward. Changes sometimes result from shifts in the broader social and political climate

to which the jury system is inextricably tied. Sometimes the changes come from within the legal system itself, perhaps from a new way of looking at a legal problem or perhaps because the jury is seen to be functioning well or not so well. Sometimes changes are brought about by the simple desire to expedite the judicial process, even at the expense of justice.

Whenever changes occur in the jury system, some people applaud them as progressive. Others, however, view them as attempts to tamper with a time-tempered and valuable institution that has served us well. They usually decry change in the status quo as one more step on a slippery slope, another sign of the demise of the jury. Our quick journey over a thousand years shows that the jury system has always been tampered with—that is the nature of evolution. This is not to say that some steps are not backward ones or to argue that there are no causes for concern. Nevertheless, the jury system appears alive and entrenched in the American, English, and Canadian legal systems—even if recent changes are not to everyone's liking.

PART II

Jury Selection

A Jury of Peers—But from an Unbiased Community

On November 24, 1963, just two days after the nation had been shocked by the assassination of President John F. Kennedy, Americans watched in horror as Jack Ruby shot and killed accused assassin Lee Harvey Oswald in a Dallas police station garage, in full view of television cameras. The world-famous attorney Melvin Belli represented Ruby at his jury trial. One of Belli's first actions on behalf of Ruby was to try to get the trial moved out of Dallas. Belli later recounted his reasons for this in a special hearing to change the location of the trial:

> Dallas was a cesspool of prejudice. Out of that pool, I argued, we couldn't get a jury that was unbiased. How was it biased? It was my primary contention that the city of Dallas itself would be on trial as much as Jack Ruby was. Dallas had been shamed by the assassination of President Kennedy, doubly shamed by letting the President's assassin be killed in the Dallas police station itself. And so, a Dallas jury had to convict Ruby in order to acquit Dallas.[1]

The judge denied the move to change the location, or "venue," of the trial. Belli described the jury that was finally selected from the Dallas jury pool as a bad one, an "entirely WASP jury eager to do its Dallas duty," composed of jurors who wanted a "ringside seat for the big show."[2] When the jurors rejected defense arguments that Ruby was insane and found him guilty of murdering Oswald, Belli blamed the jury. Right after the verdict was announced, Belli erupted in the courtroom: "May I thank the jury for a victory for bigotry and injustice?"[3]

Melvin Belli is hardly unique in focusing on the jurors to explain the outcome of a trial. As a rule, handbooks for lawyers on American trial tactics stress the importance of jury composition and the scrutinizing of prospective jurors. One such handbook begins by emphasizing "a very obvious fact: The people who constitute the jury can have as much or more to do with the outcome of a trial as the evidence and arguments."[4]

Similarly, a past president of the American Trial Lawyers Association, Robert Cartwright, like many veteran trial lawyers in the United States, believes that careful jury selection pays off. He asserts that if trial lawyers can assess the biases, prejudices, and inclinations of potential jurors, and select those jurors who will identify with and be sympathetic to their clients, then their clients will have a tremendous advantage.[5] As well as guaranteeing the practice of questioning and eliminating certain individuals from the jury, U.S. Supreme Court decisions have established the right to a jury drawn from a representative cross section of the community. Underlying these decisions is the presumption that the makeup of the jury is a critical factor in trial outcomes. Indeed, jury selection occupies a prominent and time-consuming spot in many American trials, often lasting weeks or even months in some highly publicized cases.

In other countries such as Canada and Great Britain, jury selection rarely takes more than a few minutes. Lawyers there seriously question our emphasis on selecting a jury.[6] In a recent interview study with barristers from Cardiff, Wales, the barristers expressed disapproval of excessive challenges and disdain at the American obsession with jury selection. The majority of barristers expressed the belief that the jury should be drawn at random and stated that they rarely used their right to challenge. One barrister, who had been practicing law for nine years, put it this way:

> The jury system is, or in any event is intended to be, as I understand it, a trial by your peers selected at random from all walks of life. And I think it's wrong that a person should try and engineer a better jury for himself, by exercising the right of challenges.[7]

Many barristers rejected the common American practice of questioning prospective jurors about their background and attitudes, calling it not only useless but basically improper. Pretrial questioning is rare in Great Britain. Done only under special circumstances, it is exercised when the trial judge is persuaded by independent evidence that members of the jury panel may be biased. As another barrister pointedly declared:

> Well why don't you then start questioning the defense counsel on what his views are, or the prosecuting counsel, or the judge, on what his views and attitudes are? I just don't see the need for it . . . I personally don't think it gets you anywhere at all. Because surely, certainly in this country the whole basis of the system is that you are presuming you are entrusting cases to jurors. And so you must, if you're going to ask people to do a job, then I think you must trust them. And if you're going to trust them there's no need to question them about their previous beliefs and so on.[7]

Most barristers did not favor legal changes that would allow them to find out more about the jurors before the trial. They thought that such practices were not only time-consuming but also unnecessary.

> I think if I knew what the backgrounds of the jurors were . . . I still wouldn't challenge them. I don't think I would be able to handle the American system, actually . . . because I happen to take the view that whatever one's personal prejudices, the chances are that a juror called to jury service and knowing the weight of responsibility upon him will do his utmost to discard prejudice.[7]

Who is right—American attorneys, who sometimes devote lengthy periods of time investigating prospective jurors, questioning them before the trial, and exercising numerous challenges; or the British barristers, who rarely spend time or thought on the selection process, and who trust the juries to decide the case solely on the evidence? Would the Ruby case have resulted in a different verdict had it been decided by non-Dallas jurors, as Melvin Belli would have us believe? Can attorneys actually stack juries in their favor, as the past president of the American Trial Lawyers Association contends? Just how important is the composition of the jury anyway? Answers to these questions require an analysis of the procedures, the art, and the science of jury selection.

* * *

In the United States, as we noted earlier, the foundation for the criminal jury's composition is contained in the Sixth Amendment to the constitution, which states that defendants have the right to a trial "by an impartial jury of the State and district wherein the crime shall have been committed." A similar guarantee for the civil jury appears in the Seventh Amendment. From these amendments, and subsequent decisions by the U.S. Supreme Court, three general principles for the selection and makeup of the jury have emerged.[8] First, the jury must be drawn from a representative cross section of the community. Second, the trial should be held in the district in which the crime occurred. Third, the jurors must be impartial: Potential jurors who are unable to judge the facts with an open mind may be rejected from the jury. Let's look at the first two principles.

A line of U.S. legal cases has determined that the jury must be drawn from a representative cross section of the community.[9] There is no absolute requirement that each jury must represent all groups in the community. Rather, no cognizable group may be systematically excluded from the jury panel from

which the jury is drawn. This should result in generally representative juries, at least in theory.

Supporters of the representative jury argue that a jury composed of individuals with a wide range of experiences, backgrounds, and knowledge is more likely to perceive the facts from different perspectives and thus engage in a vigorous and thorough debate. Consider the plight of a black defendant whose case is heard by an all-white jury. A representative jury that included some members of his or her race might view and discuss the evidence differently. This point was made by Richard Cloward, a Columbia University sociologist, in his testimony at a jury challenge in the 1970 trial of Black Panthers Bobby Seale and Ericka Huggins. The two were charged with murdering a police officer in Oakland, California. Cloward argued:

> [A] white juror sitting in a jury box listening to the testimony of a black witness would sift and evaluate and appraise that testimony through a screen of preconceived notions about what black people are. Now, some of those notions may be based in fact . . . and some may be notions that have some relation to fact but are greatly exaggerated, and still others of those screening biases or notions may be completely contrary to fact. None of these things would be as likely to be true of a black juror listening to and appraising and judging the same testimony. The black juror, because of more similar life experiences to the black witness would, it seems to me, appraise that testimony from a distinctively different life experience in the world.[10]

Different interpretations of the evidence could even influence the final verdict. What may appear to white jurors as a black defendant's implausible story may ring true to black jurors with greater knowledge of the context and norms of black experience. Ralph Davis, a black who served as a juror in Los Angeles, demonstrates how race-dependent context and knowledge may sometimes be crucial:

> It seemed like the only reason that they arrested the [black] defendant [who was charged with auto theft] was that someone in the gas station across the street looking out into the light in the dark could identify the run-of-the-mill black man from 90 to 100 feet away. They arrested him in the area of York Boulevard [a white neighborhood near Occidental College and Pasadena]. Well, we all know what being black is on York Boulevard. I was raised and born in Los Angeles so it is nothing new to me. If you are black and you're on York Boulevard at four o'clock in the morning, they are going to pick you up. They will pick me up on York Boulevard walking at four o'clock in the morning. This was the only thing that they seemed to have against the man, so we acquitted him.[11]

The jury's heterogeneous makeup may also lessen the power of prejudice. Biases for and against the defendant, if evenly distributed on the jury, may cancel each other out. Furthermore, juries drawn from a representative cross

section of a community are more likely by chance to have minority group representation. The very presence of minorities would likely suppress the open expression of racial and ethnic prejudices.

Drawing the jury from a representative cross section may also increase the legitimacy of the jury system and jury verdicts. For example, when blacks or other minorities discover that they as a group are underrepresented on juries, they may feel verdicts are biased reflections of community sentiment rather than fair judgments. In 1980, an all-white male jury acquitted four white police officers in Dade County, Florida, of the murder of a black insurance salesman. Anger at the verdict and perceptions of its illegitimacy sparked three days of rioting in Miami's black community.[12] We can reasonably speculate that if the same verdict had been reached by a racially mixed jury, blacks might have felt their voices and perspectives had been represented on the jury and they might have been more able to accept its decision. Regardless of whether or not the composition of the jury actually makes a difference in any particular case, people look to the composition of the jury to explain verdicts. Thus, not only for fact-finding but also for legitimation, a representative jury is desirable.

*   *   *

The ideal of the representative jury has not always been as widely accepted as it is today. On the contrary, the road to representativeness has been a long and rocky one. In the United States, from the first Supreme Court decision concerning the composition of the jury in 1880 to the most recent definitive one in 1975, the Court gradually expanded and refined its definition of the constitutional right to trial by jury. Only now does it include the right to draw a jury from a truly representative cross section of the population.[13]

The increasing representation of women on juries allows a prime illustration of this pattern. Although women have constituted roughly half of the U.S. population since colonial times, the jury has been predominantly a male bastion until the last few decades. The outright exclusion of women from juries in the United States was an inheritance of the English common law system. In England, women were excluded from juries until 1919. Indeed, the famous legal scholar Blackstone wrote in the 18th century that women were rightfully prohibited from jury service because of what he labeled the *defect of sex,* which made them incapable of the intelligent decision-making required for jury duty. In 1898, Utah became the first state to allow women to sit on juries in a state court, and a few other jurisdictions followed suit. But it was not until the passage of the 19th Amendment in 1920, which gave

women the right to vote, that women's representation on juries was more than sporadic. After 1920, women's organizations such as the League of Women Voters and the National Women's Rights Party took up the jury issue. They attempted through lobbying efforts, legislative reform, and court challenges to increase women's participation on the jury.[14] However, as late as 1966, three states—Alabama, Mississippi, and South Carolina—still prohibited women from jury service. By 1972, women were eligible in all federal and state courts in the United States. On the other side of the Atlantic, in England and Wales a property qualification for jurors effectively excluded most women from jury service until its repeal in 1972.[15]

Despite women's widespread eligibility since 1920, the truth is that until very recently women were dramatically underrepresented on juries. Legal scholar Jon Van Dyke reviewed over 200 surveys of jury panels conducted by clerks of federal district courts between 1971 and 1974. In nine out of every ten jurisdictions, women were underrepresented on the jury lists, and in many courts, that underrepresentation was substantial.[13] This lack of equal participation was a direct result of special provisions of women relating to jury service. In some states there was a practice called *affirmative registration* which put a special burden on women. Although men were summoned directly for jury service, women who wanted to serve had to go to the courthouse and formally register. The constitutionality of this practice was challenged by one Mrs. Hoyt of Florida. In that case, decided by the Supreme Court in 1961, Mrs. Hoyt killed her husband with a baseball bat. She was apparently driven to this extreme act by the double affronts of her husband's adultery coupled with his rejection of her when she said that she'd be willing to forgive and forget. She pleaded temporary insanity as a defense, but an all-male jury convicted her of second-degree murder. At the time, an affirmative registration plan for women was in place in Florida. The result was a drastic underrepresentation of women: Only ten women's names were on the jury list of 10,000 persons. Mrs. Hoyt argued that the practice of affirmative registration denied her equal protection of the law, because it precluded a representative jury. She also pointed out that in her case, women's representation on the jury might have been important since women jurors may have been more sympathetic to her case. The Court, however, denied her claim.[16]

Another widespread practice allowed women to gain exemptions from jury service simply because of their sex. Exemptions and outright exclusions were legislatively sanctioned on the grounds that jury service would interfere with many women's family and childcare responsibilities. A paternalistic approach toward women also contributed to the problem. Consider, for example, what the Mississippi Supreme Court said in a decision in 1966:

The legislature has a right to exclude women so they may contribute their services as mothers, wives, and homemakers, and also to protect them (in some areas, they are still upon a pedestal) from the filth, obscenity, and noxious atmosphere that so often pervades a courtroom during a jury trial.[17]

Only fourteen years after *Hoyt v. Florida,* the U.S. Supreme Court reversed itself in the case of *Taylor v. Louisiana* in 1975.[18] This time it was a man, Billy Taylor, who argued against the burdens placed on women under Louisiana's affirmative registration plan. He maintained that such a plan, because it led to the systematic exclusion of women, interfered with his right to a representative jury. His arguments were similar to Mrs. Hoyt's. But this time, the Court agreed with them. Changes in attitudes toward women, increasing numbers of women in the labor force, and intervening laws and Supreme Court decisions affirming the desirability of jury representativeness all contributed to the reversal of the earlier decisions permitting special treatment of women.

*　　*　　*

A strong legal commitment to representative jury panels has, therefore, been relatively recent. Yet, even with laws requiring it, there are considerable practical difficulties in assembling representative groups from the community. The first step is to select names from one or more lists of members of the community. In the past, prospective jurors were often selected by a "key man" system, whereby key members of the community, such as aldermen, ministers, and the local banker, submitted lists of names of prospective jurors to the jury commissioner. Because communities are not organized randomly, only certain subgroups were represented by the key man system. For example, in one case argued successfully before the U.S. Supreme Court, the defendants pointed out that all the women on the jury panel were members of the League of Women Voters who, furthermore, had heard lectures at which the prosecutor's views were presented. In its decision, the Court noted disapprovingly that selecting prospective jurors from membership rolls of private organizations like the League of Women Voters could make the jury "the organ of a special class."[19]

The biggest changes in procedure for selecting jurors in the United States came with the passage of the federal Jury Selection and Service Act of 1968 [20] To try to ensure that a broad range of the population would serve as jurors, the Act required that voters' lists be used as the primary source for jury panel members. However, researchers have shown that although voters' lists are preferable to a key man system in increasing the representativeness of jury

panels, they still do not produce a true cross section of the community. Voters' lists fail to represent many young people, racial minorities, and the poor and transient. Some jurisdictions have begun to supplement voters' lists with other records such as drivers' licenses and welfare rolls.[21] Nonetheless, courts have rather consistently upheld the sole use of voter registration lists in assembling jury panels.[22]

In addition to the limitations inherent in choosing jury panel members from voters' lists, other steps in assembling the jury panel undermine its representativeness. After names are selected from the voters' lists and any other supplementary lists, the jury commissioner's staff may send a jury questionnaire to each person selected. The questionnaire varies somewhat but generally includes questions on the ability of the individual to serve on the jury. The return of these questionnaires is required by law, but for a variety of reasons a substantial number are not returned. This differential return rate results in additional underrepresentation of the poor, racial minorities, and other people with high mobility.[13]

The screening of returned jury questionnaires also works against a representative cross section of jurors. Prospective jurors are sometimes disqualified (not allowed to serve) or exempted (allowed to decline serving) from jury service by a commissioner or a judge. Different jurisdictions have varying criteria for disqualifications and exemptions. Generally, if in the minds of legislators, an individual possesses a characteristic that would make him or her unsuitable for jury service, that individual may be disqualified. For instance, people with serious criminal records, police officers, and non-English-speaking people are often disqualified. Others who are qualified for jury service may find it a special hardship, such as people with domestic obligations, owners of small businesses, physicians, or nurses. In these cases, exemptions from jury service may be granted, usually by the judge. In the past, it was common for entire categories of people, such as all physicians, or all women, to be given a blanket exemption. Legislators reasoned that many people in such categories would experience hardship from jury service; it would be more efficient to exempt the whole group by statute rather than deal with their excuses one by one. But most of those offered such an exemption took it, whether or not jury service would be a hardship. This needlessly destroyed the representativeness of the jury panel. Today, many of these blanket exemptions have been eliminated. Indeed, even judges have served on juries in some jurisdictions. It is usually necessary to satisfy the court on an individual basis that jury service would pose a hardship.

There are several stages, then, to jury panel selection, each of which typically contributes to the less-than-representative character of jury panels:

voters' lists as the source of names; differential return rate of jury question-naires; disqualifications; and exemptions. Even without an intent to discriminate, the procedures used in most jurisdictions result in juries that are not typical of the population.

To make matters worse, there have been documented instances in which jury commissioners' staff have purposefully discriminated against specific groups at some point in the jury panel selection process. In one landmark case, *Thiel v. Southern Pacific Company* (1946),[23] the petitioner brought suit against a railroad company for negligence in its treatment of him while he was a passenger. The passenger jumped out of a window of the moving train. Later he filed suit for damages, arguing that the company personnel knew that he was "out of his normal mind," and should either have been refused boarding or, once he boarded, been guarded so that he did not harm himself. Mr. Thiel requested a jury trial, but asked to strike the entire panel, on the grounds that "mostly business executives or those having the employer's viewpoint are purposely selected on [the] panel." Indeed, both the jury commissioner and the clerk of the court revealed that they deliberately eliminated from the jury panel all persons who worked for a daily wage. They justified their activity on the grounds that most of the daily wage-earners would find jury service a financial hardship and would be excused anyway. Thiel's claim for damages was rejected by the jury, but later the U.S. Supreme Court reversed the decision. The Court said that such systematic exclusion, however well-intentioned, could not be upheld, or otherwise "[w]e would breathe life into any latent tendencies to establish the jury as the instrument of the economically and socially privileged."[24]

Another successful challenge to the composition of the jury panel occurred in the prison rebellion trial of the Attica Brothers. On September 9, 1971, inmates at Attica State Prison in New York took 50 guards hostage and presented a list of demands to state officials. On September 13, four days later, Governor Rockefeller sent state troopers into the prison. Altogether, 43 persons (32 inmates and 11 hostages) died in the incident. The trials of the Attica prisoners were held in Erie County, New York. The defense team challenged the representativeness of the jury panel. During a special hearing, several clerks involved in the jury panel selection testified that it was common practice to select many more men than women from voter registration lists. They justified this practice on the grounds that previous experience had shown that women frequently claimed their statutory exemption. To counteract this tendency and to ensure enough jurors to fill the court's requirements, the clerks called a larger number of men. Close inspection of jury pool name cards also revealed that the race of some black jurors had been penciled

directly onto the cards, suggesting that the clerks' decisions on selection may have been based upon race. As a result of these discriminatory practices, the trial judge invalidated almost the entire jury pool.[25]

Sometimes even when there is no intention to discriminate, the selection procedures may result in an unrepresentative jury pool. Recently, an Atlantic County grand jury indicted Ronald Long for murder, armed robbery, and weapons offenses. The State asked for the death penalty. Before Long's trial began, however, the Public Defender's office in New Jersey filed a motion challenging the method of grand and petit jury selection. Public Defenders Robert Moran and Barry Cooper worked together with David Kairys of the Philadelphia law firm of Kairys and Rudovsky and several statistical experts to examine the manner in which New Jersey jury panels were selected. They found some surprises.

Like many other jurisdictions today, Atlantic County has turned to the computer for generating its jury lists. On the face of it, the Atlantic County jury selection process appeared to be a highly complex, computer-assisted system for selecting jurors randomly from the population. Computer tapes of licensed drivers and registered voters were merged by computer to produce a source list. Then the Jury Commission Clerk divided the number of required jurors into the total number of names on the source list to derive an interval number. The computer used the interval number to make selections of names from the source list. A constant was added to the interval number if subsequent runs through the source list were required for additional names. The Clerk mailed a juror questionnaire to each person listed, and after evaluating the returned questionnaires for disqualifications or exemptions, developed an alphabetical list of qualified jurors. Subsequently, the lists were re-ordered alphabetically by the fifth letter of the juror's last name, the fourth character of the address, and the second character of the driver's license number. Finally, a judge picked at random a number for each of the jury panels. The judge's number was used as the starting and interval number to select people for the jury panels.

Although the system appeared random, the maze of lists, interval numbers, and different alphabetizing created some systematic problems. The defense team was alerted to the problems when they began noticing some peculiar patterns in the Atlantic County jury panels. One panel, for instance, contained an inordinate number of people with apparently Jewish names. Another panel had a large proportion of Italian names. Fully 10% of another panel had the last name of Williams; this constituted half of all the people named Williams in the entire jury pool. Out of a total of 4366 jurors, 292 people had another family member on the list, much greater than would be expected by chance.

The defense called mathematical expert Joseph Kadane to analyze the jury selection system and to discover what the problem was. Dr. Kadane found that several aspects of the supposedly random system worked together to create nonrandom jury selection. First, the driver's license list and the voter registration list were merged incorrectly, so that many people were listed twice. There were about 180,000 names on the merged source list, but only 130,000 people in Atlantic County between the ages of 18 and 74. Almost 40% of the people had double the opportunity to be selected for jury duty. The interval number was four times larger than it should have been, and the starting number for the computer was not randomly selected. Furthermore, constant numbers rather than random numbers were added by the computer in subsequent runs through the list, which meant that certain parts of the list (the Williams section, let us say) were frequently selected and other parts were rarely selected. When judges were asked to pick numbers at random, without realizing it, they tended to choose low numbers; thus, the selection process was not truly random. And the fifth-letter alphabetization, combined with the other problems, meant that many people in the same panel would have the same fifth letter in their last name. This explained how some panels had large numbers of Jewish names (e.g., Wiseman, Feldman) or Italian names (e.g., Ferarro, Dinardo).

Dr. Kadane testified before the Court that due to the defects of the system, he believed that the responsibility for jury service was not being equitably distributed in Atlantic County. He pointed out that the system in use was more burdensome and expensive than a true random system, which he defined as giving each person an equal chance at serving on a jury. As a result of his testimony, the judge invalidated the entire jury selection system in Atlantic County and required the Jury Commission to develop a new scheme.[26]

* * *

Another principle of jury selection is that the jury should be drawn from the community in which the offense occurred. This rule goes almost unnoticed until trial participants fear that a fair trial cannot be had in the community and demand that it be held elsewhere. When Melvin Belli pleaded to move the Ruby trial out of Dallas, the city he labeled a "cesspool of prejudice," his request was denied. What Belli was asking the judge to do in the Ruby case was to buck a long tradition of holding a trial in the jurisdiction in which the crime took place. Historically, trials have always been local affairs, an arrangement which makes it easier for the defendant, witnesses, and other trial participants to attend the proceedings. But even more important, jurors

from the community have some sense of the atmosphere in which the participants behaved. They know local norms and standards and are better able to put the disputed behavior in context. Recall how the juror Ralph Davis's knowledge of the street on which the black defendant had been picked up allowed him to take into account the probability that the defendant had been arrested simply because he was black in a white neighborhood. Jurors from another city may not have known or surmised this, and their views of the defendant's acts may thus have been incorrect. Finally, members of the immediate community are usually the ones most concerned about local crimes and other matters. They have the greatest stake in their outcomes. Observing or participating in the court process firsthand may satisfy the concerned community that justice is being done.

One can see that there are a good number of reasons for holding trials in the local community. Judges who are asked to have trials moved to other locations must balance these reasons against the possibility of a biased local jury. Judges also have to decide whether local biases are so great that normal procedures like pretrial questioning and challenges will not eliminate biased jurors. Finally, judges also have to consider the time, trouble, and expense of trials in other locations. For all these reasons, judges are reluctant to grant petitions to change the venue of a trial. For it to occur at all, the prejudicial pretrial publicity or local knowledge and continuing passions must be so inflamed to make it nearly impossible to select an impartial jury. Even in many cases fitting these criteria—like the Jack Ruby case—judges have denied motions for change of venue.

Under other circumstances, however, judges have agreed to move the trial. In the early morning hours of August 27, 1974, a night jailer named Clarence Alligood was found dead inside a locked cell in the women's section of the Beaufort County (N.C.) jail.[27] He had apparently been killed by an ice pick. His pants and shoes were outside the locked cell. Joan Little, the black woman who had been occupying the cell, was missing, and so were the jailer's keys. The event received a tremendous amount of publicity. There was an unsuccessful search for Ms. Little, but she finally turned herself in to the police in Raleigh, North Carolina. She maintained that she had been raped by Alligood and had killed him in self-defense. Her attorney, Jerry Paul, and the team of social scientists working on her defense doubted that Joan Little could get a fair trial in rural Beaufort County. They believed that, for the most part, the community consisted of extremely conservative people with sexist and racist attitudes that would interfere with a fair hearing of the facts. They also surmised that these attitudes had been exacerbated by the extensive pretrial publicity surrounding the case. Though they were convinced

that a change of trial location was necessary, they still had to persuade the judge.

Traditionally, when attorneys have petitioned for a change of venue, they have submitted two types of evidence to support their motions. First, they introduce evidence of local media coverage, including articles from local newspapers and reports of television coverage, with special note of any potentially prejudicial material. Second, they submit affidavits from local and often prominent citizens of the community, who attest to the level of prejudice and indicate that a fair trial would not be possible. While these sources of information may be helpful, they do not necessarily provide accurate reflections of community sentiment. The publication of news articles does not mean that prospective jurors have read them, been prejudiced by them, or continue to be biased by them. The opinions of community leaders often don't reflect the attitudes of an entire community.

To supplement this limited evidence, in recent years lawyers have commissioned scientifically conducted opinion polls. If designed correctly, these surveys can produce accurate evidence of the level and extent of prejudice in a community. When such polls were first conducted in the 1950s, judges were reluctant to accept them. They were skeptical about the usefulness of the polls and wary of the intrusion of social science in the courtroom. Indeed, often their skepticism was justified. Many of the surveys were not very good. Some were not true random samples of the community; others contained superficial or legally irrelevant questions. But today, with improvements in the quality and sophistication of the surveys, and a more open-minded approach by judges, survey evidence is becoming more accepted.

Joan Little's defense team, eager to explore the level of prejudice in Beaufort County, decided to conduct a survey. They wanted to show that there was a great deal of prejudice against Little, and to indicate in which nearby counties she was more likely to get a fair trial. Before the trial began, the social scientists whom they hired conducted a massive and scientifically accurate telephone survey of residents of Beaufort County and 24 other counties in North Carolina. The researchers asked residents how much they had heard about the Joan Little case, whether they had already formed a preconception of her guilt, and other questions probing racism and sexism.

Almost three quarters of the people from all the counties that were sampled said that they had heard "a lot" about the case. Beaufort County residents were no different from people in other counties concerning knowledge about the case. However, people in Beaufort and neighboring Pitt County (to which presiding Judge McKinnon was considering a change of venue) were twice as likely to have prejudged Joan Little as guilty. They were also more likely

to hold racist and sexist attitudes than residents of more urban Orange County. For example, two out of every three Beaufort and Pitt residents believed that black women had lower morals than white women, and that blacks were more violent than whites. In comparison, only one out of every three Orange County residents expressed these attitudes. On the basis of these data, the lawyers argued that a move to Pitt County would accomplish nothing, while a change of venue to a more urban area of the state, such as Orange County, would increase the chances for a fair jury. Along with the survey results, the attorneys for Joan Little also submitted copies of all local newspaper stories, a content analysis of the media coverage, expert testimony on communication in rural areas, and 102 affidavits on the state of public opinion about Joan Little.

Judge McKinnon was persuaded by all the evidence. He didn't follow the defense team's recommendation to move the trial to Orange County, but he did authorize a change of venue out of Beaufort County to urban Wake County. When he announced the change of venue to Wake County, Judge McKinnon mentioned the high level of pretrial publicity and racism as reasons for his decision. The jury subsequently found Ms. Little not guilty of all charges.

One of the present authors (N.V.) conducted research for a successful change of venue in a Canadian case. Rather than the politically volatile issues of race, gender, and prisoner's rights as in Joan Little's trial, it involved the seemingly mundane crime of fraudulent sales practices.[28] Roy Brunner was charged with fraudulently misrepresenting and selling overpriced home improvements to senior citizens. His defense lawyer was very concerned about obtaining a fair trial because Brunner had recently been convicted and was awaiting sentencing in a highly publicized fraud trial that had taken place in the same area, Middlesex County in Ontario. In that trial, known locally as the Bevlen Conspiracy Trial, the owners and employees of a formerly reputable home improvements company were found guilty of fraud. They, including the salesman Brunner, had sold overpriced housing materials to elderly persons by using high-pressure sales tactics. The trial was one of the longest and most publicized courthouse events in local memory. Over 100 articles on the case had been printed in the local newspaper. The articles were accompanied by banner headlines and contained graphic accounts of police wiretaps that recorded company employees badgering and even threatening senior citizens.

The defense lawyer feared that most of the jurors from Middlesex County would be prejudiced by Brunner's conviction in the Bevlen trial, and regardless of the evidence in the upcoming case, would decide he was probably guilty. When the survey was conducted, these hunches were confirmed. A

substantial majority of people indicated that they could not be impartial jurors in a fraud case similar to Bevlen. Furthermore, they said that they would have particular difficulty being fair jurors if they learned that the defendant had already been convicted in the Bevlen trial. These and other findings were presented to the trial judge. The research was accompanied by additional evidence that helped to corroborate the conclusions. The trial judge granted a change of venue to a different county, saying that the survey findings and the corroborative evidence had convinced him that a fair trial for Brunner might well be impossible in Middlesex County. The judge's decision was a particularly significant one, since changes in venue are even rarer in Canada than they are in the United States. Oh yes, the jury acquitted Brunner of the new charges, but he received a two-year jail sentence for his involvement in the Bevlen case.

*　　*　　*

The principles of jury selection are designed to assemble juries that will reflect the range of voices in the community and decide cases in an unbiased way. Yet, even if the jury pool is representative, and the community as a whole is relatively unbiased, that is no guarantee that the people selected for the jury will be free from prejudice. That is the problem we will consider next.

Jury Selection: Eliminating Some of the Peers

Can the individuals who sit on the jury decide a case fairly, impartially, and solely on the facts presented in court? Even if the community as a whole is relatively unbiased, some citizens called for jury duty may find it difficult to keep an open mind. Few people would argue that the defendant's mother or the victim's sister could be impartial jurors, for they have a very obvious interest in the case. As we move away from this direct interest, however, the concept of bias becomes arguable. Can a person who was a mugging victim twenty years ago judge a robbery case with an open mind? Can a man whose former girlfriend has narrowly escaped rape serve as an unbiased juror in a rape trial? Some people would argue that they probably can while others would say no. Some might go so far as to say that any person who has been a crime victim will have attitudes against almost all criminal defendants.

Similar arguments can be developed about jurors for civil trials. Most of us would accept the argument that neither the plaintiff's accountant nor a man to whom the defendant owes money are likely to be impartial jurors. But can a blue-collar worker impartially consider both sides in a case where a "little guy" is suing a large corporation? Or can an executive of a large bank? Perhaps. Perhaps not.

U.S. Supreme Court Justice Charles Evans Hughes said in 1936 that impartiality is not a characteristic of who or what a person is but rather is a state of mind.[1] Nevertheless, even the "state of mind" definition lends itself to different interpretations depending on the particular jurisdiction or the judge or the lawyer. In Canada, for example, the courts have said that we must start with an initial presumption that "a juror will perform his duties in accordance with his oath." It is assumed that normally jurors will set aside whatever biases or preconceived notions they have and follow the judge's instructions. In the United States, most courts do not take this position. While the norm is to question jurors briefly about their background and knowledge of the case, in some courts prospective jurors are questioned at great length, not only about specific biases as they relate to the case at hand, but also about

more general views and attitudes that might color the way they view the plaintiff, the defendant, or the evidence. Questioning on these very broad grounds is highly controversial, however. And in recent years U.S. federal courts have been moving from a broad and sweeping concept of bias to a more narrow, restricted definition.

*   *   *

The different faces of prejudice, and the challenges the courts face in discovering them, are illustrated in the trial of two parents charged with the murder of their infant son. In May of 1978, officials of the Ontario Children's Aid Society found 14-month-old Albert Iutzi dead on a couch in his home outside a small village situated in predominantly rural but prosperous Oxford County, Ontario. An autopsy revealed that the boy had died from a brain injury, and that he had suffered multiple bone fractures in the past. Shortly thereafter, the child's parents, Royden, age 51, and Vera, age 32, were charged with second-degree murder. Each claimed no knowledge of how the death occurred and pleaded not guilty.[2] The parents were not typical citizens in many ways. Their life-style was unorthodox. Both had worked at various odd jobs when they were not on welfare. They had lived in a series of houses throughout the county. They had no automobile of their own, but instead hitchhiked along Oxford County roads and highways. Neither would win an award for sartorial splendor. Royden was a small, thin man who had a reputation for heavy drinking and an argumentative personality. Vera was a large woman with blond, unruly hair who had a history of psychiatric problems. After her first child was born, she had consented to having it put up for adoption, not because she mistreated it, but rather because she was persuaded that she could not properly care for the child. The local newspaper carried none of this information, though it did report the death of Albert and the facts that the two parents were charged and each pleaded not guilty. As the defense lawyers representing the two defendants began to prepare for trial, they quickly realized they had problems. The defendants both reported that they had been subjected to a number of threats. Then, two law students working for the defense team were threatened with physical violence. These events convinced the lawyers that prejudice against their clients was high. They turned to one of the present authors (N.V.) and asked him to conduct a survey of the community. Like the Joan Little defense team, the lawyers wanted to build a case for a change of venue. But even if the change of venue motion failed, they wanted to know what kind of prejudices their clients were facing.

The survey uncovered a wealth of interesting, but disturbing, information. Almost 70% of the people questioned had detailed knowledge of the case. One in eight persons had direct or indirect personal knowledge of the defendants: for instance, "they once rented from my family"; "my neighbors know them"; "I worked with his sister"; "I know him pretty good"; "we saw him today across the street while I was in the restaurant and we talked about him." The spontaneous comments that people gave about the case were often highly prejudicial. Almost 40% used the terms "child battering," "neglect," and "mistreatment." People disclosed a great deal of information and misinformation about the defendants and the case. Some told the interviewers about the mother's psychiatric history, about the involvement of Children's Aid, and about another child that had been "taken away because of her mistreatment of it." Others said that the father was an alcoholic, that the parents had malnourished the child, that they had put the child in a washing machine, and that they had killed the child for insurance money. The interviewers also asked whether the facts that the defendants had been arrested and charged by the police and were now standing trial created in their mind a belief that the Iutzis must be guilty. Many persons replied yes.

These results were no surprise to the defense team in light of the earlier events that had led them to commission the research. But one additional finding was totally unanticipated. The survey also asked each interviewee to indicate whether he or she believed the mother or the father was probably responsible for the death. A substantial number of persons, more often women than men, replied that the question was "irrelevant." These people stated categorically that a mother is responsible for the welfare of her child, even if the father is the one who has killed it. Therefore, she must be guilty. In short, many what held lawyers would call a "strict liability" concept of maternal responsibility, a view that is contrary to the law.

Of course, just because a large majority of people know that a crime has occurred, or even know some details about it, does not mean that they are all prejudiced. On the other hand, in the Iutzi case many people indicated not only that they had formed an opinion about the case, but what is more, had talked with and expressed their opinions to their neighbors. Common experience, as well as a body of social psychological findings, tells us that while people can change their minds, it is more difficult to do so if they have already publicly expressed an opinion about something. Thus, people who have already formed and stated an opinion might be inclined to evaluate the testimony and other trial evidence in a way that conforms with that opinion. Similarly, a number of people indicated that they knew the defendants or

some of the witnesses, and that this might determine how they would view the testimony. For example, one woman's family doctor was a witness for the prosecution. She said that she would probably give more credence to his opinion just because he was her family doctor.

Another problem arose with those people who had information that would otherwise be withheld from the jury. The facts that Vera Iutzi had a psychiatric history or had allowed a previous child to be placed for adoption, or that Roy Iutzi had a reputation for heavy drinking, were not legally relevant to the case. The lawyers were faced with some troubling questions. Even if the judge informed the jury that their deliberations should concern only the facts that came out at trial, would those jurors who knew this additional information be affected by it? In the confines of the jury room, would they convey the irrelevant facts to the other jurors? And what about the misinformation that the survey uncovered? Would some juror bring forth as truth the rumors that the Iutzis killed the child during a drinking spree or that they had previously thrown the child in a washing machine or had killed him for insurance money?

Finally, what about the more general beliefs that some people expressed? Some held the view that a mother was responsible for her child no matter what. Could they render an impartial verdict on the mother? Others expressed some beliefs about the legal system that were less than open-minded. Can a person who believes that the police don't make mistakes and that the state doesn't charge an innocent person really hold the defendant innocent unless guilt is proved beyond a reasonable doubt? After all, some people had even expressed open distaste for the defendants' general life-style and their ethnic background. On the other hand, some people who were interviewed seemed to have open minds.

When the case came to trial, the judge did not grant the change of venue for technical reasons. But he did allow the defense lawyers to ask the prospective jurors a series of questions, based around what the research had uncovered. Thus, there was an attempt to weed out those people who could not hear the Iutzi case with an open mind. A jury was eventually chosen and the defense lawyers were satisfied that it consisted of people who would evaluate the evidence fairly. Ultimately, the jury found the father not guilty, and the mother guilty of manslaughter.

The Iutzi case helps to demonstrate many of the manifestations of prejudice. A number of people in the community had formed opinions about the case or about the defendants. Some had prejudicial beliefs about the legal system and about the responsibility of mothers. Many had information and misinformation that was legally irrelevant to the trial and which might have biased the way they viewed the evidence and ultimately their verdict. While

we want to represent the community's voice on the jury, we don't want to include people who are so biased that they cannot evaluate the case fairly.

*   *   *

The *voir dire* presents an opportunity to learn about existing prejudices on the part of prospective jurors. As we described earlier, in the United States a pretrial questioning period called the *voir dire* is a routine part of every trial. Depending on the jurisdiction, it may be as brief as 20 minutes or as long as 8 hours for an average trial. In the vast majority of trials in the United States, attorneys' questioning of prospective jurors is quite limited. However, in complex cases or cases involving extensive pretrial publicity like the DeLorean trial, the *voir dire* may take weeks or even months. For example, in the Hillside Strangler trial in Los Angeles, a case which had saturated the local media, the *voir dire* and jury selection took 49 court days.[3]

During the *voir dire*, the trial judge and/or attorneys ask questions of prospective jurors to determine their qualifications for jury service, their knowledge of the defendant and the case, and attitudes toward issues or individuals in the case that could bias their views of the trial evidence. Questions may be wide-ranging or more specifically related to the case, depending on what the trial judge allows. On the basis of prospective jurors' responses to these questions, the trial judge may determine that they would have difficulty being fair and impartial jurors, and may dismiss them with a *challenge for cause*. At one time, if prospective jurors asserted that they could judge the case impartially, they were taken at their word unless they had an obvious interest in the outcome of the case. Today many judges tend to grant dismissals on somewhat broader grounds, partly because they have become increasingly knowledgeable about psychological research on the effects of unconscious biases in jurors. Often, however, attorneys feel that prospective jurors whom the judge does not dismiss for cause are, nevertheless, likely to view their side unfavorably. Such people may be eliminated from the jury through the use of *peremptory challenges*. Peremptory challenges are solely the prerogative of the lawyers, and they may be exercised without providing reasons. Both sides are given a limited number of these challenges. The exact number varies with the jurisdiction and the type of case. A typical number is six for civil disputes and many criminal matters, and twelve or more for very serious crimes.

*   *   *

Tactically, the *voir dire* is a critical part of the jury trial. The lawyers determine the composition by how people respond to the questioning. However, in addition the jurors are introduced to the attorneys, the defendant, the judge, and many legal concepts for the first time during the *voir dire*. It is a golden opportunity to educate the jurors about why it is important to keep an open mind. Some lawyers even attempt to pretry their case during the questioning. So it is perhaps not surprising that considerable lore has developed around the conduct of the *voir dire*.

A leading trial practice manual written by F. Lee Bailey and Henry Rothblatt, for instance, advises lawyers that during *voir dire*: "As you interrogate the jurors you meet them personally for the first time. You are given a chance to start selling your defense. Your questions should educate each prospective juror as to the legal principles of your defense. . . .Their answers to your questions may be effectively used in your summation; you argue that each answer is in reality a promise."[4]

Skillful questioning often enables attorneys to introduce and hopefully defuse the impact of damaging facts about their client and case. For instance, if the defendant has a prior criminal record, her attorney might ask whether the prospective juror will follow the law and not hold it against her, especially to infer that she is necessarily guilty in the present case. Usually, jurors will agree to follow the law. This simple exchange has a number of ramifications. First, the attorney has introduced in advance the client's criminal record, avoiding a more prejudicial "surprise" introduction by the prosecutor. Indeed, the defense's credibility may actually increase in the eyes of the jurors, since a damaging fact has been freely admitted. Second, the lawyer has educated the jurors about the proper use of the criminal record. Third, the lawyer has obtained a public promise not to be biased by the defendant's prior convictions. Some experimental research by psychologists suggests that this trial tactic might in fact reduce prejudice resulting from a criminal record.[5] These studies show that instructions to disregard evidence are more effective when they are given before potentially prejudicial evidence is introduced than when they are given after it. The *voir dire* question period may thus be an ideal time for a lawyer to forewarn jurors about facts that are prejudicial to the client's case.

While the primary purpose of the *voir dire* is to discover prejudiced jurors, the difficulties in achieving this goal are legion. Many judges permit only very limited questioning of prospective jurors, and these constraints on the scope of questions may interfere with the discovery of bias. Some judges conduct the questioning themselves, and do not allow the lawyers to ask additional questions. Prospective jurors are often expected to volunteer information about their own biases and to judge for themselves whether they

could be impartial jurors. But people vary greatly their ability or willingness to do so. While some people may be quite aware of their prejudices, others may be honestly unaware of them. There are obvious social pressures not to admit either to oneself or to others that one is prejudiced. Compounding these problems is the fact that some prospective jurors actually lie on the stand. In one study, jurors were interviewed after the trial. A number of them openly admitted that they had intentionally suppressed or distorted damaging information about themselves during the *voir dire*.[6] In the trial of American Indian activists at Wounded Knee, sociologist Jay Schulman testified that his surveys had revealed that three-quarters of the people in the jurisdiction were aware of the events at Wounded Knee and had followed them closely in the mass media. Yet during the questioning in the courtroom, only 40% of the jury panel members claimed they had followed the case. Schulman concluded that many people said that they were not aware of the events at Wounded Knee precisely because they wanted to serve on the jury.[7] Schulman also reported that during later personal interviews with him, a third of the prospective jurors admitted that they had consciously lied during *voir dire*.

This lack of juror candor, when combined with varying degrees of awareness about their own biases and the limits on questioning, presents a substantial challenge to attorneys. Yet many have responded creatively to the challenge. For instance, Bailey and Rothblatt, recognizing the unwillingness of people to admit their prejudices, described how attorneys should interrogate jurors about racial bias:

> Approach matters of prejudice delicately. Suppose the defendant is a Negro. . . . You would be wasting your time if you asked: "Will you be prejudiced against the accused because he is a Negro?" The "no" you receive is meaningless, as few will admit to their prejudices. Instead, you might inquire: "Have you had any experience—such as with Negroes, or with anybody who had used a knife— that might keep you from sitting on this case?" The juror's answer and the way it is given (tone, hesitancy, etc.) will give you insight into his true feelings.[8]

Many attorneys argue that they will be able to discover deeply held prejudices only if they are allowed wide latitude in the range and scope of their questioning. Consider the trial of black Communist Angela Davis in 1972. Ms. Davis had twice been fired from her job as a professor at the University of California. The first time she was fired for being a Communist. The courts ruled that her membership in the Communist Party was not a legitimate reason for dismissing her. Back at work, she was fired again, this time for "unprofessional conduct" because she spoke at political rallies. Then, on August 7, 1970, she was implicated in a sensational escape attempt in a Marin County, California courthouse that left one judge and two convicts

dead and several others wounded. Although no one claimed that she had actively participated in the convicts' escape attempt, the men used guns that were registered in her name. A week later, a warrant was issued for her arrest. She fled California, fearing that prejudice against her was so great that she could not receive a fair trial. Later, she was picked up in New York and returned to California for trial on charges that she had aided and abetted the men in the escape attempt and on conspiracy charges. In the trial, Ms. Davis acted as her own co-counsel and used a number of different lines of questioning to probe the potential racism of prospective jurors. For example, in questioning one jury panel member on employment matters:

> Q: About how many workers would you say you come into contact with . . . daily?
> A: Oh, probably in the neighborhood of 100 or more.
> Q: Well, out of those 100 or so workers, approximately how many are black?
> A: Well, in the particular group that I am in, there has been a black girl. She just quit last month to be a housewife.
> Q: How old is the black girl?
> A: Gosh, I don't know—20—25 years maybe.
> Q: Well, the reason I was saying is as you probably know, that one of the ways in which racism has expressed itself in this society is that black people are called boys and girls. I don't know whether that was what you were—
> A: No, no.
> Q: I just wanted to bring it out.[9]

Other attorneys have found repeated, rephrased versions of questions an effective method of discovering prejudice. The case of Black Panther leader Huey Newton offers an example. On October 28, 1967, at 5:00 am, two white Oakland police officers stopped Newton and a companion in their car. A shootout ensued, leaving one officer dead and Newton and the other officer wounded. Newton was charged with murder and assault on the police officers. As the case came to trial, prejudice against blacks and the radical Black Panther party was strong. Newton's attorney, Charles Garry, used the *voir dire* to try to uncover the biases of the potential jurors. In one instance, Garry repeatedly questioned an elderly, retired printer who appeared to have a problem accepting the premise that defendants are entitled to a presumption of innocence. The *voir dire* went on at some length. In reply to Garry's questions, the man would say that he could not decide on Newton's innocence until he heard the evidence. Garry argued to the judge that the man was presuming the defendant's guilt and should be excused. The prosecutor opposed this interpretation. He said it was just a matter of semantics because the man was foreign-born. The judge appeared to be agreeing with the prosecutor. Finally, Garry turned to the printer again and the following exchange settled the matter:

Garry: Mr. —, again I ask you that same question which you have answered three times to me now—
The Court: No. Please ask the question without preface.
Garry: As Huey Newton sits here next to me now, in your opinion is he absolutely innocent?
Answer: Yes.
Garry: (Raising his voice dramatically) But you don't believe it, do you?
Answer: No.
The Court: Challenge is allowed.[10]

These examples from well-known trials provide us with some information about how attorneys attempt to develop evidence for challenges for cause. Unfortunately, we know little about how frequently such challenges occur, and how judges reach the conclusion that prospective jurors are so biased that they cannot serve. In one three-year study of New Mexico courts, judges dismissed about 1 in 20 jurors for prejudice.[11] How well that proportion holds for other jurisdictions is still a matter of conjecture.

* * *

There is a lot of controversy about the appropriate conditions for conducting the *voir dire*. Should it be limited or wide-ranging? Should the attorneys or the judge alone question prospective jurors? Should questioning take place in or out of the presence of the entire jury panel? David Kairys and his colleagues at the National Jury Project[12] argue that attorneys should be allowed to ask questions. They assert that judges do not do a good job. Judges ask leading questions, suggest appropriate replies, and do not probe fully for the existence of bias. Kairys and his colleagues also contend that jurors are so awed by the judge that they shape their answers to please the judge rather than tell the truth. Thus, questioning by the judge alone may interfere with the already monumental task of discovering prejudice in jurors. In contrast to the Jury Project position, other people argue that attorneys abuse the *voir dire* by trying to indoctrinate jurors to their side of the case; persuasion attempts should take place during the trial itself, not during jury selection.

In addition to the attorney–judge questioning debate, other contentious issues involve the scope of *voir dire* questioning, whether it should be done in a group or individually, and whether prospective jurors should be interrogated in or out of the presence of other potential jurors. These practices differ greatly from court to court. Some intriguing comparisons of trials with different *voir dire* methods suggest that, for the purpose of eliminating prejudiced jurors, individual, private, extensive questioning by attorneys is the superior method. In an affidavit he submitted in a 1974 civil case, psychologist

Richard Christie argued that this method should be used because it was better able to expose the biases of prospective jurors. To substantiate his claim, Christie compared the number of successful challenges for cause in several well-known trials. In three trials in which the judge conducted group questioning and the questions were narrow in scope, the judge dismissed a juror for cause an average of only 1.7 times per trial. In three *voir dires* that Christie labeled "intermediate," the judge conducted both group *voir dire* and individual questioning of jurors. Attorneys could suggest questions to the judge, but except for pretrial publicity issues, the questions were not extensive. In these three intermediate trials, an average of 6 challenges for cause were successful. The greatest success, however, was in a case in which prospective jurors were questioned individually by the judge and the attorneys, and a wide latitude of questioning was allowed. In that case, 27 prospective jurors were dismissed for cause by the judge.[13] Similarly, during another trial where the judge permitted attorneys individual and extensive interrogation of prospective jurors, 41 people were successfully challenged for cause.[13] Of course, these results may not be due exclusively to the type of *voir dire*, since the judges may have allowed extensive questioning by lawyers primarily because the cases involved more prejudice than the narrow and intermediate cases. Yet, psychologists Michael Nietzel and Ronald Dillehay[14] discovered a similar pattern in Kentucky when they compared death penalty trials with different *voir dire* procedures. Cases in which attorneys were able to question prospective jurors privately and extensively yielded the highest number of successful challenges for cause, while those with more limited *voir dires* resulted in the fewest dismissals of jurors for cause. These results are tantalizing. They suggest that an attorney-conducted *voir dire* may result in a less biased jury than one conducted by a judge, since more individuals are eliminated for prejudice through this method than with any other.

*   *   *

In contrast to the challenge for cause, which is the prerogative of the judge, the peremptory challenge is the exclusive province of the attorney. Even if the judge is satisfied that a prospective juror is not biased, the lawyer for either side may eliminate that person from the jury through a peremptory challenge. Because attorneys do not have to give a reason for a peremptory challenge, it strikes some people, especially some of the eliminated jurors, as unfair. But law professor Barbara Babcock maintains that the peremptory challenge is valuable because it allows defendants some choice about who will sit in judgment on them. Suppose that you are involved in a legal case

and you are convinced that a particular prospective juror is biased against you, even though the judge doesn't share your insight. The option of eliminating that person through a peremptory challenge may help you to accept the verdict as reasonable even if it should not be in your favor.

Given the difficulty in spotting bias and the consequent difficulty of proving it to the trial judge, the peremptory challenge may serve a valuable supplementary role in rejecting potentially biased jurors. But problems confront attorneys attempting to exercise their peremptories in an effective, intelligent way. In contrast to highly publicized cases, in many ordinary trials lawyers do not have the time or are not allowed extensive *voir dire* questioning. In these cases, information about jurors is often limited to their names, obvious physical characteristics like gender, race, and appearance, as well as occupations, leaving lawyers little on which to base their challenges.

Given these constraints, attorneys oftentimes display remarkable ingenuity in using what's available to develop rules for challenging jurors. Gender and occupation frequently form the basis for exercising challenges. A comparison of trial tactics manuals reveals a wealth of advice that is often contradictory, however. Take the example of the sex of the juror. Clarence Darrow offered the categorical advice to avoid women in all defense cases.[15] Others recommend choosing women for the defense if the principal witness against one's client is female, under the assumption that women are somewhat distrustful of other women.[16] Another view hints that "women's intuition" may assist an attorney who can't win a case on the facts alone.[17] Moreover, other lawyers have volunteered that old women wearing too much makeup are usually unstable.[17] Then, of course, the challenge to Darrow: the common belief that women are more sympathetic than men to criminal defendants.[18]

In many jurisdictions, prospective jurors are required to indicate their occupation, and this category gives rise to some of the more creative rules for challenging. According to one expert, lawyers should challenge cabinetmakers because they want everything to fit together neatly.[19] Bailey and Rothblatt[16] counsel defense attorneys to avoid bank employees, management, and low-salaried white-collar workers. Since these individuals are trained to give or take orders, they expect others to conform as well. In contrast, salespeople, actors, artists, and writers have been exposed to a wide variety of experiences, are not easily shocked by crime, and are likelier to forgive indiscretions in others. One piece of advice that appears in several different manuals: Look for jurors whose minds can be molded, who will not resist your arguments, and who are not expert in the matters of the current case. Hence, advice to the budding young lawyer is often based on plain old-fashioned stereotypes, and conflicting or outdated ones at that.

The desire for the naive juror is strong and possibly universal. In a mock jury selection exercise that she conducts, one of the present authors (V.P.H.) assigns students to either prosecution or defense lawyer teams. She provides them with a jury list containing limited information about each prospective juror, including age, race, and occupation. Each team is allowed to eliminate up to six people from the jury list for a specific case. Invariably, people with knowledge and familiarity of law and criminal justice are removed by either the prosecution or the defense. The students explain that they just can't take a chance that the person may hold a strong and contradictory view of the case. Because of their expertise, such people would have higher prestige and credibility than other jurors. Thus, they would be particularly dangerous if they disagreed with your team.

Interviews with lawyers also give us some idea about what they desire in jurors. Some of their confessions provide a disturbing commentary on the adversary system.

Attorney Herald Price Fahringer frankly admits that jury selection involves some deception. Lawyers begin the selection process by claiming to the jury panel that their only wish is for fair and impartial jurors. Yet they do not desire impartiality but rather favorability. Fahringer argues that it is the duty of attorneys to select people for the jury who are likely to decide in favor of their clients. In jury selection, he claims, "[w]e lie to them and they in turn lie to us."[20]

In two different studies, researchers have tried to discover what rules lawyers use for selecting jurors by presenting the attorneys with lists of hypothetical jurors and asking them which jurors they would prefer in certain cases.[21] The researchers discovered that lawyers indeed relied on simple demographic variables such as age and gender in making their hypothetical decisions, although the factors they used varied for different cases. Attorneys also frequently disagreed about whom to challenge. As in the trial tactics manuals, one lawyer's juror is another lawyer's peremptory challenge.

Regardless of the foundation upon which attorneys exercise their challenges, the use of challenges can make a big difference in the composition of the jury. Studies have shown that almost one-third of all prospective jurors are eliminated by peremptory challenges.[22] Defense attorneys usually exercise two or three times as many challenges as prosecutors. One study showed, for instance, that defense attorneys peremptorily challenged an average of 22.7% of prospective jurors, compared to 7.4% dismissed by the prosecutor.[11] Why do defense attorneys usually exercise more challenges? Perhaps they believe that most people initially favor the prosecution and are biased against the defendant. A more cynical reason is that defense attorneys represent specific

clients who privately retain them; they therefore may challenge more aggressively to preserve the appearance of working assiduously for their clients. Also, state laws usually provide the defense with more peremptory challenges than the prosecution.

While prosecutors typically do not challenge as frequently as defense attorneys, an ominous pattern has been noticed by some observers: Prosecutors are more likely to peremptorily challenge minorities off the jury than are defense attorneys. Several black defendants have appealed their convictions on the grounds that most or all of the prospective black jurors were peremptorily challenged by the prosecutor.

In the leading case of *Swain v. Alabama*, decided in 1965,[23] the Supreme Court, in a close decision, refused to overturn the conviction of a 19-year-old black man on Death Row. Robert Swain was convicted by an all-white jury of raping a 17-year-old white woman and was sentenced to death. Eight blacks were on Swain's jury panel, but two were excused and the prosecutor peremptorily challenged the remaining six. Furthermore, no black had served on a trial jury in Swain's county since 1950. In rejecting Swain's plea, the Court did say that if a prosecutor systematically excluded members of a racial group in case after case no matter what the circumstances, then it would violate the Constitution. However, the defendant had the burden of proving that systematic discrimination had taken place, and Swain had not done this to the Court's satisfaction. The burden of proof is heavy; in the twenty years since *Swain,* just a few defendants have successfully proven such systematic discrimination.[24] Swain's case is not an isolated one. Legal scholar Jon Van Dyke studied New Mexico courts over a period of several years and found prosecutors disproportionately challenged blacks, Hispanics, and young people.[11]

In several states, defendants have successfully appealed prosecutors' discriminatory challenging practices on the basis of their state constitution's guarantee of an impartial jury. In the 1978 case of *People v. Wheeler,*[25] black defendants in California stood trial and were found guilty of murdering a white man. The prosecutor eliminated all the blacks from the jury through peremptory challenges. The California Supreme Court held that the prosecutor's behavior had denied the defendants their right to an impartial jury which was required by the California Constitution. The Court held that if defendants can develop some evidence of systematic exclusion, then the burden shifts to the prosecutor to show that the peremptory challenges were *not* made on the basis of, for instance, race, but rather on more justifiable grounds. If the prosecutor cannot justify the peremptory challenges, then the jury must be dismissed. In California and a few other states, then, the level

of proof of systematic exclusion is not as strict as that required by the U.S. Supreme Court.[25]

*   *   *

With evidence accumulating that attorneys exercise their peremptory challenges on the basis of simple factors like race, age, gender, occupation, or on a variety of conflicting and dubious rules, we come to our final question. Just how effective are attorneys in their attempts to create favorable juries? Can they stack the jury in their favor? Harvard law professor Alan Dershowitz has disparagingly noted: "Lawyers' instincts are often the *least* trustworthy basis on which to pick jurors. All those neat rules of thumb, but no feedback. Ten years of accumulated experiences may be ten years of being wrong."[26]

False stereotypes can easily develop and even flourish under typical *voir dire* and challenge procedures. Attorneys are usually forced to exercise their peremptories on the basis of only limited information about prospective jurors. They never receive feedback on their choices, since those challenged jurors are eliminated. On the other side of the coin, the jury renders its verdict as a group. Attorneys thus seldom learn whether their hunches are correct.

Given the basis on which most of these hunches are formed, there is good reason to suspect that many of them are inaccurate. The sorts of information attorneys usually have available to them—a prospective juror's age, race, gender, and occupation—have been shown in a number of studies to be very poor predictors of verdicts and other decisions. Through jury simulation studies, psychologists have examined whether personality and demographic characteristics make a difference in reactions to and decisions about cases. In these jury simulation studies, researchers have sometimes found differences in perceptions of cases and verdicts due to age, race, gender, education, previous jury service, authoritarianism, moral reasoning ability, and attitudes toward the death penalty. However, with few exceptions (death penalty attitudes constitute a notable exception that we will discuss later), the way in which these characteristics influence verdicts varies from case to case and study to study.[27] For example, in the majority of studies there are no significant differences in the way men and women perceive and react to trials; yet a few studies find women more defense-oriented, while still others show women more favorable to the prosecutor.[28]

Another way of looking at the importance of personal characteristics is to ask this question: If all we knew about an individual were a specific attribute of him or her, how well would we be able to predict the verdict the person would reach in a trial? Social psychologist Steven Penrod took this approach.

He collected demographic and attitudinal information from 367 members of a Boston jury pool, and then asked all of them to reach verdicts in four different hypothetical cases. He used statistical techniques to determine the extent to which the verdicts could be predicted just from knowledge about the jurors' characteristics. His analyses revealed that knowledge about a juror's age, race, and gender was almost useless in predicting how people would decide cases.[29] Other researchers using similar methods have also found demographic variables to be only negligibly correlated with verdicts.[30]

A 21-month study of jury trials in Birmingham, England has confirmed the results of these simulation studies.[31] Researchers John Baldwin and Michael McConville collected background data on the 3,912 members of 326 juries in Birmingham, and compared the verdicts reached by juries varying in composition along the dimensions of age, gender, and occupation. Baldwin and McConville found no discernible differences in verdicts reached by juries of different demographic makeups.

A slight margin of success has been achieved by researchers who attempt to match attitudes toward specific types of cases with verdicts in those cases. In two different projects that we will discuss in detail in a later chapter, attitudes about rape as a crime were modestly related to decisions in hypothetical rape cases.[32] These findings suggest that an extended *voir dire*, during which prospective jurors discuss their attitudes toward the case at hand, would best be able to uncover preexisting biases.

All the psychological research conducted to date indicates that, especially under conditions of limited *voir dire* where attorneys are forced to rely on obvious personal characteristics, lawyers will be only minimally effective in securing more favorable juries. This conclusion is buttressed by the findings of an inventive project by scholars Hans Zeisel and Shari Diamond that provides a more direct evaluation of attorney effectiveness in exercising peremptory challenges.[33] As we pointed out above, the impact of the lawyer's peremptories is unknown, since challenged jurors are eliminated and the jury decides as a group. However, in Zeisel and Diamond's study of twelve actual trials, prospective jurors who had been challenged by the prosecutor or the defense attorney sat in court during the trial. Like the real jurors, they were asked to render a verdict. Zeisel and Diamond also interviewed the real jurors immediately after the trial and asked them what verdict they had favored before deliberations began. Then they compared this information with the challenged jurors' decisions. They constructed a profile of what the initial jury vote would have been if the challenged jurors had been allowed to remain on the jury. Zeisel and Diamond concluded that in at least two or three of the twelve trials, the final verdict might well have been different if the chal-

lenged jurors had not been eliminated. Thus, in at least a few cases, attorney challenges seemed to be effective in securing a more favorable jury. Zeisel and Diamond also used the challenged jurors' votes to calculate to what extent individual lawyers were effective in eliminating prospective jurors who would have later voted against their case. The lawyers' abilities were dramatically different. Some attorneys were indeed good at spotting unfavorable jurors, while others might have done as well in exercising their challenges by flipping a coin.

*   *   *

Just how important is the composition of the jury? We now know that people vary in their orientation and decisions about trials, and that the jury's composition, while not the major determinant of verdicts, may sometimes make a difference in specific cases. Yet our methods for securing an impartial jury, one uninfluenced by biases and prejudices, are not the best. We have reason to doubt lawyers' abilities to peremptorily challenge unfavorable jurors, and judges' skill in dismissing biased jurors. It is understandable that in their difficult quest for an unbiased jury within the constraints imposed upon them by the courts, attorneys have looked to social science for some assistance.

CHAPTER 6

The New "Science" of Jury Selection

In June of 1980, after 15 weeks of testimony, a federal jury deciding an antitrust suit awarded M.C.I. Communications Corporation $600 million, to be paid by the American Telephone and Telegraph Company. Antitrust awards are automatically tripled for punitive purposes, which meant that M.C.I. was to receive the largest antitrust judgment ever—the stunning amount of $1.8 billion. Although the attorneys for the winning side were jubilant, they were not really surprised by the decision. Before the trial, they had engaged jury researchers who used sophisticated social science techniques to determine which jurors would be most favorable to M.C.I., and to predict how jurors would react to the evidence.

A Chicago research firm conducted a telephone poll of local residents and supplemented it by personal interviews. In their interviews they asked questions designed to reveal whether the respondents, if they were jurors, would be likely to side with M.C.I. or with A.T.&T. They also obtained the demographic characteristics of these individuals. With computer analyses of these responses, the researchers developed demographic profiles of people who were favorable and unfavorable to M.C.I.'s case, knowledge that would later be of benefit in selecting jurors for the trial.

Next, the firm paid individuals of varying sympathy toward M.C.I. to meet on three successive evenings. On each evening, a mock jury composed of eight of these individuals listened to M.C.I.'s attorneys present abbreviated verions of both M.C.I.'s and A.T.&T.'s sides of the dispute in a minitrial. The researchers and attorneys then watched the mock jurors deliberate on the case through a one-way mirror. What they learned from behind the one-way mirror affected how the attorneys presented their side before the real jury.

M.C.I. was suing A.T.&T. for damages they alleged were due to A.T.&T.'s monopolistic practices. By law, A.T.&T. was required to share its long lines with other communication companies, and this information was presented to the simulated juries. The first evening, from behind the one-way mirror, the observers watched while the mock jurors debated heatedly about the fairness

of this law. After all, some jurors argued, why should A.T.&T. have to share its lines with competitors if it owned the lines? The attorneys learned from their experiences. The next evening, they emphasized to the mock jury that they were to decide the M.C.I.–A.T.&T. case according to the letter of the law, regardless of their personal views about its fairness. That night, the jurors did not have much trouble accepting the law.

Another lesson from the observations may have played a role in netting M.C.I. the largest antitrust award in history. In the first evening's presentation, the attorney representing M.C.I.'s side argued that M.C.I. had suffered $100 million in lost profit from A.T.&T.'s monopolistic behavior. The first mock jury decided in M.C.I.'s favor and awarded it exactly $100 million. Noting the similarity, the attorneys wondered what would happen if they avoided mentioning a specific figure. The next night they experimented, and left it to the jury's speculation how much A.T.&T. had cost M.C.I. With no exact dollar amounts to guide or constrain them, the second mock jury's award was $900 million.

Thus, from the community surveys and the mock juries, the M.C.I. attorneys learned what kinds of jurors to look for and to eliminate during the selection process. They also obtained tactical clues about how to present their case to different types of individuals. Morton Hunt, a journalist who has written about the M.C.I. case, likened it to "putting juries on the couch." In a sense, though, in M.C.I.'s attempt to put its jury on the couch, the M.C.I. team was doing more precisely and with scientific assistance what lawyers have tried to do for centuries: stack the jury in their favor. The M.C.I. team may have been *too* successful. The jury award was judged to be excessive and on appeal it was overturned. A second jury evaluating the damages awarded M.C.I. only $37.8 million.[1]

*   *   *

The techniques used by the M.C.I. team are the product of several decades of the participation of social scientists in the jury selection process. We have already described how many lawyers exercise jury challenges based on inadequate information. As early as the 1950s, some attorneys hired experts to help them make decisions in selecting jurors. Well-known trial attorneys F. Lee Bailey and Melvin Belli hired a "hypnoanalyst" in the highly publicized trials of doctors Carl Coppolino and Sam Sheppard to evaluate prospective jurors and to make recommendations for challenges.[2] Experts also helped develop effective *voir dire* questions in the 1968 trial of Black Panther Huey Newton as well as in other trials that touched on sensitive political and racial

issues. Psychologists assisted in the jury selection process during the 1960s on a case-by-case basis by helping frame questions for prospective jurors and evaluating their responses.

Although there were these early uses of experts in the jury selection process, what is often called "scientific" or "systematic" jury selection had its origins in the 1972 conspiracy trial of Catholic priests Philip and Daniel Berrigan and 5 other anti-Vietnam War protesters.[3] The charges against the defendants included conspiracy to raid draft boards, blow up heating tunnels in Washington, D.C., and kidnap Secretary of State Henry Kissinger. The federal prosecutors had a good deal of leeway in deciding where the defendants would be tried, and they settled on Harrisburg, Pennsylvania, the capital of the state and a very conservative community. By the time the case came to trial, it had already been the subject of extensive publicity. Sociologist Jay Schulman, whose sympathies were with the Berrigans and their codefendants, believed that jurors from the Harrisburg area were likely to be already prejudiced against the Berrigans. Schulman later described how he came up with the idea for systematic jury selection: "I kept thinking . . . 'There must be something I, as a social scientist, can do to help my friends. But what?' The answer—I could use my skills to get a fair jury."[4]

Schulman consulted with two other social scientists, Richard Christie and Philip Shaver, and together with the assistance of some dedicated graduate students, they designed a telephone survey of the Harrisburg area. In the survey, the researchers asked questions about issues in the upcoming trial and obtained demographic information from respondents. They supplemented the telephone survey with in-depth, face-to-face interviews. From this work, they were able to develop demographic profiles of the kinds of persons likely to be sympathetic or hostile to the Berrigans. Some of their findings surprised the defense attorneys, who initially doubted whether such surveys could tell them anything they didn't already know. For instance, the lawyers had presumed that college-educated individuals would be liberal and thus desirable defense jurors. Yet the research demonstrated that Harrisburg residents with a college education were conservative. Armed with the survey findings, the lawyers carefully questioned during *voir dire* those prospective jurors with unfavorable demographic profiles. If such jurors were not excused for cause, the defense attorneys used their peremptory challenges to eliminate them. The outcome of the case: a victory for the Berrigans and their friends, and an auspicious beginning for the new techniques of jury selection.[5]

Since that time, systematic selection techniques have been employed and refined in numerous trials. Many of the early trials in which they were used were trials with political overtones: the Vietnam Veterans Against the War

case, the Attica Prison rebellion trial, the Wounded Knee trial of Indian activists, the trial of former U.S. Attorney General John Mitchell and Maurice Stans, and the trial of Joan Little.[6] Schulman and his associates started a nonprofit organization, the National Jury Project, which conducted systematic jury selection in a number of these trials. Today, several research firms engage in jury selection on a full-time basis and use social science methods to benefit corporate clients in civil trials. The techniques were employed in the famous obscenity trial of Larry Flynt, the publisher of *Hustler* magazine, and his codefendants.[1] Thus far, the use of special jury selection techniques has remained largely an American phenomenon. Because other countries place less emphasis on jury selection, there is less potential elsewhere for interest in these methods in selecting a jury.

Although it is often an expensive undertaking, "scientific" jury selection techniques are likely to be used with greater frequency in the future, at least by those who can afford them. Exactly what are the techniques? Do they deserve the label "scientific"? Or is the more modest label of "systematic" more appropriate? Can they really make a difference in a jury's decision?

*   *   *

The centerpiece of systematic jury selection is a public opinion survey of citizens from the area of the trial. Often, a large survey is conducted by telephone in efforts to obtain a random selection of voting residents. The telephone surveys are frequently supplemented by longer face-to-face interviews with selected participants to explore issues in greater depth.

The surveys contain questions relevant to a specific case. The community survey for the Joan Little trial that was discussed in an earlier chapter, for example, asked people whether they believed Little had killed her jailer in self-defense, and inquired about attitudes toward black people and black women in particular. Specific questions about the trial are asked rather than more general questions because psychological research indicates that more specific questions are better indicators of what individuals will actually do. While the particular questions about each trial vary, respondents are always asked to provide demographic information about themselves such as age, gender, race, education, occupation, religion, and political party.

The data obtained from the community survey serve a number of functions. Most important, the pattern of differential opinions in the community is used to construct demographic profiles of "good" and "bad" jurors, just as in the M.C.I. case. This is accomplished by the use of sophisticated statistical techniques. Surprisingly, a "good" juror in one jurisdiction might well be a

"bad" juror in a different jurisdiction, even for very similar trials.[7] Psychologist Richard Christie pointed this out by comparing data from the trial of the Berrigan Brothers and those of a similar case, the Vietnam Veterans Against the War.[8] While both trials involved antiwar protest, the Berrigan trial took place in Pennsylvania whereas the Vietnam Veterans trial was held in Florida. Women in the North were *more* likely than men to be open-minded toward the antiwar defendants, but in the South were *less* open-minded than men.[9] Because the attitudes of community members often differ between jurisdictions, it is important to conduct surveys of the specific community with questions aimed at a particular trial.

Community surveys provide other valuable information to attorneys, giving them leads in formulating questions to ask during *voir dire* and in determining what trial tactics are likely to be effective with the jury. In one civil case, for example, research uncovered a good deal of opposition to the plaintiffs and their ideas. Yet, most survey respondents said that they believed that the plantiffs deserved a fair trial. The astute attorneys for the plaintiffs changed their trial strategy to emphasize the concept of fairness.[9]

The scientists working on the Joan Little trial have also pointed out that these surveys enable attorneys to estimate just what proportion of the population will be favorable to their clients. During jury selection, the defense attorneys in the Little trial challenged some moderately acceptable individuals, relying on the survey results which indicated that there was a strong probability that more favorable jurors were yet to be picked from the jury lists.[10]

What many people see as the most ominous aspect of pretrial work on jury selection is using information networks to obtain facts about the prospective jurors. In the United States, the jury panel list is available to the defense and the prosecution prior to trial. Direct contact with the jurors might well constitute illegal jury tampering, but it is not forbidden to contact people who know them, such as neighbors or business associates, to find out more about them. For instance, researchers might ask neighbors about jurors' personality, political attitudes, and whether the jurors have expressed opinions about the case. Or they might drive by jurors' homes to look for bumper stickers or other signs that would reveal the jurors' political leanings.

Despite its Big Brother aura, investigation of jury panel members is not the recent invention of modern jury researchers. Attorneys have, for many years, inquired into the lives of jurors as part of pretrial investigation work. Prosecuting attorneys, for example, routinely have the police check their files to determine whether jury members have arrest or conviction records. They have also gone much further. In the 1950s, racketeer Frank Costello was charged with income tax evasion. Before the case came to trial, government

prosecutors obtained information on individual jurors from the confidential files of the Internal Revenue Service. The government did not want jurors who had ever had any problems with the IRS, presumably because such jurors might be sympathetic to Costello's plight. A federal appeals court that reviewed Costello's case after he was convicted did not find the prosecutor's tactics unacceptable. There are also documented instances of prosecutors conducting their own information networks by having police officers contact the neighbors of prospective jurors. In Britain, the public was outraged to learn that the police had conducted secret investigations of prospective jurors in a number of cases with political overtones.[11]

Because defense attorneys are not privy to police files, they rely on personal knowledge that they or their friends have about potential jurors. In smaller communities, the reputation of many prospective jurors may be known. In larger jurisdictions, attorneys may rely on networks of interpersonal relationships. The structure of communities is not random. With knowledge of local politics, civic and business associations, and friendships, one can often readily locate individuals who know prospective jurors. Richard Christie has pointed out that this can be a risky procedure on several grounds. Many people in key positions are unwilling to cooperate with the defense; moreover, the information obtained about jurors may be erroneous. Furthermore, if potential jurors find out that they are being investigated, they may become resentful; and there is often little time between obtaining the jury list and the trial in which to gather accurate information.[7]

Information about prospective jurors also comes from observing the jurors as they sit in court awaiting *voir dire* and as they answer *voir dire* questions put to them by the judge and the attorneys. Some attorneys realize that there may be valuable information in subtle nonverbal or voice cues given off by the jurors. Recall Bailey and Rothblatt's advice in questioning jurors about prejudice during *voir dire*: "The juror's answer and the way it is given (tone, hesitancy, etc.) will give you insight into his true feelings."[12] Experts on body language have systematically observed nonverbal behavior of potential jurors in some trials. For instance, in the Joan Little trial, a body language expert observed body movements and posture, vocal intonation and hesitancy in speech, and eye contact for clues about prospective jurors' veracity and anxiety. The expert then rated them on a five-point scale of favorability to the defense.

Psychologists have also helped attorneys by rating prospective jurors' authoritarianism. Authoritarianism is a personality trait that is linked to racism, political conservatism, a punitive orientation toward defendants, and "prosecution proneness," the tendency to want to see accused persons convicted.[13]

When the *voir dire* questioning is conducted by the judge, authoritarianism ratings are based on potential jurors' reaction to the judge as an authority figure. Submissive responses and nonverbal behavior can indicate undue deference to authority. With extended *voir dire* questioning, the statements of potential jurors may also be analyzed for evidence of authoritarian values.

Juror ratings are based on probability judgments. Thus, a rater might conclude that an individual exhibits characteristics of a high authoritarian and is likely to be unfavorable to the defense. Because of the probabilistic nature of their judgments, raters can sometimes be wrong. Richard Christie worked with the defense team in the Vietnam Veterans Against the War trial. The VVAW had obtained permits for peaceful demonstrations during the 1972 Republican National Convention in Miami, Florida. Just prior to the opening of the convention, however, leaders of the VVAW were charged with conspiracy to disrupt the convention by violent means. When the VVAW case came to trial, Christie sat in the courtroom and rated the authoritarianism of prospective jurors. He and his co-workers also conducted valuable posttrial interviews with all the jurors, and attempted to validate their pretrial judgments about which jurors would be sympathetic to the defense. Many of their predictions about jurors' attitudes and the positions taken during jury deliberations were accurate, but one or two jurors deviated markedly from the predictions. A 20-year-old female student, for instance, had come across as calm and intelligent during *voir dire* questioning by the judge. Because she also was young and a student, Christie concluded that she would be a low authoritarian. However, as the researchers learned in their lengthy posttrial interview with her, nothing could have been further from the truth. She came from an extremely conservative family and was an ardent advocate of Ayn Rand's philosophy. Every night of the month-long trial, this juror made extensive notes of the prosecution's case but took no notes of defense arguments. She was able to use these notes to support her pro-prosecution position during jury deliberation.[7]

For more than forty years, social psychologists and sociologists have studied the dynamics of interaction in small groups, including the phenomena of leadership selection, the formation of friendships and alliances, and the resolution of conflict. Psychologists have used the findings from this research on group dynamics to predict how certain potential jurors will interact if they are selected for the jury.

One consistent finding from the group dynamics literature is that the status, power, and privileges individuals hold in society are usually reflected in their roles in the small group. Persons of high status—men, whites, those with prestige occupations, higher education, and age—are more often the

leaders of the jury than those with lower external status. During jury selection it is worth paying special attention to the attitudes of high-status individuals, since they are likely to be extremely influential in determining the verdict.

The findings of group dynamics helped the defense team for the VVAW calculate who was likely to be jury foreperson and how subgroups would form in the jury.[7] These insights determined several of their jury selection choices. The defense team's strategy centered around the fact that Juror No. 1, a college-educated white woman who was married to a university administrator, appeared to be a natural leader. She was rated by the defense expert as low in authoritarianism, and she had not been challenged by the prosecution. According to network information sources, she was politically conservative but had a reputation for fairness. Among the potential leaders on the jury, she appeared to be the most favorable to the defendants. Therefore, the defense team used peremptory challenges to eliminate high-status males who might be leadership rivals to Juror No. 1. They also tried to ensure that Juror No. 1 would have some allies on the jury, since she would be less likely to capitulate to others if she had social support.

Another discovery from research on group behavior, that high authoritarians succumb more easily to group pressure than low authoritarians, also proved useful to the defense team. There were two young men, labeled "rednecks" by the defense team, both of relatively low status, whose demographic profiles and courtroom ratings indicated that they would be favorable to the prosecution. They were also very inarticulate, a characteristic which lessened their ability to be persuasive in the jury deliberation. The defense team assumed that although these two rednecks would be unfavorable to the defendants, they were unlikely to do much harm. Therefore, the defense did not challenge them.

In addition to the opinions of experts, the intuition of trial attorneys and clients also plays an important role in deciding whom to challenge in systematic jury selection. As we saw earlier, such views and intuitions are of unknown value. However, the insights of veteran trial lawyers, based on often extensive experience with jury trials, add an extra level of perception to the proceedings. Finally, on some occasions, others with acute powers of perception are asked to give their insights about jury selection. For example, a psychic named Richard watched potential jurors in the Joan Little case and made judgments of their auras, karma, and psychic vibrations. While the research team would not comment on the scientific merit of the psychic, they noted that he had conferred considerable publicity onto the case and helped to focus the nation's attention on the trial.[10]

When it comes to making a final decision, the research team uses a number of approaches in selecting jurors. They use demographic profiles of ideal jurors from community surveys, they learn about prospective jurors from information networks, they rate jurors on their behavior in court, they decide on the best strategies in terms of group dynamics, and they use a bit of their own and their clients' intuition. The research team in the Joan Little trial reported that all the different sources pointed to the same decision for nine out of every ten jurors. The defense would not accept a juror until all members of the team were unanimous in approving the person.[10] Thus, in the final decision process in systematic jury selection, a heavy emphasis is often placed upon team consensus about the acceptability of jurors.

*   *   *

An intriguing new development in jury research was illustrated by the M.C.I.–A.T.&T. case. It involves the use of mock juries—groups of individuals thought to mirror the characteristics of the jury that will actually hear the case. Prior to a trial, mock juries are typically presented with an abbreviated version of the case that the actual jury will hear. The mock jurors then deliberate to a group verdict. The deliberations are observed or taped, and members of the mock juries are interviewed after they reach a decision in the case. On the basis of this information, the research team makes suggestions to the attorneys about what kinds of jurors to seek or to challenge and what trial tactics will be most effective with different types of jurors. These recommendations are often incorporated into trial strategy, as in the M.C.I.–A.T.&T. case.

The mock juries bear a strong resemblance not only to the groups studied by experimental psychologists but also to the "focus groups" of market researchers. In testing or evaluating products and advertisements, market researchers often gather together small groups of individuals who are selected to represent different segments of the market. A discussion leader guides group discussion about people's thoughts and reactions to the product. Market researchers favor focus groups because they believe that group discussions reveal people's reactions to products in more depth and detail than standard interviews. Typically, large-scale interview studies and focus groups are used in conjunction with each other. In the sense that attorneys are trying to sell a "product," that is their "brand" of the case as opposed to the competitor's brand, trial lawyers are confronted with a task similar to that of the market researcher: how to get the public, or the jury, to buy their goods.

The M.C.I. team presented different versions of their case to mock juries on three successive nights, revising their tactics on the basis of the previous evening's experiences. In another trial, psychologist Saul Kassin adopted a different strategy in his work with the plantiffs in the "Chevymobile" engine-switch case.[14] General Motors had installed Chevrolet engines rather than the standard Oldsmobile "Rocket" 350 engines in some 1977 models. The plaintiffs argued that GM breached its warranty by making the engine switch without informing consumers. However, the defendant GM maintained that the engines were comparable products and that such interchanging of parts was standard practice in the auto industry.

The plaintiffs' attorneys contacted Kassin and asked him to conduct some mock jury research to aid them in organizing their trial strategy. He began by recruiting eighteen randomly selected Chicagoans who were paid $100 each for their participation in a day-long research study. To avoid biasing them in favor of the plaintiffs, the participants were not told who was sponsoring the project until the end of the day.

After the eighteen participants were divided into three six-person mock juries, they watched a live mock trial, which was presided over by a judge in a federal courtroom. Two of the plaintiffs' attorneys represented their own side, while two others took the adversary's side. The trial, which lasted about five hours, included a *voir dire,* opening statements, examination of witnesses, a lunch break, closing arguments, and the judge's instructions. Then the participants individually and privately recorded the verdict and award they deemed appropriate. Next, they deliberated in their juries until a unanimous verdict was reached. The deliberations were recorded for later analysis. After the jury decisions were made, each participant filled out an extensive questionnaire tapping reactions to different witnesses, issues, and arguments of the case. They also rated how important various arguments had been in determining their decision. At the end of the session, all participants were told the purpose of the study and were interviewed by the attorneys, who asked about the impact of their style and other evidence in the case.

Kassin reports that the information from the study proved invaluable to the attorneys in refining their trial strategy. For example, the plaintiff's argument that GM tried to cover up the engine switch turned out to be extremely important. The mock jurors who believed that argument were very likely to side with the plaintiffs. In contrast, support for some other arguments the attorneys made, such as gas mileage differences between Chevrolet and Oldsmobile engines, was unrelated to jurors' verdicts. Kassin therefore recommended focusing on the coverup claims and paying little attention to the gas mileage issue. Attorneys also learned how they and the witnesses were per-

ceived by the mock jurors, which led the attorneys to modify their style and demeanor in some instances.

Moreover, the research conferred information on the finer points of jury selection. One mock juror, an employee of an import company, pointed out during the deliberation that the practice of interchanging component parts was common in her business. This, of course, supported the defendant's contention that interchanging parts was acceptable in the auto industry. Hence, this woman's mock jury decided in favor of the defense. This all served to alert the plaintiffs' team to avoid jurors with a similar occupational background.

One trial consulting firm, Litigation Sciences, used a special form of the mock jury, the "shadow jury," in consulting for an antitrust case.[15] The case was brought by California Computer Products of Anaheim against IBM. The IBM attorneys were concerned about the jury's ability to understand the complex evidence in the case. They hired Litigation Sciences to help in IBM's defense. The researchers began by recruiting a shadow jury composed of six persons who were roughly similar in background and abilities to the actual jurors who had already been selected. The six shadow jurors sat in court during the course of the trial, and each evening they telephoned the researchers to report on their impressions of the day's proceedings. Because the plaintiffs had to present their entire case first, the defendants, through the research team, were able to learn how the shadow jurors were reacting to the plaintiffs' case and whether they were confused about the evidence. It just so happened that the judge directed a verdict in favor of IBM after the plaintiffs finished presenting their side. But if the case had run its course, IBM attorneys would have used the knowledge gleaned from the shadow jury in presenting their side of the case. Questions have been raised about the usefulness of the shadow jury, particularly about whether the procedure detrimentally diverts the attention of the trial lawyer and whether the information gained outweighs the potential disruption of normal court proceedings. To our knowledge, the shadow jury has not been used since.

The mock jury serves still another purpose. By providing information about the likely verdict, it gives attorneys some information about the probability of winning the case. If the prospects of winning are unfavorable, they may be encouraged to plea-bargain, or to settle out of court prior to the trial. If the prospects are favorable, they may be encouraged to reject settlement offers altogether.

*   *   *

It is important to ask whether all of these jury selection techniques are really effective. Many well-publicized cases in which such techniques have

been employed have ended with favorable awards, acquittals, or, at worst, convictions on lesser charges. Litigation Sciences advertises in its promotional brochure: "To date, where our advice and recommendations have been employed, our clients have achieved successful results in over 95 percent of the cases in which we have been involved." The attorneys in these cases, along with the mass media and some jury researchers, often claim that the favorable decisions were due to the use of scientific jury selection. After Joan Little was acquitted, her defense lawyer, Jerry Paul, boasted to the news media that he had "bought" the verdict with a large defense fund, used particularly to support a team of jury selection experts. At the end of a highly publicized Texas murder trial, two of five defense lawyers and an advisor to the prosecutor credited the acquittals to jury selection techniques rather than to the evidence presented at trial.[16]

There are good reasons, however, to be skeptical about such claims for the effectiveness of "scientific" jury selection methods.[17] The success rate in such cases may not be due to the jury selection techniques but rather to other features of the cases. Most of the early trials in which the techniques were used were of a political nature, and centered on charges of conspiracy. Most legal experts argue that conspiracy is a very difficult charge to prove.[18] Additionally, in many of these trials, the evidence against the defendants was weak. A case in point is the Joan Little trial. While some people credited her acquittal to the survey and systematic techiques, trial Judge Hamilton Hobgood stated that the case against Joan Little was one of the weakest he had seen in 20 years on the bench.[10] Similarly, researchers Hans Zeisel and Shari Diamond analyzed the systematic jury selection used in the trial of former Attorney General John Mitchell and Maurice Stans. Although Mitchell and Stans were acquitted, Zeisel and Diamond concluded that the selection techniques themselves were useless.[19] Finally, most attorneys who have the drive and the resources to employ scientific jury selection techniques have probably prepared other aspects of their cases exceptionally well. Outstanding case preparation rather than the selection techniques may be responsible for the favorable results.

It is also important to point out that some of the individual techniques used in "scientific" jury selection are probably unreliable. Whether body language bears any relation to jurors' verdicts, for example, is still open to question. When psychologists interpret cues to predict how an individual juror will behave, they go out on a limb. Research by psychologists themselves has demonstrated that psychological ratings and other measures are often inaccurate in predicting future behavior.[20]

Some jury researchers have pointed out another potential confounding factor with systematic jury selection techniques. The research team in the Joan Little trial suggested that the selection procedures might well have had side effects, and that the side effects, rather than the systematic selection tactics, contributed to the not guilty verdict.[10] The techniques could have operated as a "placebo," or self-fulfilling prophecy. Both defense and prosecuting attorneys expected scientific jury selection to work. These expectations encouraged the defense team and discouraged the prosecutors. The jurors chosen by the experts might also have felt very special and favorably inclined toward the defense. Finally, the very extensive *voir dire* may have alerted jurors to their own biases and may have made them more committed to being impartial.

The critical issue is whether these new jury selection techniques by themselves are more effective than a good attorney using traditional selection techniques. Does the employment of a systematic approach make a difference above and beyond what an attorney normally does?[21]

It is doubtful whether we will ever have a definitive answer to this key question, and certainly not in the immediate future. For methodological as well as ethical reasons, it would be difficult if not impossible to test with certainty the impact of systematic selection techniques in the courtroom. However, theory and research in psychology indicate that the social science approach should be more effective than traditional techniques, at least in some cases. In traditional selection, attorneys often rely on general hunches and demographic variables, whereas with systematic selection the relationships between demographics and favorability to a case are established through a community survey about a specific trial. Systematic selection also has an advantage in that it combines many different ratings, whereas in traditional jury selection, an individual attorney works alone. By using multiple indices, and requiring that they all point in the same direction, one can develop more accurate predictions.[22] Moreover, extensive *voir dire* is characteristic of these trials. As we saw earlier, extensive *voir dire* appears more effective in discovering juror bias than limited *voir dire*. Taking all these factors into account, we would say that systematic jury selection should in theory indeed be more potent than traditional jury selection, especially with limited *voir dire*. Though postrial interview studies with actual jurors have revealed some mistakes, they have validated many predictions made by jury researchers.[22]

How useful are mock juries in helping lawyers to develop trial strategies? Since evidence rather than juror characteristics is the prime determinant of jury verdicts, testing the impact of different presentations or pieces of the

evidence with mock juries could potentially have a substantial effect on the outcome of a case. The major drawback with mock juries is that it is difficult to know whether the reactions of the mock jury will be the same as those of the actual jurors. They are, after all, not clones. There is no guarantee that the members of the mock jury will respond the same way as the members of the real jury. This problem can never be totally eliminated. However, it could be minimized if care is taken to ensure that the mock jury members are as similar as possible to those likely to serve on the actual jury, a reasonable number of mock juries are used so that effects based on specific individuals can be observed in proper perspective, and mock juries are substantiated and analyzed in connection with other techniques such as community surveys that reliably reflect the jury pool at large.

A final point: The particulars of the case will determine whether social science methods can be effective. In cases in which the evidence is strong either way, neither the composition of the jury nor the insights derived from mock juries are likely to make much difference. In homogeneous communities where one prospective juror is very similar to another, systematic selection is also likely to be of little use.[22] If people know little about the case in advance of the trial, or do not have decisive views about it, it may be difficult to obtain a good assessment of how the jury will respond. In contrast, when there are strong relationships between demographic variables and reactions to a case, the use of systematic techniques should be more effective.[23] Social science research could be most effective in trials where jurors' political views may strongly influence their verdicts. In brief, techniques such as community surveys and information networks are likely to be more effective than traditional attorney selection when the evidence is ambiguous, when the jury pool is heterogeneous, when demographic variables are strongly related to reactions to the case, and when the trial contains political or other issues likely to polarize jurors.

On balance, jury consultants using the tools of social science may aid the attorney in selecting the jury and in developing trial strategies, at least in some cases. However, the consultants, often abetted by the mass media and by some of the lawyers who have employed them, have claimed too much. Their prognostications, like other attempts to predict complex human behavior, are prone to substantial error. The use of the label "scientific" jury selection to describe what they do has contributed to the misunderstanding about systematic approaches to jury behavior. "Scientific" creates a mystique, an impression of accuracy and precision, that the techniques cannot deliver.

*   *   *

Assuming that these new techniques produce some benefits, should we use them? Are jury researchers undermining the possibility of a fair trial by tipping the scales of justice to the side that employs them? Does the use of the techniques destroy the public's trust in the rationality of the jury decision-making process? Should those with the kind of money to afford this research have such an advantage over their opponents? These and other ethical questions have been central to many critiques of the use of social science in the courtroom.[24]

Scholar Amitai Etzioni, for example, argued that systematic jury selection should be prohibited because it gives an unfair advantage to one side.[25] Even people who use the techniques have voiced concerns about the ethical questions. The Joan Little jury researchers, for instance, expressed apprehension that the techniques, which are very expensive, will increase the already large disparity in the quality of defense between the haves and the have-nots. If both sides use jury selection experts, the net effect could be for each side to cancel the other out while increasing the overall cost of trial by jury. Using the techniques, justice may not always be served, and some guilty defendants could be acquitted.[10]

Another question underlying the ethical issue is when does impartiality end and favorability begin? Many early jury researchers justified their involvement in political trials on the grounds that it was otherwise impossible for the politically unpopular defendants to get a fair trial. Yet the field of jury research has undergone a transformation. Such research is increasingly being used by large corporations and wealthy clients, who already have tremendous resources at their disposal and who make no bones about wanting a favorable rather than an impartial jury.

Other critics have focused not so much on the trial itself as on the public perception of the trial. They maintain that the legitimacy of the trial and resulting verdict are undermined by the use of systematic techniques. The image of social scientists is also tarnished by their participation in the adversarial attempt to obtain favorable juries.[9]

Most, though not all, of these criticisms appear to stem from two sources: the belief that it is somehow improper to "select" the jurors who will sit on a case, a belief reminiscent of the criticisms of the British barristers; and a general mistrust of the adversary system. To the extent that "scientific" jury selection systematizes what attorneys do anyway, criticisms of its use are largely attacks on the adversarial roles played by attorneys in the jury process. As we discussed earlier, the ideal goal of jury selection is a fair and impartial jury; the aim of the *voir dire* and challenge process is to secure such a jury. Within the adversarial context, it is presumed that each side will eliminate

those prospective jurors most favorable to the other side and that the end result will be an impartial jury. Yet this assumes equal resources and skills for the two sides. The viability of the adversary system to ensure a fair and impartial jury and trial, in jury selection as well as in other stages of the trial, is sorely tested when the adversaries possess unequal resources. In this light, the major ethical problem with social science in the courtroom is not the techniques themselves but rather the fact that in our society the condition for equality of resources is most often not met. Jury experts may exacerbate the impact of such disparities. There are no easy answers in this ethical quagmire, since the issues extend beyond the techniques themselves to the nature and functioning of the adversary system itself. But the ethical issues must constantly be confronted by those who conduct and by those who benefit from the new developments in jury selection.

PART III

Jury Decisions

CHAPTER 7

Inside the Jury Room

From the start, the murder of the Scarsdale diet doctor captured the popular imagination. Partly it was the fame of the victim. Dr. Herman Tarnower, a respected internist and cardiologist, had become a household name with the 1979 publication of his bestseller, *The Complete Scarsdale Medical Diet.* Partly, it was sympathy for the defendant. Jean Harris, headmistress of the exclusive Madeira School for young women, had been Tarnower's lover for 14 years. Some observers saw her rather than Tarnower as the real victim. Those who had experienced sexual jealousy, or had been subjected to contemptuous behavior on the part of a former lover, took particular interest in this case. The love triangle included the 69-year-old bachelor Tarnower, his long-time lover Harris, who was 57, and her younger rival, Lynne Tryforos, Tarnower's nurse and secretary, a woman half his age, with whom he'd been spending more and more time. The public was intrigued too by the highly emotionally charged events leading up to the tragedy: Tarnower's rejection of Harris, Harris's depressions, drug-taking, and desperate attempts to regain his favor; Harris's agonizing five-hour drive from the Madeira School in Virginia to Tarnower's home in Purchase, New York, on the night of the fatal shooting.

During the three-month trial, Harris took the stand to maintain her innocence, claiming that she had wanted Tarnower to kill *her* and that his death by her hand was accidental. As these and other details emerged, public attention focused increasingly on the jury. What would they do? How would they evaluate the competing claims of prosecution and defense? Would they be prejudiced by Harris's arrogance on the stand, or by Tarnower's status or infidelities? There were eight women jurors. Would they, the press wondered, take Harris's side and the four male jurors identify with Tarnower's point of view?

Interest in the jury mounted when they retired to deliberate. The jury failed to reach a verdict within the first few hours, as many had expected. As their deliberations extended to days, interest became even more acute.

There were only a few clues about what was transpiring. On the first day of deliberations, the jurors asked that all the exhibits be given to them. The next day, they asked that all the testimony about the shooting be read to them. On subsequent days, they also asked for a repetition of the testimony concerning Mrs. Harris's actions on the day of the shooting. On several occasions, they asked the judge to clarify the legal meaning of "intent" which they had to find in order to convict the defendant of second-degree murder.

After eight days and nearly 48 hours of deliberation, the jury filed in to report its verdict. It's said by experienced court watchers that jurors who reach verdicts of not guilty usually look at the defendant as they come into the courtroom, while juries set on conviction studiously avoid eye contact. One courtroom observer noted that these jurors averted their gaze from Jean Harris as the foreman announced that they had found her guilty of the most serious charge against her, second-degree murder.[1]

Usually one learns almost nothing about what goes on behind the sacrosanct door of the jury room. During deliberations, the door is locked. No one can go in the jury room, and jurors can't go out. Normally, we are left to infer or imagine the issues in debate and the clash of personalities, the key arguments or pieces of evidence on which a verdict stands or falls. But the Harris case was different. A number of jurors agreed to interviews after the trial. The account of how jurors reached their verdict was front-page news.[2]

The picture that emerged from these interviews was one of active, dedicated jurors who took their task extremely seriously. Like most juries, the jurors were divided when they began their deliberations. According to one report, four jurors initially felt Mrs. Harris was not guilty, while the others believed she was guilty or were undecided. The key evidence that ultimately helped to unite the group and convict Harris was her own testimony. Harris said on the stand that she was holding the gun to her own left temple, about to commit suicide, when Tarnower seized it and accidentally shot himself in the hand. There were numerous reenactments of the night of the shooting during deliberations, with jurors "roleplaying" Tarnower and Harris. The Yonkers bus mechanic who served as jury foreman, Russell von Glahn, put on the bloodstained pajama top riddled with bullet holes that the diet doctor had worn that night. Then the jurors tried to re-create the events of the shooting the way Harris described them, and to square her account with the actual physical evidence. According to one juror, Mrs. Jackson, a New Rochelle clerical worker, "We re-enacted it a couple of ways. Von Glahn put on the pajama top and came toward us, like the testimony said. We also had the gun. Two people stood in front of each other and tried it like it was told. We couldn't see how he could have come in back of her and gotten shot in the

hand." In the end, Harris's version of the event as a thwarted suicide was just not believable. The reenactments raised serious doubts in the jurors' minds about the truth of Harris's version of the killing, and contributed strongly to their ultimate decision. Harris's defense attorney later attacked the jurors' reenactments during deliberations as "playing detective." But the jurors were fulfilling, through their role-playing, the duty with which they had been charged: evaluating the credibility of all the testimony.

Glimpses like these behind the door of the jury room are rare. Posttrial interviews with jurors are often limited to cases of national prominence; even then some or all of the jurors will not reveal what went on, or the judge will suggest that jurors not talk to reporters about the case. While some jurors have written entire books about their experiences,[3] whether their recollections are entirely accurate is open to question. For instance, one juror remembered that the initial vote in the Harris trial had been eight to convict and four to acquit, yet another juror reported that three jurors initially favored conviction, four favored acquittal, and the rest were undecided.

Although it would be interesting indeed to listen in on actual deliberations like those of the Harris jury, it is against the law. In the 1950s, as part of a large study of trial by jury, researchers obtained the permission of the judge and counsel and tape-recorded the jury deliberations in five Kansas civil cases. Even though the recordings were made only for research purposes, when the fact of the tapings became known to the public, there was a huge outcry. The taping was censured by the United States Attorney General and the researchers had to appear before the Subcommittee on Internal Security of the Senate Judiciary Committee. Over thirty jurisdictions then passed laws specifically forbidding the recording of jury deliberations.[4]

Because direct access to jury deliberation is illegal, social scientists have used other tools to discover what goes on in the jury room. In the jury simulation approach, researchers ask subjects to role play jurors. Often the researchers videotape or tape-record jurors' mock deliberations. By analyzing these discussions we can make an educated guess about what probably happens in the jury room. There are limitations to this method too, of course. Even if people are asked to decide a case, they might approach the case differently as part of a psychology experiment than if they were part of a real jury. Ultimately, we will never be absolutely sure about what goes on behind those locked doors. But the indirect knowledge we do have from jurors' own voices and from these simulation studies—has given us a pretty good idea.

Even before an actual jury retires to the privacy of the jury room, forces unconnected with the evidence presented at the trial are at work that will affect the goings-on of deliberation. Over the course of the trial, the jury

undergoes a metamorphosis from a collection of twelve individuals into an enclosed group. Alliances between members develop during recesses, over lunches, while carpooling, and even as a result of the location of the jurors' assigned seats. The social forces that promote this transformation are especially strong during an extended trial.

However, during the presentation of evidence, jurors are forbidden to discuss the one thing that is on everybody's mind: the case itself. So jurors explore similarities and differences among themselves by discussing "safe" topics like food, politics, current events, or sports. Views on these subjects provide clues to the jurors about the perspectives of their fellow jury members on the forbidden topic, the trial.

The civil case of *California Computer Products of Anaheim v. IBM* demonstrated these dynamics at work.[5] Jurors in that case never even deliberated. The judge directed a verdict for IBM after he concluded that the case against them was so weak that it should not go to the jury. Despite the fact that the jury had not deliberated, interviews conducted with jurors after the trial showed that three well-defined subgroups had already emerged: the pro-IBM group, the pro-Cal Comp group, and a third group of moderates who did not signal in any way what position they would have taken in the deliberations. The IBM group members were mostly political conservatives who believed in the value of free enterprise. Discussing current events, economics, and politics during the trial, they looked down on the Cal Comp group members, whom they considered their intellectual inferiors. In contrast, the Cal Comp group, whose natural leader was a Catholic female factory worker, talked mainly about food. They considered the IBM group as pretentious. In the last group—those who would not articulate which side they were on—sports dominated the conversation. Thus, even without deliberations, jurors in this cutoff trial had formed subgroups and alliances that would have provided networks of support during deliberation.

Once the case is concluded and the jury is sent off to deliberate, the first item of business is selecting a group leader, a foreman or forewoman. Sometimes local court procedures require that the first person selected for the jury automatically becomes the foreperson. If jurors select the foreperson themselves, usually only a few minutes is devoted to the process. Often, one juror will ask: "Who wants to be foreman?" A juror may nominate himself or herself or agree to the task when his or her name is suggested, usually by someone he or she has formed an alliance with during the trial. Interestingly, the first person nominated typically becomes foreperson.

Even though selecting a foreperson takes only a few minutes, the process is not as unstructured as it appears. Status in the jury room mirrors status in

the outside world. More often than not, the chance of leading the jury is highest for a white male with a college degree or postgraduate work, in a high-status occupation, and with previous jury service. Women are selected as the foreperson much less frequently than one would expect from their numbers on the jury. It's not odd that the term jury *foreman* strikes us as a *natural* term for jury leader.[6] Studies of selecting the foreperson in mock juries have revealed other interesting patterns. For example, whoever speaks first at the start of the deliberations is likely to be picked to lead the jury. Whoever sits at the head of the table (as opposed to the sides) is likely to be picked. Perhaps people look up to whoever is sitting at the end of the table, or it may be that people who pick the end seats are by temperament and status most likely to lead the jury. Indeed, high-status men are often the ones to speak first and to pick the end seats.

That isn't to say that only high-status men lead juries. Indeed, a celebrated counterinstance occurred in the trial of black Communist Angela Davis. The jury selected a woman, Mary Timothy, for that case. Even though women are not typically chosen as leaders of juries, the selection of Mary Timothy was probably no accident. Compared to a number of the other jurors, she had high external status. A college graduate, she worked at Stanford University carrying out medical research. Moreover, her husband was a lawyer. In addition, as you will see, she had already formed alliances during the trial with vocal members of the group. Witness, below, the support of Bob, a high-status male, who spoke first in the deliberations to nominate her. On her own, however, she had already shown her inclination for leadership by photocopying a suggested outline for jury deliberations and distributing copies to other jurors at an earlier stage of the trial. In Mary Timothy's account of the jury deliberation, she described how she was picked as foreperson, which gives us an intriguing glimpse into the selection process.

> No one wanted to sit down. No one knew how to get started. With all the others milling around the room, I wondered where I should sit . . . I went over to get a drink of water and when I straightened up from the fountain, the rest of the group had moved en masse to the table and were pulling out chairs and taking seats. I joined them and found that the only empty chair was at the head of the table. Each of the jurors had instinctively avoided that seat. I hesitated. I didn't want it to appear that I was assuming that I would be selected, or that I wanted the job, or that this was a fixed election.
>
> As I stood looking around the table, trying to avoid sitting in the only empty chair, Bob called out, "Mary, come sit here!" and he stood at the head of the table pulling out that chair for me to use. I sat down and he remained standing and started to speak. "I would ask the group's indulgence because I am the senior member, and would you allow me the honor of speaking first as we start our deliberations?"

There was no objection—in fact, everyone seemed pleased that he took the initiative and got things moving. He spoke briefly, saying that he knew that we were all aware of the importance of the role that we, as jurors, were playing in this historic trial and that he felt it was time to add another footnote to history and select a woman to be foreman of this jury—and he would suggest that Mary Timothy be the one.[7]

A number of jurors assented immediately. But one juror objected and nominated Jim, an Annapolis graduate and ex-Navy officer who worked as an airport flight controller. A secret ballot produced eight votes for Mary and four for Jim, hence Mary Timothy became the foreperson. Diplomatically, after the vote, Mary leaned over to Jim and asked him to stay beside her and help her with any difficult spots she couldn't handle alone. He agreed.

Occasionally, getting started proves to be a challenge for juries. Days, weeks, even months go by while jurors are required to sit passively in the jury box while attorneys, witnesses, and judges carry on the show. Forbidden to discuss the case, the jurors are constantly cautioned not to jump to conclusions. When finally it comes time to act, judges do not give jurors much guidance on how they are supposed to go about their task. Furthermore, few jurors have had any past experience on juries. It is no wonder, then, why jurors are sometimes initially bewildered as they first sit down to deliberate.

The confusion can be acute for jurors when they begin organizing the complex task before them, as the Juan Corona case in the early 1970s demonstrated. Corona, a Mexican labor contractor in Yuba City, California, was charged with 25 separate counts of murder. At that time, this was the largest alleged mass murder ever attributed to one individual in the United States. With the trial lasting almost five months, the evidence presented to the jury was massive. One hundred and seventeen witnesses had given testimony and 980 exhibits had been introduced. The courtroom itself was reserved for the jury deliberation since the exhibits would not fit into the regular jury chambers. When the time to deliberate came, the jury was at a loss as to how to start the proceedings.

Ernie Phillips, a retired Air Force sergeant who was selected as foreman, asked others how they should proceed. "[W]e can either start by talking about the evidence, meaning the knives, the gun, the blood, the vehicles, and so on, or we can start with the first body that was found and then proceed to the second body, the third body, and so on through all twenty-five. Are there any suggestions?"[8] Faye Blazek, a retired teacher, raised her hand, and said, "Well, I've been thinking during lunch, and the biggest trouble I see is the evidence. . . . [W]e can't possibly deliberate from an evidentiary point of view. I believe we'll have to go by the victims."[9] Several jurors agreed

immediately, but then Jim Owen, a naval metals inspector, stood up and said, "[H]ow can we possibly do it by the victims? There are twenty-five and not all the evidence pertains to all twenty-five dead men. Some evidence only relates to one or two of the victims. Going by the phases [of evidence] makes more sense. . . . What I'm trying to say is . . . do we consider all the victims as a whole, or do we consider all the evidence relating to all the victims or to each separate victim?"[10] After further befuddled discussion, Ernie concluded: "we're back where we started from . . . how do we begin?"[11]

At an impasse, the jurors finally decided to ask the judge for help. They notified the bailiff that they wanted to ask the judge an instructional question. As required by law, the judge reconvened the entire court—the defense attorney, the defendant Juan Corona, the prosecutor—and the courtroom filled up quickly with interested observers and representatives from the news media. Everyone's eyes were on the jurors. The crowd wanted to know what question the jurors would ask so early in their deliberations. Would it reveal how they were leaning in the mass murder case before them? The jurors felt overwhelmed. All they had wanted was a little informal conversation with the judge. But what they got was a packed courtroom and intense scrutiny.

The judge asked Ernie for the jury's question. Ernie stammered out that they were having trouble deciding the manner in which to try each case, whether evidence should be considered collectively or whether to proceed from victim to victim separately. Rather than answering directly, the judge called Corona, the defense attorney, the prosecutor, the court reporter, and the clerk into his chambers for consultation. The jury waited for what seemed like an interminable time.

The court finally reconvened. The judge, back in his place, stated:

> I believe that this one instruction provides the answer which you seek, and I will read this instruction. . . . Each count charges a separate and distinct offense. You must decide each count separately on the evidence and the law applicable to it uninfluenced by your decision on any other count. The defendant may be convicted or acquitted on any or all of the offenses charged. Your findings as to each count must be stated in a separate verdict.[12]

The judge then sent the jurors back to their deliberations, and pounded the gavel, dismissing the court.

Returning to the jury room, the jurors felt embarrassed and angry. They had wasted everyone's time, including their own, and they all agreed that the judge had been absolutely no help at all. They had hoped for some assistance, but they couldn't have gotten less help if they'd planned it. The rigidity of the proceedings, the hidden discussion in the judge's chambers, the formal instruction read by the judge—all these things seemed to conspire to prevent

them from communicating and getting the direction they needed. After some angry talk, they bantered a bit about the case. Tension eased, and they took the plunge: They began discussing the first murder victim.

The Corona case was unusually complex. In fact, juries may begin their deliberations in a diverse number of ways. A popular option is to poll the jury. Polling occurs most frequently at the beginning and toward the end of deliberation. It's done in several ways, as a Chicago study of mock juries deciding a civil suit illustrated.[13] In that study, over one-third of the juries used the *go-around,* in which jurors in turn announced their verdict preferences. Another third used *secret ballots.* Two other ways, used less frequently and typically employed later in the deliberation, were a *show of hands* and *verbal dissent,* in which only those jurors who opposed a motion or vote spoke up. When groups were far from being unanimous, the jurors typically used the go-around and secret ballots. But as groups approached unanimity, they employed a show of hands and verbal dissent more frequently.

Whichever polling method is used can affect deliberation and even the verdict itself. In the Chicago study, juries who made more use of the secret ballot were more likely to end up with a hung jury. Furthermore, juries that took polls before beginning to deliberate were the fastest to reach their verdicts. Juries that delayed voting until unanimity was reached were the slowest to reach a verdict.

A detailed study of simulated jury deliberations revealed that the manner of beginning the discussion is associated with different styles of deliberation. Professors Reid Hastie, Steven Penrod, and Nancy Pennington analyzed the content of jury deliberations and discovered two distinct approaches. In the "verdict-driven" deliberation, juries often began with a public ballot. Jurors aligned themselves with others who held similar positions, and embarked on deliberation by citing evidence in support of their positions. Throughout the verdict-driven deliberation, statements about which verdict jurors preferred and polling were frequent. In contrast, the beginning of the "evidence-driven" deliberation was devoted to a general review of the evidence rather than the identification of verdict preferences. Instead of mentioning only facts supportive of their own positions, jurors engaged in a general assessment of the evidence and tried to develop a joint account of the events related to the crime. Polling the jury occurred much later in the deliberation.[14]

Most juries are similar to that of the Harris trial: They are rarely unanimous from the start of the deliberation. To reach unanimity, jurors must weigh the strengths and weaknesses of all their different perspectives concerning the evidence. In the first stages of deliberation, jurors generally focus on the trial testimony. Later, they shift to discussion of the judge's instructions

on the law, the different verdicts they might reach, and the task of applying the law to the facts.[14] The period of open discussion and conflict is the heart of deliberation. The substance and pace of such discussions, according to jury researchers, seem erratic and disorganized:

> There is at first . . . the sense of buzzing, booming, confusion. After a while, we become accustomed to the quick fluid movement of jury discussion and realize that the talk moves in small bursts of coherence, shifting from topic to topic with remarkable flexibility. It touches an issue, leaves it, and returns again. Even casual inspection makes it evident that this is interesting and arresting human behavior. It is not a formal debate; nor, although it is mercurial and difficult to pick up, is it just excited talk.[15]

Talk of evidence dominates the deliberations. In one study, for example, over half the comments jurors made were devoted to specific testimony or other facts; another quarter concerned the judge's instructions about the law.[14] Jurors mention evidence they feel is important or confusing, solicit various views of the evidence, and confront the perceptions of others regarding the strength of the evidence.

These points can best be illustrated by letting the jurors speak for themselves. In a mock jury study one of us (V.P.H.) conducted, subjects listened to a tape-recorded summary of the facts and applicable rules of law in a case of robbery.[16] They then deliberated in groups of six until they reached a verdict. In this case involving a holdup at a food store, the cashier and the store manager were in the store at the time of the robbery, and both subsequently identified the defendant in a police lineup. A passerby was able to get the license number of the getaway car that was later linked to the defendant. Other testimony indicated that the defendant had borrowed the car from a friend at about the time of the holdup. The passerby was not able to pick the accused man out of a lineup, however. The defendant, contending that he had not committed the robbery, claimed to have been at a movie by himself at the time of the holdup. In the group discussion excerpted below, two mock jurors, Mr. C. and Ms. F., initially favored a guilty verdict, while the rest, Mr. A., Ms. B., Mr. D., and Ms. E., initially favored a not guilty verdict.

> Mr. D.: If the woman outside could have identified him the same as the other ones, maybe this would collaborate it, but she couldn't.
>
> Mr. C: Should we perhaps think about the policeman's testimony? He stated that the cashier and the owner of the store were upset, but that in his opinion, they were not too upset to be rational enough to observe carefully and with some certainty identify the accused. I mean I'm just saying, perhaps it should be considered.
>
> Mr. A.: One thing that bothers me about this is that the whole thing took 15 to 20 minutes which is a long time, and you know they would have had a fairly

reasonable length of time to observe the man, but—with him being disguised by a stocking, I think that's enough to distort the facial features. And I think too that, you know, you're so fearful that they're going to fire at you that you really don't notice that much.

Ms. E.: He had the gun at her back all the time, so she wouldn't have been looking at his face that much.

Mr. A.: Right.

Ms. E.: I guess the manager would have, some of the time.

Mr. C.: Well, she would have had the chance to see him I think when she was at the cash register.

Ms. E.: Yes.

Mr. C.: It's true there may be a few problems, but there was a positive identification.

Mr. D.: First of all, he borrowed his friend's car, right? And he knew that if that car was spotted they could trace him back to that car. Anybody in their right mind logically would not borrow somebody's car to be traced. They usually steal a car. This is ridiculous.

(General agreement.)

Mr. A.: And he wouldn't park in the parking lot of the supermarket either.

Mr. D.: No, this is stupid. It doesn't make sense. I mean a person would have the brains to think better than that.

Mr. C.: Right.

Ms. F.: I think in a moment of—you know when something like that happens, all the adrenalin in your—like when the robber came in—all the adrenalin—you remember things more vividly than you would normally. Because of the unusual circumstances.

Ms. B.: I just don't think they had an opportunity to identify him, with the stocking mask, with the kind of clarity that you would need to make that kind of identification. Now if the person standing outside the store had seen him come out, take off the stocking mask, get into the car, and then identify him, but we don't know that. That person couldn't identify him.

Mr. C.: It seems that there's evidence that the roberry was planned in that the robber had a gun and the mask. And he knew about the safe apparently. There was some plan behind it. It does seem curious that—

Mr. D.: Excuse me. This could be a set-up.

Mr. C.: Who would be setting him up?

Mr. D.: The robber, you see—

Mr. C.: But if it's—but, well, I think maybe we're going a little too far afield.

Mr. D.: Yeah, too far.

Mr. A.: There was a case in the States a couple years ago that was very circumstantial. It was two young brothers that were poor, and it was very circumstantial. The same kind of thing as this case. They had a car similar to the suspects. They looked alike—the same general description, the slight build. And they're still in prison. Because they couldn't afford a good lawyer. And there's all kinds of evidence to prove that they did not do it. That's why I would rather go the other way, and vote not guilty.

Mr. C: Well, it's true that this business of identity is really a crucial thing, and there are suspicions that mistakes are often made. I must say that I find the evidence

of the identification, the cashier and the manager, together with the circumstantial evidence linking him with the car, and linking that car with the area of the crime, now I admit that there are gaps in the story for sure, but I do find the collective evidence pretty strong, and I think it doesn't raise a reasonable doubt in my mind.

There are a number of interesting features of this deliberation. The discussion does tend to jump from one point to another and then back again. The two sides, Mr. C. and Ms. F. on the one hand, and the not guilty faction of Mr. A., Ms. B., Mr. D., and Ms. E. on the other, made comments largely consistent with their views. For instance, Mr. C. talked about the fact of a positive identification, the police officer's testimony that the victims were not so upset that they couldn't identify their assailant accurately, and the evidence linking the defendant with the crime. Ms. F., who also favored conviction, talked of the way the adrenaline rush during the robbery would enhance memory. The exactly opposite point was made by Mr. A., of the not guilty faction, who argued that fear of being shot would make the victims notice very little! Mr. D. claimed that the whole thing could be a setup, and that someone in his right mind would not borrow a car to commit a robbery. Instead he maintained that robbers usually steal cars, a statement to which everyone agreed.

While the argument that defendants aren't stupid enough to do what they're accused of may seem farfetched to us, such a view is apparently a common reaction and has been noted in other jury simulation studies.[17] Defenders of socialite Claus von Bulow, who was convicted in his first trial of the attempted murder of his millionaire wife, Sunny, raised this very point. The jury found that von Bulow had injected a dose of insulin into his wife, which caused her to slip into a coma from which doctors say she will never recover. After the verdict, von Bulow's supporters maintained that a man like von Bulow, noted for his intelligence, would never have bungled the insulin injection as he did. If he had wanted to kill Sunny, they maintained, he would have succeeded! Therefore, he could not have been the culprit.[18] His supporters may have been right; the first jury verdict was overturned by an appeals court, and in 1985 a second jury acquitted von Bulow.

Also of note in the deliberation excerpt is Mr. A.'s story about another case involving circumstantial evidence in the United States. According to Mr. A., there was "all kinds of evidence" to prove the accused men were innocent but they were convicted nevertheless. Therefore, Mr. A. was voting not guilty in the present trial. As in this example, jurors frequently bring personal knowledge as well as more direct personal experiences to bear on the case at hand.

One thing is obvious even from this brief excerpt: All jurors do not contribute equally to the discussion. In theory, every juror is supposed to have an equal say in the deliberation and verdict, but in practice there are vast differences in how much jurors talk. In this jury deliberation, Mr. C. clearly dominates the discussion, followed by Mr. D. and to a lesser extent Mr. A. But Ms. B. and Ms. F. are almost silent; each contributes only a single comment.

Research studies show that the amount of group participation is related to the characteristics of the individuals themselves. Just as external status is reflected in the selection of the foreperson of the jury, it is reflected too in who participates the most during deliberation. On the average, men speak more than women, as they do in this deliberation. Those with more education and higher-status occupations also tend to dominate the discussion. Likewise, the foreperson, usually male, is regularly one of the most active participants.[6] Research with simulated juries reveals that most juries include several people who virtually never participate in the deliberation. They have little impact on the group decision-making process; their only contribution may be to take part in the balloting. Typically, these low participators are members of large factions, that is, groups of people who share the same verdict preference. Indeed, one of the most striking patterns of participation is that the larger the faction to which a juror belongs, the less likely that juror is to speak. If only one or two jurors represent a certain position, they tend to be very active in the deliberation; but if a large number of jurors espouse a position, they each tend to speak less.[14]

As differences of opinion about the case are brought out into the open, deliberation increasingly focuses on areas of conflict. During the beginning stage of the deliberation, many comments are directed to the group at large. However, subgroups soon develop, composed of jurors who support the same view of the case. As these factions form, the mode and content of conversation shifts.[14] Now, jurors ask one another about the bases for opposing views, challenge the divergent perceptions of other jurors, and justify their own stands. This kind of conflict can make jurors uncomfortable. Not only are they locked in a room with virtual strangers with whom they disagree, but also they must reach consensus or deadlock the jury before they are released.

While most conflicts center on the evidence, personality conflicts among jurors are not rare. Publications by jurors after trials typically include at least some derogatory statements toward fellow jurors. Consider the following comment made by one juror: "Somehow, by offering the faint suggestion that he might *eventually* change his mind, Juror 6 seemed more stubborn, quixotic, and self-indulgent than he had when he was proclaiming that he would never

vote for acquittal."[19] Another juror reported that, during the course of deliberations, she was "subjected to verbal abuse, anti-Semitism, and accusations of being weak-willed and uncooperative."[20]

Occasionally, instances of personal conflict, so severe that they disable the jury, come to the attention of the court. The level of apparent animosity among jurors in one Delaware trial was so great that the Delaware Supreme Court reversed the jury's murder conviction of the defendant and ordered a new trial. The jury's problems came to light during the trial when the forewoman of the jury requested two private conferences with the trial judge. As the forewoman explained during the first interview:

> We have a problem on the jury. Let me see how I can express it. We have one jury member—for some reason or other she feels as though we are antagonistic to her. We ask her, "Well, what—what is your opinion?" And she says, "I'm tired." . . . Let me see what else. She quite often does not sit with the jury. She sits off to the side. In other words, she is not around the table.[21]

The trial judge met with the juror in question, Juror 4, who put the problem this way:

> [I] think the other jurors are a little upset with me—okay?—because I'm having problems with a few words, or the wording of some statements, and I think that because of this, they are having—they are maybe getting a little uptight with me.
> Now I can't say—I can't just do something because somebody wants me to do it. I have to feel like it's the right thing to do as far as I'm concerned. Now, if that goes along with everybody else, fine, but if it doesn't—I'm not going to use the word intimidated. Anyway I don't feel as though I can be forced into something I don't feel right about.[22]

The judge told Juror 4 to write down any questions about legal instructions and submit them to the forewoman, and the judge would answer the questions in court before the entire jury. No questions were forthcoming, however. Instead, the forewoman asked to meet again with the trial judge. During this second interview, she stated that a "heated discussion" had occurred during which Juror 4 told the other jurors to disqualify her and get an alternate.

When this information surfaced, the defense attorney called for a mistrial, arguing that the animosity among jurors and the judge's interviews with individual jurors could have intimidated some jury members, thus compromising the defendant's right to a fair trial. While the trial judge denied the mistrial motion, the Delaware Supreme Court agreed with the defense attorney that unlawful juror intimidation was a "reasonable probability" and tossed out the conviction.

Cases of disabling animosity, like the one just described, are rare. But Juror 4's plight—of being in the minority with the rest of the jury trying to convince her to talk or to change her mind—is experienced, albeit in muted, milder forms, by many jurors. Pressures to conform to the group are strong.

Most juries begin with a majority favoring one alternative or another—usually conviction. To reach unanimity, the minority will have to either convince everyone else they're wrong or change their own stances to conform with that of the rest. Many people have seen Henry Fonda's brilliant portrayal of the single juror holding out for acquittal against his eleven convicting colleagues in the film *Twelve Angry Men*. During the deliberations, Fonda convinces all eleven of his opponents that he is right and they are wrong. Despite the fact that the jury begins its deliberations with eleven of twelve for conviction, the final verdict is a unanimous "not guilty." It makes for a gripping movie, but outcomes like this one almost never occur in real life. Research studies have shown time and again that the best predictor of a jury's final decision is the distribution of opinion among the jurors at the start of the deliberations.[23] A jury beginning with eleven votes for guilty, like Henry Fonda's jury, would almost inevitably deliver a conviction. Indeed, jurors are much more likely to defect from a smaller faction than a larger one. It is only when a minority juror has initial support, in the form of other jurors with similar views, that the probability that a juror will sway the majority or hang the jury improves.

While the first ballot vote will often reveal what the final verdict will be, it is not completely predetermined. In one study of Wisconsin jurors, about a third of all the jurors said that they had changed their minds at some point during the deliberation.[74] And minorities *do* sometimes prevail. Furthermore, the criminal trial jury operates with what some have called a "leniency bias": Minority jurors arguing for acquittal are more often successful than minority jurors pressing for conviction. This is no doubt due to the high standard of proof required for conviction, "beyond a reasonable doubt." Apparently, it is easier to raise a reasonable doubt than to squelch reasonable doubts. Finally, if there are several charges against a defendant in a criminal trial, or the jury is asked to award damages in a civil trial, minority jurors can sometimes effect a compromise on the verdict or the amount of award.

Despite the fact that oftentimes jurors in the minority will eventually conform, they still retain a considerable amount of power during deliberation. Since the typical rule is that juries must be unanimous, the dissenting or unformed opinions create pressures. This may be illustrated by forewoman Mary Timothy's description of the jury deliberations during the Angela Davis trial.[25] The jury's first formal vote took place on the second day of deliber-

ations, and showed nine not guilty and three undecided on the key charge of criminal conspiracy. Each of the three undecided jurors, Michelle, Stef, and Winona, said she would like to go off by herself for a few minutes to resolve her own thoughts about the case. The majority quickly agreed and resorted to a game of cards. After half an hour or so, the undecided jurors returned, declining further discussion. A second secret ballot was taken and revealed, to the majority's shock, eleven votes for acquittal—and one for conviction. As forewoman Timothy recounted the episode:

> What had happened? What had I done wrong? Whose vote was it? Was this going to be a hung jury?
>
> Before the enormity of it had sunk in, Winona spoke up, "I am the one that voted guilty. I want you all to stop and listen to me. I came in here thinking one thing and there has been so much said, now I don't know what to think. There are things that I want to say and I feel that I have been pressured terribly. I voted *guilty* to make you stop and listen to me!"
>
> We stopped! Boy, did we stop! No one said a word.
>
> Then Ruth took over. She agreed with Winona and said that we had been rushing but that we had plenty of time—and what was it you wanted to say, Winona?[26]

After extended discussion with Winona about the parts of the case that disturbed her, the third vote was unanimous for acquittal.

Like the Angela Davis jury, most juries reach a verdict. Sometimes, cases are so clear-cut that all jurors agree easily, almost immediately on a joint decision. More often, spirited and dedicated discussion among jurors with conflicting views forges common ground with which they can all agree. But occasionally, in about one case in twenty, jurors wade unsuccessfully through the morass of evidence and the maze of differing perspectives. Despite repeated and earnest efforts to resolve conflicts, they find the gulf is too wide: They simply cannot reach unanimity. The result is a deadlocked jury.

There is quite possibly no more demoralizing experience for jurors than the inability to reach a verdict, particularly after a lengthy and tiring trial. Often, anger is expressed at the end of the deliberation at the "holdouts" who are preventing the jury from delivering a unanimous verdict. Minority jurors who insist on voting their consciences may still experience the sting of disapproval. Members of hung juries typically report their feeling that they have let the court down.

But have they? Remember that minority jurors will not hang the jury without some initial support. We can infer that trials resulting in hung juries almost always produce some substantial differences of initial opinion among jurors. Jury researcher Hans Zeisel has called the hung jury a treasured, paradoxical phenomenon. It is treasured, he explains, because it symbolizes

our legal system's respect for the minority view that is held strongly enough to thwart the will of the majority. However, it is also a paradox: The hung jury can only exist in moderation, since a great number of hung juries would disrupt the court system to an unacceptable degree.[27]

Once the eventual verdict is clear, or once jurors finally agree to disagree, the jury deliberation enters its final phase: reconciliation. Their task essentially accomplished, jurors move to heal rifts caused by the open conflict of the deliberation, to assert solidarity with one another, and to commit themselves to the final group decision. Comments exchanged across opposing factions no longer predominate. Rather, much of the conversation is directed to the group as a whole. Laughter at their shared experiences, and light-hearted talk, are common. One juror, for example, reported that after a verdict was reached in a controversial New York trial of several Black Panthers:

> We began to chat, to write our addresses down; it was Steve, of course, who would make them up into a list and send a copy to each of us. I reminded my friends that they were welcome to come to my apartment for a drink as soon as we were released.[28]

The jury's deliberation is at an end.

*   *   *

While the dynamics of the deliberation process can be captivating, some researchers have questioned their importance. They point out that jurors often make up their minds during the trial, and that usually the majority prevails. Some have compared the deliberation to the development of exposed film: "It brings out the picture, but the outcome is pre-determined."[29] There is in fact much support for this view. Nevertheless, the deliberation serves some important functions. It allows collective pooling of jurors' memory and encourages thorough consideration of the evidence and the law which helps them to interpret the evidence.[30] Jurors proceed through fact-finding in a careful, methodical manner. It also helps to clarify and solidify initial positions. For instance, in one study 10% of the jurors were undecided at the beginning of deliberation, but by the end each and every juror had developed a strong preference for a particular verdict.[14] In short, even if its impact on the ultimate verdict is modest, deliberation helps to assure the integrity of jury decision making.

Jury Competence: Twelve People of Average Ignorance?

In the fall of 1982, lawyer Norman Perl, along with three investigators from his law firm and former Aetna Insurance adjuster Willard Broune, stood trial in Minnesota on nineteen counts of mail fraud and conspiracy.[1] Perl, representing women injured by Dalkon Shield contraceptive devices, had filed many claims against Aetna Insurance and the A.H. Robins Co., developer of the Shield. Perl had placed Broune on his own payroll at the same time that he was negotiating with him as the adjuster of the women's cases. The government charged Perl with fraud on the grounds that the financial relationship with Broune negated adversarial responsibility to give "loyal and undivided services" to his two clients, that is, the women and the insurance company. The case was complicated by the fact that the government did not allege that Perl agreed to settlements that were too low for his clients or that Broune settled for amounts that were higher than Aetna should have paid. Lasting eleven weeks, the trial was marked by acrimony between prosecution and defense lawyers and arguments about the admissibility of evidence. Everyone, lawyers and observers, agreed that it was a complicated case.

The jury eventually acquitted Perl, but when *Minneapolis Tribune* reporter Dave Anderson interviewed some of the jurors after the trial, the legal competence of their verdict was called into question. One juror reported that during their deliberations, some of the jurors discussed how long a sentence Perl would get if he was found guilty, despite the fact that the judge had specifically admonished them not to take possible punishment into account. All of the jurors who were interviewed said that they had focused on the conspiracy charge because they decided that if there was no conspiracy there could be no fraud. Eventually, they decided that there was no conspiracy because there was no evidence that the fraud was planned in advance. The jurors' analysis of the relationship between the fraud and the conspiracy charges and their belief that it had to be planned in advance were contrary

to the instructions that the judge had given them—and contrary to the law. Some jurors also stated that it was difficult to ignore the judge's periodic admonitions to disregard certain statements. As one juror said, "You can't really disregard what the judge tells you to when the trial lasts so long, because you can't remember what thing you were supposed to forget."

The picture that emerges from the Perl trial interviews is that of a jury bewildered by the law, the evidence, and the histrionics of the lawyers. Was there a miscarriage of justice? Is the behavior of the jury during the Perl trial typical? Many critics of the jury would say yes to both questions.

A major criticism of those who would abolish or curtail trial by jury is that jurors are not competent to decide the complex legal and factual issues germane to many trials. This charge is directed most often against the jury in civil cases, but it is applied to the criminal jury as well. In a frequently cited quotation, Dean Griswold of Harvard Law School said in 1963:

> The jury trial is the apotheosis of the amateur. Why should anyone think that 12 persons brought in from the street, selected in various ways, for their lack of general ability, should have any special capacity for deciding controversies between persons?[2]

The English scholar Glanville Williams set forth a similar opinion in his remark asserting that "it is an understatement to describe a jury . . . as a group of twelve men of average ignorance."[3] A series of recent U.S. court cases such as *In re U.S. Financial Securities Litigation* (1979) and *In re Japanese Electronic Products Antitrust Litigation* (1980) have been fought around the issue of whether the Seventh Amendment to the Constitution protects the right to a jury trial in complex civil cases. The basic issue in these cases is whether juries possess the intellectual capacity to provide a rational evaluation of the evidence.[4]

The debate over jury competence, like many other jury issues, often invokes strongly expressed opinions by lawyers and judges. They base their claims on personal experience with juries. The difficulty is that one can find proponents on both sides arguing with equal vehemence that their position is the correct one. It is possible, however, to attempt to test the various hypotheses about jury competence by empirical means. We will describe some of these empirical studies and report their conclusions after we analyze qualitatively arguments on both sides of the debate.

The critics who argue that juries are incompetent are really making a comparative judgment with a particular alternative in mind. After all, few people, if any, would argue that trials are unnecessary, and few would want to see trial outcomes determined by the ordeal or by a flip of a coin. The

alternative to the jury is to have the judge try the case alone and render the verdict. (Another alternative could be a panel of judges or a mixed panel composed of judges and laypersons as is the practice in some of the legal systems of Europe[5]; but this alternative is seldom considered in Anglo-American jurisprudence.) The position of critics opposed to the jury, therefore, is this: A judge, who has formal training and experience in law and in the logic of evidence, is far more likely than twelve men and women taken off the street to be able to decide a case accurately and according to the law.

Federal Judge Jerome Frank, a widely respected jurist and scholar, was unsympathetic to the jury, especially in civil cases. In *Skidmore v. Baltimore & Ohio Railroad* (1948)[6] he outlined his reasoning. There are three elements that enter into a verdict: the facts of the case as presented at the trial; the law; and the application of the law to the facts. Judge Frank argued that we seldom know if the jury gets the facts straight, since all they are required to do is indicate whether the verdict is for or against the plaintiff (or in criminal cases whether the defendant is guilty or not guilty). Unlike judges, jurors do not explain the basis of their decision. Regarding the law, he argued, the jurors are ignorant of it and must have it explained to them by a judge. In his words: "[W]hile the jury can contribute nothing of value so far as the law is concerned, it has infinite capacity for mischief, for twelve men can easily misunderstand more law in a minute than the judge can explain in an hour." Further, Judge Frank argued, as to the application of the law to the facts, the general verdict merges law and facts so that we cannot know what was done: "They may have applied it in a wholly wrong way, or they may have failed to apply it at all." Frank's position was that judges, while not totally immune to logical errors or to emotional appeals, are more skilled in fact-finding—and they understand the law.

Defenders of the jury system set forth several arguments against the position taken by Judge Frank and other critics. One argument is that judges and juries do essentially the same thing but by different paths. The great trial lawyer, Louis Nizer, had this to say about judges and juries:

> Although jurors are extraordinarily right in their conclusion, it is usually based upon common sense "instincts" about right and wrong, and not on sophisticated evaluations of complicated testimony. On the other hand, a Judge, trying a case without a jury, may believe that his decision is based on refined weighing of the evidence; but . . . he, too, has an over-all, almost compulsive "feeling" about who is right and who is wrong and then supports this conclusion with legal technology. Because Judges, sometimes, consciously reject this layman's approach of who is right or wrong and restrict themselves to the precise legal weights, they come out wrong more often than the juries.[7]

Added to Nizer's arguments are the additional points that the jury is composed of twelve people compared to a single judge, and the collective wisdom of twelve heads is usually superior to that of one individual.

Another argument acknowledges that indeed juries and judges may differ, but it asserts that the reason is that juries frequently apply a measure of fairness and equity to a case that a judge, preoccupied with the fine points of the law, will ignore.[8] For example, newspapers recently carried an article about a woman who shot her common-law husband. For fifteen years she had suffered physical abuse and threats of death from him. He threatened to kill her if she reported the assaults to the police. Finally, she purchased a gun. When her husband again attacked her in a drunken rage, she took the gun and shot him in the leg. Because of the premeditated nature of her act, a judge would have felt compelled to follow the letter of the law and find her guilty, but the jury acquitted her. In short, the jury differs from the judge on the values it brings to the case and on the freedom to apply those values.

These conflicting arguments about jury competence are simply opinions, and opinions do differ. There are, however, some basic research questions that arise from the debate. Do juries and judges actually differ in their verdicts? If so, in what ways do they differ? Can the differences be ascribed to lack of jury competence, or to some other factors? Social scientists have, in fact, provided at least partial answers to these questions.

*   *   *

In the 1950s, the University of Chicago Law School's Jury Project undertook the task of discovering if and how juries differed from judges. The logic of their research strategy was simple. Since judges preside over the trial and hear the same evidence as the jury, one need only to ask the judge how he or she would have decided the case and then compare the judge's hypothetical verdict with the actual decision of the jury. The researchers enlisted over 500 judges across the United States to participate in the study. The judges eventually returned data on 3576 criminal trials. At the end of each trial the judge filled out a detailed questionnaire. The completed questionnaire described the nature of the case, the nature of the evidence, the jury's verdict, the verdict that the judge would have reached, reasons why the judge differed with the jury (if he or she differed), and other relevant information. The results were published by Professors Harry Kalven and Hans Zeisel in a 1966 book entitled *The American Jury*.[9] It is a landmark study that is continuously discussed in the literature of social science and law. It has been frequently cited in Supreme Court and lower court decisions as well.

Professors Kalven and Zeisel compared the differences in the number of convictions and acquittals between judges and jurors. In any criminal trial, the jury is faced with one of two alternative decisions: to acquit or to convict the defendant. The judge has the same two alternatives. Kalven and Zeisel simply compared the number of times the judge and jury agreed or disagreed in the sample of 3576 trials. The results of their study show that the judge and jury agreed on the verdict 78% of the time. In 64% of the cases both judge and jury agreed that the defendant was guilty, and in 14% they agreed that the defendant should be acquitted (64% + 14% = 78%). But these figures mean that the judge and jury disagreed on the remaining 22% of cases. The nature of the disagreement was interesting. Had the judges tried the cases themselves, that is, without a jury, there would have been substantially more convictions. Specifically, in 19% of the trials the jury acquitted when the judge would have said guilty. In only 3% of the cases did the jury convict when the judge would have acquitted (19% + 3% = 22%). In brief, judge and jury disagreed on the verdict in one trial out of every five; and when they did, in the vast proportion of the times the jury was more lenient than the judge.

Does the agreement rate between judge and jury differ in civil trials? Perhaps in civil cases there is even greater disagreement. Kalven and Zeisel also compared jury verdicts with judges' opinions in some 4000 civil trials.[10] Rather than a verdict of guilty or not guilty, however, both jury and judge had the option of finding for the plaintiff or for the defendant. In one sense, judge/jury agreement was remarkably similar to the criminal cases: they agreed on the verdict 78% of the time. In 47% of all cases both judge and jury found in favor of the plaintiff and in 31% they both found in favor of the defendant (47% + 31% = 78%). The disagreement, however, was more balanced than it had been in the criminal cases: 10% of the time the judge favored the plaintiff when the jury favored the defendant, and 12% of the time the judge believed the defendant should have won but the jury chose the plaintiff.

Thus, Kalven and Zeisel provided some hard statistics bearing on the jury competence debate. Though judge and jury would have reached the same verdict in four out of five trials, they disagreed on the fifth. For criminal trials the pattern of disagreement shows that the jury was usually more lenient toward the defendant than was the judge. For civil trials, the disagreement pattern was more evenly balanced between plaintiff and defendant.

With just these results, however, a jury critic might say, "Well, fine, what Kalven and Zeisel's findings suggest to me is that in one-fifth of the cases, the jury probably just didn't understand the evidence while the judge did." The research was designed, however, to provide other data bearing on this criticism. The reasoning of Kalven and Zeisel was ingenious and yet

elegantly simple. Trials differ in the degree of the complexity of evidence. Sometimes the evidence is straightforward and simple; other times it is complicated and difficult to follow. For each trial, the judge was asked to indicate whether the evidence was very difficult, somewhat difficult, or easy to comprehend. If the judge and jury disagreed on the verdict because the jurors had not understood the evidence, then surely disagreement would occur in cases in which the evidence was complex and difficult. If the disagreement was due to some other factors, then there would be no relationship between the difficulty of the evidence and disagreement. Kalven and Zeisel in fact found no relationship between "evidence difficulty" and judge/jury agreement. Judges and juries agreed just as much in easy cases as in difficult cases. This finding was supported by other data. For example, the judges were also asked to give their opinion of why the jury rendered a decision that differed from their own. Though the judges offered a wide variety of possible reasons, they virtually never said the jury did not understand the case. Kalven and Zeisel therefore concluded that, by and large, the jury does *not* misunderstand the evidence.

What then does account for the judge/jury disagreement? A number of factors were found to explain why jurors were often more lenient than judges. If the defendant had no prior criminal record, the jurors were likely to give him or her the benefit of the doubt. The jury was also more likely to interpret the standard of "beyond a reasonable doubt" in the defendant's favor. Sometimes the disagreement arose because of jury sympathy toward the defendant. Sometimes they apparently disagreed with the law itself.

Another factor that must be considered is that defendants usually may choose whether to have a jury trial or a trial before a judge. No doubt defendants tend to select trial by jury when they believe that the jury will view their case more sympathetically than the judge. In other cases where defendants think they may have a better chance before a judge, they may elect to be tried by the judge. If there were not these selection factors, and juries judged all cases (not just the ones that the defendant submitted to them), the leniency of juries might be less or could even disappear. Thus, the leniency Kalven and Zeisel discovered may be more a function of the types of cases brought before juries rather than the jury's greatheartedness.

More attention will be given to these sources of disagreement in following chapters, but the bottom line is that *The American Jury* concluded that it was not jury incompetence that caused disagreement between judge and jury.

Two other social scientists, Baldwin and McConville, conducted a study of jury trials in England that is somewhat more negative toward the jury's competence than that of Kalven and Zeisel.[11] Beginning in 1974 they examined 370 criminal trials in Birmingham, plus a number of trials in London.

About one-third of all jury trials in Birmingham ended with an acquittal for the defendant. This is very similar to what Kalven and Zeisel found.

Like Kalven and Zeisel, Baldwin and McConville obtained the views of the trial judge after the trial, but they also obtained the views of the prosecution and defense solicitors and the principal police officer involved in the case. Not surprisingly, these groups differed somewhat on their views of the case, with defense solicitors showing the most marked pro-defendant bias and the police officers the most anti-defendant bias. There was, nevertheless, some consistency in their viewpoints. Judges, for example, expressed some doubts about whether the verdict was justified in about 38% of the acquittals, while even defense solicitors expressed some doubts in over 17% of them.

Before the study began, the British researchers met with a group of judges to discuss the content of the questionnaire. Unfortunately, the judges requested the deletion of questions requiring judges to say whether a jury verdict was proper, or even whether it was contrary to expectations. Thus, Baldwin and McConville could not ask many of the questions Kalven and Zeisel asked of their judges. They had to rely on judges and other respondents to volunteer any doubts that they had about jury verdicts.

Nevertheless, there were some remarkable similarities in the results of the two studies. British judges expressed no doubts about the jury verdict in the majority of cases. Judges identified the evidence (strength of prosecution and defense cases) as the most important factor contributing to jury verdicts. In some cases, the judges believed, juries appeared to apply a fairness rule rather than the rule of law. Like the juries studied by Kalven and Zeisel, Birmingham juries took a merciful view of the facts or considered the surrounding circumstances in acquitting some defendants.

When English judges voiced doubts over verdicts, they were much more likely to disagree with jury acquittals than with jury convictions, as were the American judges. However, when Baldwin and McConville looked at those cases in which judges and others had expressed disagreement with the jury, they could find no clear-cut pattern to explain them. Some acquittals for which judges voiced doubts were decided on sympathy or equity grounds. But for most acquittals there was no obvious explanation for the differences.

In slightly more than 5% of the cases where the jury convicted rather than acquitted the defendant, the judge or the other experts expressed doubts about their decision. This difference is not much at variance with Kalven and Zeisel's finding that in 3% of cases the judge would have acquitted when the jury convicted. The explanations for disagreement which were given by the judges and others in these English cases varied, but two stood out. First, they believed that juries sometimes did not appreciate the high standard of proof

needed to convict. That is, the judge would have had a stricter standard regarding "proof beyond a reasonable doubt." Second, they believed that sometimes the juries did not comprehend the evidence or the judge's instructions on the law. But these were a small minority of overall cases.

The English and American juries differ in many ways, and the crimes they are asked to judge may differ as well. But despite Baldwin and McConville's expressed concerns about the jury, the similarity between the English findings and those of *The American Jury* appear much greater than any differences.

Sociologist Martha Myers recently conducted some research on 201 criminal juries in Indianapolis, Indiana.[12] She found that jury verdicts were usually based upon the amount of evidence brought forth at the trial, and that juries discriminated between types of evidence. They did depart from the judge's instructions, but only in special circumstances, as for example, when the cases involved a serious offense, a young victim, or an unemployed defendant. However, their departures from the law were limited, and not due to incompetence but rather the jurors' perceptions of what was fair and just.[13]

A closer look at jury decision-making processes also confirms the jury's strength as a fact-finder. In one jury simulation study we discussed previously, Professors Hastie, Penrod, and Pennington analyzed the jurors' memory for the facts and the law. They discovered that individually, jurors' memory was only moderate. However, the jury's collective memory was impressive. The researchers credited each jury with remembering a fact or a legal rule if any juror knew it. As groups, juries remembered 90% of the evidence and 80% of the judge's instructions correctly. Part of the reason for the jury's competence, then, may be its ability to combine the individual memories and perspectives of jurors.[14]

*   *   *

While the overall report card on jury competence may be good, other research does suggest that jurors may have trouble with specific instructions. The jurors in the Norman Perl trial, for example, did apparently get confused about the law, and they had trouble disregarding evidence that the judge had told them to ignore. Some lawyers believe that the nature of the problem resides in the complexity of the law—legal concepts cannot be reduced to simple lay language. Judge Frank further articulated this idea in his *Skidmore* critique:

> . . . often the judge must state . . . [the legal] rules to the jury with such niceties
> that many lawyers do not comprehend them, and it is impossible that the jury

can. Judge Bok notes that 'juries have the disadvantage . . . of being treated like children while the testimony is going on, but then being doused with a kettleful of law during the charge that would make a third-year law student blanch.'[15]

What did Judges Frank and Bok mean? Many courts have developed "pattern" or standardized instructions that judges use to explain the law to jurors. In California the following instruction is given in civil cases of negligence:

Instruction BAJI 3.11

One test that is helpful in determining whether or not a person was negligent is to ask and answer whether or not, if a person of ordinary prudence had been in the same situation and possessed of the same knowledge, he would have foreseen or anticipated that someone might have been injured as a result of his action or inaction. If such a result from certain conduct would be foreseeable by a person of ordinary prudence with like knowledge and in like situation, and if the conduct reasonably could be avoided, then not to avoid it would be negligence.

If you had to read through this legal instruction more than once to understand it, and still aren't exactly sure how it might be applied in a specific case, you have a lot of company. In the past few years, psychologists, psycholinguists, and lawyers have collaborated in a number of research projects intended to determine if jurors understand such instructions.[16] They have given people called for jury duty passages of instructions, orally or in writing, and then asked them to explain what the passages mean. Not surprisingly, given the convoluted language and special legal terms, jurors' comprehension is often very low.

Defenders of the jury have several responses to such findings. First, the jury decision really derives from the deliberations of twelve people. Any lack of comprehension on the part of individual jurors may be corrected through group discussion. Second, even if they still do not fully comprehend the instruction, the jury's decision is based upon common sense, and usually ends up at the same place as the law intended it to be. Third, they also argue that the problem lies with the instructions rather than with the jurors. The instructions should be changed, not the jury system. Jury critics, of course, disagree with this last suggestion. They claim that if you change the instructions you'll change their meaning. In this view, law is too complex to be reduced to the language of the people in the street. But is it?

Robert and Vera Charrow rewrote the California instructions by using knowledge from the field of linguistics.[17] Compare their revised version with the original.

Modified BAJI 3.11

In order to decide whether or not the defendant was negligent, there is a test you can use. Consider how a reasonably careful person would have acted in the

same situation. Specifically, in order to find the defendant negligent, you would
have to answer "yes" to the following two questions:
   1. Would a reasonably careful person have realized in advance that someone
might be injured as a result of the defendant's conduct?
   And,
   2. Could the reasonably careful person have avoided behaving as the defendant
did?
   If your answer to both these questions is "yes," then the defendant is negligent.
You can use the same test in deciding whether the plaintiff was negligent.

Research was conducted to compare the modified version with the original version. The jurors' comprehension was dramatically better with the
revised instruction.

Researchers Amiram Elwork, Bruce Sales, and James Alfini conducted
similar work with the negligence instructions used in Michigan.[18] They too
rewrote the passages, but going further than Charrow and Charrow, they
attempted to assess the effects of these changes in the context of a simulated
civil trial. Jurors viewed a realistic videotaped trial. Some of them received
the regular Michigan negligence instructions, some received the modified
instructions, and some received no instructions at all. The jurors were tested
for their ability to evaluate the evidence and apply it to reach what would be
considered a "correct" verdict under the law. The jurors who received the
regular Michigan instructions performed no better than jurors who received
no instructions at all! However, those jurors who received the rewritten instructions performed substantially better.

Attorney Lawrence Severance and psychologist Elizabeth Loftus have
shown that similar improvements can be made on instructions in criminal
trials. The form of their research was very much the same as that of Elwork,
Sales, and Alfini, and their findings were similar.[19] However, they took the
additional step of having groups of lawyers review the revised instructions
to ensure that they were legally accurate and not likely to be criticized by
appeals court judges. Thus, their study showed that not only can juror comprehension be improved, but it can be done without losing legal accuracy.

Some procedural changes might improve juror comprehension as well.
For the most part, jurors are given little advance knowledge about what is to
come in the trial or how it should be evaluated. They are simply sworn in
and the trial begins. Only after all of the evidence is presented and the
arguments are made by the opposing lawyers does the judge instruct them on
aspects of the evidence and the law. The usual rationale given by judges for
this procedure is that the jurors will be less likely to forget instructions if
they are delivered just before deliberations begin rather than at the beginning

or in the middle of the trial. It is probably valid reasoning insofar as it goes, but it ignores the possibility that instructions could be given earlier in the trial as well as at the end. Elwork, Sales, and Alfini also experimented with this approach and found that when instructions were presented at both the beginning and end of a trial, simulated jurors were better able to distinguish relevant evidence and remember it.[20]

Another procedural change that might aid jury comprehension is to allow jurors to take notes. In the majority of jurisdictions in the United States and Canada, note-taking is forbidden. Judges explain that if jurors take notes, they might miss some important testimony. Furthermore, note-takers might have undue influence in the jury room. They might be trusted more than other jurors who rely on memory, even if their notes are inaccurate.

Psychologists Larry Heuer and Steven Penrod conducted an experiment in Wisconsin courtrooms to explore how jurors, judges, and attorneys would react to such procedural changes. Working together with Wisconsin's Judicial Council, the researchers randomly assigned actual jury trials to be conducted with innovative procedures. Both civil and criminal cases were used. Overall, while the techniques had only modest impact on juror comprehension, the jurors, judges, and attorneys reacted more or less favorably to them.

In half of the Wisconsin test trials, jurors were permitted to take notes. Approximately two-thirds of them did so. Interestingly, 70% of the note-takers took less than five pages of notes during the entire trial, with about the same attention being given to the plaintiff's or prosecutor's case as to the defense's case. The jurors reported that the notes were moderately helpful. In the few instances in which jurors' notes disagreed, discussion resolved the inconsistency. Contrary to the claims of opponents of jury note-taking, jurors did not find note-taking distracting, and note-takers had no greater influence during deliberation. Wisconsin Judge Thomas Barland collected and reviewed the notes from eight trials. He found that within each trial, jurors' notes were in strong agreement. Discovering that most notes were well-organized and very articulate, the judge concluded that jurors "had far better notetaking capacity than I had realized."

One novel procedure the Judicial Council studied was allowing juries, within carefully prescribed procedures, to ask questions about trial testimony, instead of being only passive observers, as is usually the case. Judges participating in the project had allowed juror questions in just 1% of their previous trials. During the experiment, in 33 trials, jurors could submit questions for the witnesses in writing to the judge after the testimony and cross-examination of the witnesses had been completed. The attorneys could object to the questions out of the hearing of the jury, and the judge ruled on whether or not

the questions should be posed to the witnesses. In the 33 trials, jurors asked a total of 88 questions, or 2.7 questions per trial. Attorneys objected to 15 of the questions; most of the time both sides objected to the same question. The judges ruled that all of the 15 questions could not be asked. Jurors asking questions said they did so to clear up confusion or to get at something they felt was being concealed. The jurors who were allowed to suggest questions were more satisfied that witnesses had been questioned thoroughly, and that the jury had sufficient information to reach a responsible verdict.

To discover whether these and other techniques helped jurors understand and remember the evidence and the law, the researchers had the jurors take a short multiple-choice test after their trial. Most of the time the procedures did not strongly affect jurors' understanding and memory. But in criminal trials, among jurors who could ask questions, those who were given preliminary instructions about law by the judge or those who were allowed to take notes scored significantly better on the multiple-choice test compared to jurors not allowed to use these techniques. These results suggest that combined use of these procedures could indeed enhance the jury's competence. Judges concerned about jurors following the evidence and the law in a particularly complex trial might want to use some or all of these procedures.[21]

*   *   *

Even if jurors fully comprehend the instructions, they may still have difficulty following them. For instance, under the law, whether the defendant in a civil case has or does not have liability insurance should have no bearing on the verdict. It is probably a good rule. We all know that the insurance company has the means to pay generously. This might affect our judgment of whether the defendant is liable, and, if so, how much in damages the plaintiff should receive. Therefore, a rule of evidence says that the fact that the defendant has insurance coverage should not be a part of the trial. Occasionally, however, the fact slips out inadvertently during testimony. Perhaps a witness will mention, incidentally, that she heard the defendant say that he was glad that he had total insurance coverage. If such a slip does occur, the defendant's lawyer will probably object, and the judge will then instruct the jurors to disregard this information. One researcher reported an experiment which attempted to test whether such judicial admonishments are effective.[22] People called for jury duty in Chicago and St. Louis were asked to listen to a tape-recorded trial of an automobile accident. The defendant was clearly liable; the main task for the jury was to decide damages. As jurors listened

to the trial, some simulated jurors learned that the defendant was covered by insurance, while others were told that he was not covered. In half of the juries that learned that the defendant had insurance, an objection was raised by the defense attorney, and the judge admonished the jurors to disregard the insurance information. For the other half, no objection was made or further notice taken of it. After the trial was completed, the various juries deliberated and rendered their awards. Those juries that were informed that the defendant had no insurance returned an average award of $33,000. Those juries that learned that there was insurance coverage but had not been told to disregard it returned an average award of $37,000. The third group of juries, those that learned about the insurance but were admonished to disregard it, should have returned an award less than $37,000 if the legal instruction was effective. However, in fact they rendered awards averaging $46,000. The admonishment not only failed to have the intended effect, it exacerbated the problem! The jury deliberations had been tape-recorded for the study, and they yielded some interesting information. The jurors who had been admonished to disregard the insurance apparently attempted to follow the judicial admonition; either they did not discuss the insurance at all, or if someone brought it up, other jurors said that it was not to be considered. Thus, the cause of the boomerang effect was complex and subtle. Even though the jurors did not actually discuss the matter, their attention had been drawn to it and it remained in their minds, unconsciously affecting their verdicts.

A similar inability of juries to follow instructions has been demonstrated in criminal trials when a defendant's prior criminal record is brought to the attention of the jury. A legal rule of evidence states that the record of previous convictions is not to be used to prove that the defendant committed the crime with which he or she is now charged. The rule's purpose, of course, is to protect the legal principle that a person should be considered innocent until proven guilty, and he or she should not be convicted on the basis of past criminal conduct. If the accused person decides not to testify, the criminal record is never mentioned. However, if he or she does testify in order to counter the prosecutor's evidence—and most defendants do testify on their own behalf—an exception to the rule is invoked. The prosecutor can mention the defendant's prior criminal record to the jury to demonstrate that his or her testimony is not necessarily trustworthy. Presumably, people with criminal records are more likely to lie than those without criminal records. (The validity of this assumption is clearly debatable, but nevertheless the rule is an old one and prevails in most courts.) However, if the criminal record is made known to the jury, the judge must give the jurors special instructions that the criminal record can only be used by them to assess the credibility of the defendant's

testimony, not his or her actual guilt. How effective is this "limiting instruction"?

One of us (V.P.H.), along with Anthony Doob, conducted some research to test whether jurors followed the limiting instruction.[23] We presented a case of burglary to simulated jurors who deliberated in four-person juries. Some of the juries were informed that the defendant had a prior criminal record, while other juries were told nothing about it. Those that were told about the criminal record were also given a limiting instruction: The record was not to be used to determine if the defendant was guilty; it was only to be used to determine credibility, that is, whether he was to be believed as a witness. In all of the juries where no mention was made of the criminal record, the verdict was not guilty. On the other hand, among the juries that heard about the criminal record, 40% returned a verdict of guilty. This finding could, of course, be due to the fact that in light of his criminal record, the juries attributed less credibility to the defendant's claim of innocence. If so, the juries would have been operating the way that the law intended. However, by analyzing the tape-recorded deliberations, we found that this was not so. Record and no-record juries did not talk about the defendant's credibility differently. Instead, juries with the criminal record information were likely to discuss it as evidence that the defendant committed the crime. In comparison with juries with no such information, they gave the other evidence bearing on his guilt more importance.

We are thus led to the conclusion that jurors may not always be able to follow the law as it is intended to be followed. But a couple of other considerations should put this finding into context. First of all, some of the problems that jurors have with limiting instructions or disregarding evidence may stem from the confusing form in which the instructions are given. In the study described earlier, Severance and Loftus discovered that juries found the limiting instruction about the defendant's criminal record to be one of the most confusing aspects of a trial. Jurors would frequently ask the judge for further clarification of its meaning. Severance and Loftus rewrote the Washington State pattern instruction on this rule and tested its effects on some of their simulated juries. In comparison to the standard limiting instruction, the revised instruction proved not only easier to comprehend, but the jurors were also more likely to be able to apply the rule correctly. The problem, therefore, may at least partly reside in how the law is delivered by the judge rather than incapacity on the part of the jurors to follow the instructions.

Revised instructions, however, may not totally solve the problem. It is often asking a lot of human beings simply to ignore an accused person's

criminal record in dealing with guilt. After all, if we learn that a person accused of a break-and-enter offense has been convicted four previous times on similar charges, it is difficult not to draw the inference that he or she is guilty this time, regardless of what the law says we should do as jurors. The real issue, however, is whether the views of the judges themselves would be colored by such knowledge if they decided the case instead of the jury. Critics of the jury would like us to believe that because of their training, judges are immune from such natural psychological inferences. The fact is, however, that judges are not immune, whatever the critics or the judges themselves would like to think. A large body of research literature has demonstrated that judges are about as susceptible to such inferences as the rest of us.[24] Thus, as with the problem of general jury competence, the question regarding evidence instructions should not be: Are juries incompetent? Rather, the question should be: Are juries significantly less competent than judges?

The issue of jury competence is also at the core of a highly controversial— and still unresolved—debate about the ability of jurors to evaluate psychological testimony about eyewitness identification. Even some of the people who would normally defend the jury on other grounds, take the position that the jury is not competent to judge the merits of eyewitness evidence—at least without some expert assistance.

In about 5% of trials, the primary, perhaps the only, evidence against the accused person is the fact that he or she is identified as the culprit by people who were at the scene of the crime. The prosecutor asks the witness, "Can you identify the person you saw robbing the bank?" and the witness points a finger at the defendant. At least as far back as the celebrated trial and subsequent executions of Sacco and Vanzetti in Massachusetts in 1921, legal experts have been concerned with the compelling impact of eyewitness identification. Sacco and Vanzetti were convicted primarily on the basis of an eyewitness whose identification of them was suspect. There are in fact a sizeable number of documented cases in the United States and elsewhere in which a person convicted primarily on the basis of eyewitness testimony was later shown to be innocent. For example, in Canada Norman Fox was convicted of a vicious rape and sent to prison. Although he had an alibi and there was other evidence that pointed to his innocence, the rape victim positively identified him as her assailant. After spending eight and one-half years behind bars, continuously protesting his innocence, in 1984 new evidence came to light proving that another man was guilty of the crime. Fox was released and pardoned.[25] Psychologists have investigated eyewitness unreliability, documented its occurrence, explored the reasons that cause witnesses to be un-

reliable, and assessed its impact on jurors. Literally dozens of research articles and a half-dozen books on this single subject have appeared in the past few years alone.[26]

The jury is a crucial element in concern over eyewitness unreliability. The distinguished legal scholar John Wigmore noted over three-quarters of a century ago that the central question is whether jury verdicts are improperly influenced by it.[27] If juries can distinguish between reliable and unreliable eyewitness evidence, then the issue of eyewitness unreliability is of no importance because the jury can give eyewitness testimony proper weight.

Some psychologists argue, however, that jurors are too inclined to believe eyewitnesses. One of the first studies to test this notion was an experiment by Elizabeth Loftus, in which she had simulated jurors read a transcript of a robbery–murder case.[28] For some of the jurors the evidence against the accused person was only circumstantial; there was no eyewitness. For other jurors an eyewitness identified the accused person. For a final group of jurors an eyewitness was also involved, but later in the trial that witness was discredited. Evidence was produced showing that the witness could not possibly have seen the accused person as she had claimed. When there was no eyewitness, only 18% voted guilty, but when there was one, a substantial 72% did. If the jurors were responding reasonably and logically in the condition with the discredited eyewitness, their verdicts should have been similar to those with no eyewitness evidence. A discredited eyewitness should have approximately the same effect as no eyewitness at all. Instead their verdicts were more similar to those of the undiscredited eyewitness; a whopping 68% voted guilty. Hence, Loftus's research supports the thesis that jurors are overly susceptible to eyewitness identification evidence. Other studies have confirmed that, sometimes, jurors do have a tendency to believe even discredited eyewitnesses.[29]

Psychologists have uncovered other problems. One group of researchers found that jurors' beliefs in the accuracy of various witnesses was related to the apparent confidence of the witness. But confidence is a misleading indicant, since research has shown that it is not actually related to accuracy. Other studies suggest that jurors' "common sense" beliefs about eyewitness testimony are often wrong.[30] Most jurors, for example, tend to believe that the stressful condition of being a witness to a crime is likely to sharpen one's memory and increase one's accuracy. In fact, psychologists have found just the opposite to be true.

To correct this apparent susceptibility to unreliable eyewitnesses, many researchers, as well as legal scholars and practicing trial lawyers, have proposed that an expert, such as a psychologist, testify about eyewitness reliability

during the trial.[31] They argue that such expert testimony can educate the jurors about the pitfalls of eyewitness reports and prepare the jurors to evaluate eyewitnesses with a more critical eye. Recent research studies using simulated juries have lent some support to these arguments, though there are grounds upon which the studies may be criticized.[32]

On the other hand, none of the studies of actual jury performance has shown eyewitness evidence to be a pervasive problem. Kalven and Zeisel's study of judge/jury disagreement did not cite eyewitness identification as a problem significant enough even to be mentioned in their exhaustive examination of jury performance. Myers's study of Indiana juries concluded that juries assigned little weight to evidence from eyewitnesses. Even Baldwin and McConville, whose conclusions were sometimes critical of the jury, observed that identification evidence was rarely relevant to experts' dissatisfaction with jury verdicts.

The laboratory studies are not completely consistent either. For example, one of us (N.V.) and two colleagues twice failed to replicate the Loftus finding, though in a third study we found evidence that simulated jurors gave too much weight to the testimony of a discredited eyewitness.[33] At this point in time, the controversy over jurors' reactions to eyewitness testimony must be considered unresolved.

* * *

Based on the various studies examining different aspects of the jury, we can conclude that the jury has not been shown, as a general matter, to be incompetent. We can never really know if even the jury in Norman Perl's trial was incompetent. No doubt sometimes juries are. Yet, the data from studies of hundreds of jury trials and jury simulations suggest that actual incompetence is a rare phenomenon. Juries do differ sometimes from the way judges would have decided, but it is on grounds other than incompetence.

Mr. Prejudice or Miss Sympathy:
A Thirteenth Juror?

Some hard facts, as we have just seen, appear to contradict those critics who claim that the jury is incompetent. Judges agree with the jury in four cases out of five, and in the remaining case the disagreement can seldom be attributed to the jurors' intellectual ineptitude. Yet, that remaining case is troublesome because the jury goes in a direction that is different from that which a learned expert—the judge—would have taken. How do we explain this disagreement? Can we explain it? It is certainly important to make an attempt because opponents of the jury will not have exhausted all of their arguments against it.

In fact, the incompetence charge is only one argument against the jury. Critics have also claimed that the jury is swayed by subjective emotions, that its verdicts are often based upon unwarranted and irrational sympathies and prejudice. Judge Frank summarized the subjective emotions charge in a memorable and frequently quoted phrase:

> [P]rejudice has been called the thirteenth juror and it has been said that "Mr. Prejudice" and "Miss Sympathy" are the names of witnesses whose testimony is never recorded but must nevertheless be reckoned with in trials by jury.[1]

Famous trial lawyers have often made statements that are quite consistent with Judge Frank's view. Clarence Darrow asserted that

> Jurymen seldom convict a person they like, or acquit one that they dislike. The main work of a trial lawyer is to make a jury like his client, or, at least to feel sympathy for him; facts regarding the crime are relatively unimportant.[2]

Percy Foreman, known for his showmanship as a defense lawyer in murder trials, voiced a similar view.[3] Foreman's philosophy was that "[i]t is the object of the defense to prejudice the minds of all persons possible. My clients want freedom, not justice." In the courtroom, Foreman's strategy was to put someone other than his client on trial, whether it was the district attorney, the police, the prosecution witness—or the victim. He defended Ethel May

Simpson, a barmaid, who confessed to killing her husband with six shots from a revolver. Foreman discovered that there were many reasons why the man had "deserved" killing. He had poisoned dogs, stomped a puppy to death, and wrung the neck of a parakeet. On the day of his death he had threatened to kill his wife and throw her in the river. Foreman dramatized these facts at the trial with the result that, in his words, "the jury was ready to dig up the deceased and shoot him all over again." The verdict was not guilty.

Texts on trial techniques also frequently stress appeals to sympathies and prejudice.[4] Lawyers are admonished to select jurors who "will most naturally respond to an emotional appeal." It is claimed that "the jury tries the lawyers rather than the clients" and that "without realizing it, the jurors allow their opinions of evidence to be swayed in favor of the side represented by the lawyer they like." Such views have even had the imprimatur of the courts. The Supreme Court of Tennessee, for example, once concluded that "tears have always been considered legitimate arguments before a jury" and "indeed, if counsel has them at command, it may be seriously questioned whether it is not his professional duty to shed them whenever proper occasion arises. . . ."

Clearly, then, it is alleged that the jury is swayed by sympathies and prejudice. But is it true? If so, how often does it occur? What is its nature? Or has the reputation of the jury been sullied by unfounded slander, libelous accusations, and bombast from lawyers with inflated notions of their oratorical skills?

Kalven and Zeisel's study again forms a starting point. Of the one case in five where judge and jury disagreed, the jury was six times as likely to be lenient as it was to be harsh. Similarly, Baldwin and McConville concluded that about one-third of English jury acquittals were questionable and that between 5 and 10% of convictions were questionable. Thus, in terms of sheer frequency, Miss Sympathy, if she exists, is more often juror number thirteen than Mr. Prejudice.

*   *   *

The folklore of trial lawyers is filled with anecdotes of jury acquittals because of the "blond and beautiful" defendant whose appearance captivates the all-male jury or about the defendant's mother who broke down in tears as she testified at the trial, causing most of the jurors to cry with her. The judges in Kalven and Zeisel's study agreed that Miss Sympathy was sometimes found sitting in the jury box. In a petty theft case, the judge observed that the jury was sympathetic to a young defendant who was clean-cut and whose mother was with him during the entire trial.[5] In an embezzlement case, the

judge observed that while the evidence pointed toward guilt, the defendant was attractive, she claimed to have tuberculosis and wore a white mask throughout the trial, she had a loyal, well-liked husband and a twelve-year-old son, and even provided for her mother. The jury voted not guilty.[5]

The issue of verdicts based on sympathy is especially important with respect to the criminal jury. We live in a period where there is much concern about law and order. Opinion polls, which attract the attention of newspapers, judges, and politicians, continually show that "crime in the streets" is a concern of the average North American. People want the legal system to crack down on crime. If the jury is letting guilty criminals go free because of sympathy for them, what does this say about the jury as a tool of justice? Some years ago Sir Robert Mark, who later became Commissioner of the Metropolitan Police Force in London, launched a fierce attack on the English jury system precisely because he believed that it was helping to put professional criminals back on the streets. He accused defense lawyers of pandering to the sympathies and incompetence of jurors so they would return not guilty verdicts. Sir Robert did not have any evidence for his claim—beyond his own personal impressions—but his prestige and eloquence caused other critics to jump on the bandwagon with cries to curtail trial by jury.[6] Even though they have not been made as explicit, similar concerns possibly underlie recent U. S. Supreme Court decisions which curtailed some powers of the jury. The charge that juries respond to emotional factors is, therefore, not a trivial one.

As we think more deeply about the Miss Sympathy issue, we can see that she has at least two faces. One is the positive or empathetic feelings toward the criminal defendant. The other is the negative feelings about unappealing qualities of the victim. The victim might be viewed as immoral, degenerate, as almost deserving of being a victim, a fact which causes the jury to view the defendant in a less harsh light than it would if the victim was neutral or even an attractive character.

The notions embodied in the idea of Miss Sympathy appeal to our common sense notion of human reactions. The handsome, remorseful young man, the matronly kind widow, the handicapped war veteran is more likely to receive the benefit of our doubts than someone without these qualities. Conversely, if the victim is a mean, quarrelsome sort, or a former prostitute, we may lean toward the defendant. These views are also consistent with psychological research on interpersonal attraction which has demonstrated that we are attracted to people who are beautiful or who hold attitudes and beliefs that are similar to our own; and we are sometimes repelled by people who are ugly or dissimilar.

Probably because of lawyers' folklore, common sense, and the body of

research on interpersonal attraction, social psychologists have conducted a large number of studies attempting to assess the sympathy hypotheses.[7] Most of these research projects have been simulation studies; they relied on college students who rendered individual verdicts rather than deliberated in a group as real jurors do. However, the studies have attempted to tease out factors that might affect the sympathies: for example, the sex of defendants, their socioeconomic status, their moral character, their attractiveness, and their attitude similarity to the juror. Interestingly, the studies are often contradictory. Some studies, for example, have found socioeconomic status (e.g., poverty or wealth, and level of education) of the defendants to have an effect while others have not. There are a few consistent findings. Jurors in these experiments are more likely to convict when the defendant is of lower moral character or if the victim is of higher moral character. When defendants have incurred severe injury during the criminal act, jurors are inclined to treat them more leniently. Defendant attractiveness appears to have no general effect except in instances where the attractiveness might facilitate the defendant's ability to commit the crime. An example would be the extraordinarily handsome man who preys upon and defrauds lonely widows. Yet, after conducting a systematic review of many of these studies, Francis Dane and Lawrence Wrightsman were led to the conclusion that "it remains difficult to state that extralegal characteristics [i.e., sympathies involving the defendant or victim] are of sufficient strength to override the legal evidence presented during a trial."[8]

But what do studies of real juries indicate? Kalven and Zeisel also examined the Miss Sympathy hypothesis in their study of the American jury and found that sometimes she was present,[9] at least if we accept the presiding trial judge's interpretation. Defendants who were older or young sometimes engendered chords of sympathy. After a trial involving aggravated assault, the judge commented that "[the] defendant was an old man. He made a rather pathetic appearance." In a case involving an acquittal for drunken driving, the judge expressed his belief that it was because the defendant was an elderly tenant farmer who had no criminal record and was an honest, hard worker. In a grand larceny trial that resulted in an acquittal, the judge commented: "not a bad looking youngster—sympathy for youth from a less-chance home. Father dead two years."

Females were also occasionally alleged to be the recipients of sympathy: "I believe that in this case [drunken driving charge] the jury was sympathetic with a woman who had no previous record and whose testimony showed she was not a heavy drinker"; the defendant charged with making an illegal sale of liquor was an "attractive young lady tried to an all male jury." Sometimes,

males who were exceptionally attractive were also the recipient of jury largess: "jury was composed of nine women [and three men] who felt sorry for the young good looking defendant" accused of burglary.

On the other side of the coin, defendants with severe disabilities or disfigurement also engendered sympathies. In a case involving indecent exposure, the judge wrote that the defendant "came into court with crutches. He was a crippled polio victim. He cried on the stand and obtained the jury's sympathy." In a trial for statutory rape, the defendant "had lost a leg in Korea and presented a sorry spectacle." Also, if the defendant appeared remorseful for the act, the jury again might be inclined to vote not guilty.

Finally, Kalven and Zeisel's research uncovered a number of cases where, according to the judge, the jury ignored the evidence because of the defendant's spouse, or children, or other family members. In a trial for theft: "The fact that the wife of one of the defendants was present and made a good appearance and seemed extremely agitated and concerned [plus t]he fact that she lost control of emotions in a quiet and inoffensive manner contributed to [the acquittal]." In a robbery trial, the defendant was middle-aged and the judge concluded that the "jury [was] probably impressed by the fact that he was a belated college student with wife and children; they were unable to overcome their sympathy in [a] belief that the defendant should be given another chance."

So do we conclude that the jury has a bleeding heart? Let's not rush to such judgment. First of all, the examples reported above were from several thousand trials that were studied in *The American Jury*. Kalven and Zeisel conducted some calculations and as a result concluded that sympathy for the defendant was a factor in only a small proportion of the cases. In those 19% of cases where the jury was more lenient than the judge, defendant sympathy was a factor about 20% of the time. Thus, 20% of 19% yields a figure of about 4% of all trials. In short, Miss Sympathy isn't around all that often.

Second, it is important to observe that the fact that the trial judge believed that sympathy for the defendant was a factor in the verdict does not mean that it was the only factor. In many of these cases, Kalven and Zeisel discovered that sympathy played an important role primarily in cases where the evidence was equivocal. Sympathies for the defendant may have had their impact only because there was already reasonable doubt in the minds of the jurors.

We should also ask whether the jury was acting so unreasonably even if they allowed their heartstrings to be plucked. Certainly some of the acquittals reported in *The American Jury* seem consistent with a sense of justice. Why shouldn't the crippled polio victim have been given a second chance or the

elderly, hard-working tenant farmer, or the middle-aged belated college student? Apparently, twelve members of the community (the jurors) decided that an errant member of their community should be given another chance. Their decisions are at least arguable even if advocates of strict decisions based upon the evidence will disagree.

A few words about sympathy as it applies to the civil jury are also in order. We have focused our attention on the criminal jury only because that is where hard data exist. Nevertheless, it is a commonplace belief among trial lawyers that, especially in personal injury cases, appeals to sympathy help to win cases. Many lawyers are very insistent upon the desirability of having a badly injured victim testify or at minimum make an appearance in the courtroom. It makes a noticeable impact on everyone, including the judge as well as members of the jury. And they sometimes build upon these feelings to make their point. Moe Green, a noted trial attorney, provided an interesting example of this tactic. In a case where he represented a plaintiff who had lost both arms, he recalled in his summation to the jury:

> The only thing I said [to the jury] was that, it would be an insult for me to tell them what it could mean to have both arms off; and all they had to do was close their eyes and think of all the things during the day requiring at least one arm. Then I paused and said, "You know, I had lunch with him. He eats like a dog." Then I continued my summation.[10]

We don't know if Mr. Green's appeal to sympathy was responsible for a verdict in favor of the plaintiff. Indeed, in relaying the story, Mr. Green argued that it was not an appeal to sympathies, it was factual: "It just occurred to me that I had eaten with this man, and he had no arms and he had to get down and eat like a dog. I said it, that's all, and the jury knew it." From this perspective, then, an appeal to sympathy was perfectly appropriate because in a civil case the jury should take such factors into account in awarding damages. Morever, trial judges are likely to be swayed by the same emotions, even if they insist they are not. Recall from the last chapter that in civil cases, as well as criminal cases, there was a very high agreement rate between judge and jury. We do not have much systematic data on the particulars of civil jury performance, but what we have learned about the criminal jury makes us inclined to argue that the burden of proof rests on critics of the civil jury rather than its defenders.

*   *   *

What about Miss Sympathy's opposite, Mr. Prejudice? In assessing his presence, we must begin with the observation that in only 3% of the trials in

Kalven and Zeisel's study was the jury more severe than the judge. Martha Myers's study of Indiana juries would appear to lend support to this figure. Baldwin and McConville estimated the figure to be between 5 and 10% in their English juries. However, even though the numbers may be small in percentage terms, their importance is not diminished. In any country that prides itself on a legal system that provides justice for everyone, even one verdict based on prejudice is of concern.

Racial bigotry cases immediately come to mind when we think about prejudice, though there are other forms as well. In the 1950s, Dale Broeder interviewed jurors after a number of civil and criminal trials and found some striking instances of prejudice.[11] In one case a twenty-three-year-old black male, Mr. Johnson, was charged under the Dyer Act with aiding and abetting the interstate transportation of a stolen car. Although one black woman was a member of the jury, two of the other jurors were not hesitant to voice their prejudices. Near the very beginning of the deliberations, the two argued for conviction on the theory that "niggers are just no good." Each then told of several instances of criminal or immoral conduct by blacks that they claimed to have known personally. During the six hours of deliberation they consistently used the terms "jig" and "nigger" in referring to the defendant. Several of the other jurors were less blatant in their expressions, but readily admitted their prejudice to Professor Broeder. One confessed that he saw nothing wrong with convicting someone because of their race even if the evidence was not overwhelming. He attempted to justify his position: "Niggers have to be taught to behave. I felt that if he hadn't done that, he'd done something else probably even worse and that he should be put out of the way for a good long while." Although the trial took place several decades ago, in the 1980s we've all heard Mr. Prejudice still expressing similar sentiments on the front lawn of a Chicago suburb, on the main street of Lawrence, Kansas, or in a restaurant off Wall Street.

Kalven and Zeisel also found evidence of racial prejudice, especially when the charges involved interracial sex.[12] In a Mann Act case the trial judge commented. "It is my opinion that the jury probably did not take time to consider the evidence but merely based its decision on the fact that a colored defendant was on trial for white slavery involving colored and white prostitutes." In another case the judge observed: "This defendant did not take the stand, but because of his association with white victims . . . he may have made a bad impression on the jury." A young black male was charged with indecent exposure. The undisputed fact was that the manager of the movie theater, using a flashlight, discovered the boy masturbating in the dark. The judge would, however, have found the defendant not guilty because indecent

exposure requires actual exposure to the public. Yet the jury was offended by the conduct and would not accept this legal distinction: "The jury could not get the morals of the case out of their minds. They saw only a colored boy masturbating in the theatre with white women and children in the audience."

More contemporary research using jury simulation has found similar effects of race in sex crimes. A study by psychologist Dennis Ugwuegbu, for example, found that white jurors were more likely to find a defendant culpable of rape when he was black and the victim was white than in other racial combinations.[13] Blacks, on the other hand, were more likely to judge that a white defendant was culpable when the victim was black. Another study by Hubert Feild, to be discussed in more detail later, also found that black defendants in a rape case simulation were treated more harshly than white defendants.[14] However, in both these and some other studies,[7] race was a factor only when the evidence for guilt or innocence was very close. Race did not affect verdicts when the evidence was more clear-cut in favor of guilt or innocence. It appears that racial prejudice is expressed only in the cases where guilt or innocence is a toss-up.

There is, however, the possibility of a more subtle and invidious form of racial discrimination. Sociologists have coined the term "institutional racism" to refer to conditions where racial bias occurs as a result of the organization of society's institutions rather than intentional discrimination on the part of the persons who form the white majority. For example, as we discussed earlier, the jury selection process might produce juries that are predominantly white and middle class rather than racially and ethnically mixed. Professor Daniel Swett has provided us with a good example of what can hapen in the case of *The People v. Young Beartracks*.[15]

Young Beartracks was charged with first-degree murder in the death of Chicago Eddie following a poolroom argument. The killing took place in a black community and Beartracks, Eddie, and all of the major witnesses were black. The judge, the jurors, the arresting officers, and the lawyers were white. Beartracks admitted shooting and killing Eddie, but he claimed self-defense on the grounds that Eddie had been the aggressor and had been about to attack him with a razor. At the trial, Beartracks and a number of the witnesses to the event all testified that just prior to the killing, Eddie had put Beartracks "in the dozens." Yet, attempts to get the witnesses to clarify what they meant by "in the dozens" were met by blank stares and seemingly irrelevant statements. There were other problems of communication as well. One witness, for example, denied that he had ever had felony and misdemeanor convictions. He was asked if he had ever served time in a correctional

institution, and he responded, "No Sir, but I was a steward in the merchant marine for twenty years." When the prosecutor introduced evidence indicating that he indeed did have both felony and misdemeanor convictions and had served time in prison, he readily admitted that this was so.

In the end the jury returned a verdict of second-degree murder, with a sentence of five years to life. Several members of the jury were later interviewed and asked about their opinion of the testimony and how they had arrived at their verdict. The interviews showed that most of the testimony had been incomprehensible to them. Furthermore, the black witnesses, in the jurors' eyes, were either morons who could not understand or speak English or were unconscionable liars. Because Beartracks claimed self-defense, which, to the jurors, had not been proven or disproven, they compromised on a verdict of second-degree murder rather than first-degree murder (which would have resulted in a mandatory death sentence). Of course, had self-defense been proven, the correct verdict would have been not guilty. And in truth the testimony from the witnesses built a strong case for self-defense—but neither judge nor jury were capable of understanding it.

In the United States the social and economic conditions that created the black ghetto have also resulted in the development of a language and culture which is often very distinct from that of the white community. Often whites do not understand the vocabulary of blacks and vice versa. In court the meaning of "in the dozens" was never clarified. In black ghetto communities, putting someone "in the dozens" is an extreme form of verbal aggression. It is a duel of insults that has no limits: "appearance, food habits, sexual behavior, mental ability, and physical characteristics of the participants, their siblings, parents, and other kin all become the subject of extreme vituperation—the more profane and obscene, the better." The loser in such a contest is the person who either resorts to violence or runs away. Young Beartracks's life may well have been in jeopardy when he killed Eddie. Furthermore, a principal witness to the event was discredited by the white jurors because he did not understand the words "felony," "misdemeanor," and "correctional institution." Neither judge, lawyers, nor jurors seemed to have considered this possibility.

Although extreme, *People v. Young Beartracks* is not such an unusual case. Swett provided a second example of a young black put on trial for assault and battery. Some evidence suggested that the defendant, Basher, had acted in self-defense, but the jury, after much difficulty, found him guilty of assault. The problem was that in appearance and demeanor, Basher typified the white community's stereotype of an antisocial, hostile, belligerent black male. According to an observer of the trial:

> [Basher's] way of life, demeanor, attitudes, manner of speaking, and many
> other things are different [from those of the jury]. For example, if Basher had
> had his hair cut shorter, if he had shaved closer and had been aware of the effect
> of his speech on the jury, he might have gotten off entirely. On the stand, Basher
> slipped into slang and jive talk . . . and had a certain air that could be easily
> mistaken for arrogance . . . among his own peers this was the natural way. . . . His
> mannerisms, according to the [District Attorney] bespoke his guilt.

In 1968 Black Panther Huey Newton was put on trial for the murder of a police officer. The jury consisted of eleven whites and a middle-class black. At the trial a crucial piece of evidence involved the meaning of a statement attributed to Newton shortly before the killing. He was alleged to have said he was going to "take care of business." Some argued that this may have meant killing the policeman but others said it had an entirely different meaning in slang. Newton was convicted.

We have personally observed a number of trials of Canadian Indians where charges ranged from assault to murder. It is clear that the language, style of expression, demeanor of witnesses, and the cultural context of the incident are often very different from those the white judges and juries are accustomed to—and difficult for them to understand. Social scientists have documented similar problems with other ethnic groups, including Spanish-speaking Americans.[16]

Social psychologists and sociolinguists have recently begun to demonstrate that the kinds of problems shown in these examples involving members of ethnic groups apply to other categories of people as well. Women and people with low social status may be discriminated against because of their language. Research has revealed that often, particular styles of speaking are associated with the speaker's sex, social class, or ethnic background. What is more, we evaluate a person's credibility by his or her speech style.

John Conley, William O'Barr, and Allan Lind went into courtrooms and observed the speech styles of witnesses.[17] They discovered that witnesses of low social status, that is, poor and uneducated, used what may be called a "powerless" style of speech. Women, regardless of social class, were also more likely to use the powerless style. On the other hand, well-educated, white-collar men tended to use a "powerful" style. Consider the answers of persons with powerless and powerful speaking styles to the following questions:

> Q. Approximately how long did you stay before the ambulance arrived?
> A. (Powerless): Oh, it seems like it was about, uh, twenty minutes. Just long
> enough to help my friend, Mrs. Davis, you know, get straightened out.
> A. (Powerful): Twenty minutes. Just long enough to help get Mrs. Davis
> straightened out.

Q. How long have you lived in this town?
A. (Powerless): All my life, really.
A. (Powerful): All my life.
Q. You know your way around?
A. (Powerless): Yes, I guess I do.
A. (Powerful): Yes.

After uncovering these differences in speech style, the research team created scripts of witness testimony. Actors then delivered the testimony in two versions—once as a powerful speaker and once as a powerless speaker. Videotapes were made of the testimony and played before simulated jurors who were asked to evaluate the witness. When the same testimony was presented in a powerless instead of powerful speech style, the witnesses were judged to be less convincing, less competent, less trustworthy, less intelligent, and less likely to be telling the truth.

The team of Conley, O'Barr, and Lind has shown more rigorously what the account of Young Beartracks's trial already suggested. Language affects how jurors perceive and evaluate witnesses. Given that the effects can be shown with white actors varying their speech styles, imagine how much more pronounced the effects must be when the witness speaks with the vocabulary of the black or Spanish urban ghetto.

There are some lessons to be gleaned from these examples. First, jury prejudice *could* be more pervasive than studies such as that of Kalven and Zeisel would suggest. Their approach to studying the jury relied upon cases where judge and jury disagreed. But in Young Beartracks's trial, for example, it is unlikely that the judge disagreed with the jury's verdict. He was as ignorant of the real facts as the jury. In the Basher case it is probable that a white judge would have had no more understanding of Basher's appearance and demeanor than the jurors. The overwhelming majority of judges, as many studies have documented, are white, male, middle class, and conservative in outlook and in their life experiences. Their legal training prepares them for the language and culture of the white middle class. We need a criterion other than the judge's opinion to assess the incidence of jury prejudice because judges are as susceptible as jurors.

A second lesson is that our definition of prejudice needs to be a broad one. It is quite possible that the jurors in the trials of Young Beartracks and Basher were not overtly prejudiced. They may have been trying to be impartial and fair—but they (and the judge) lacked the ability to understand the essentials of the case. From this perspective, prejudice came not from negative feelings toward the defendants but from inability to understand black language and culture.

A third lesson harkens back to our earlier discussion of the need for juries that are representative of the community. There is a partial remedy for jury prejudice. If the jury in Beartracks's trial had contained a few members from the black community, the verdict might have been different. In the jury room those jurors might have been able to explain to the others the implications of being put "in the dozens." Their perspective and knowledge would have increased jury competence to deal with the issues. Indeed, in such an event the jury would have been far more competent than the white middle-class judge. Similarly, more black jurors in Basher's trial would have been able to understand and explain Basher's behavior on the witness stand. At the very least they could have provided dissenting views during the deliberations. Indeed, we know of one case involving a black defendant in which a lone black juror persuaded two other jurors that the circumstances of the crime, which took place in a ghetto, created a reasonable doubt about guilt; the ultimate result was a deadlocked jury.[18]

The presence of minority group members on the jury will also help to inhibit the expressions of blatant prejudice that Professer Broeder described. Broeder's investigations were carried out in an earlier period of race relations. While people today still harbor such prejudices, they are less likely to express them openly in a racially or ethnically mixed group. There is evidence that the presence of minority group members makes majority group members more sensitive and willing to consider opposing points of view.

Finally, there are two further implications of more broadly representative juries. One is that jury conviction rates might increase. In the same way that the phrase "in the dozens" pointed to grounds for self-defense for Young Beartracks, in other trials that crucial insight into the meaning of language and culture might point toward guilt. We can easily think of a different Beartracks trial where the evidence pointed toward not guilty by reason of self-defense except that a number of witnesses testified that just before the shooting, it was Beartracks who put Chicago Eddie "in the dozens."

The other implication is that more representative juries would possibly increase the incidence of disagreement between judge and jury. The jury would have insights about the meaning of the evidence that were beyond the knowledge of the judge. The judge would, therefore, favor one verdict and the jury another—and the jury would be correct. In fact, some current dis-content with the jury may arise from just this factor. Despite the fact that the goal of truly representative juries has not been met, juries are today more representative and heterogeneous than in the 1950s when Kalven and Zeisel conducted their research for *The American Jury*.

*   *   *

Aside from racial and ethnic prejudice, can it be that defendants who are unattractive or who can be described as disreputable or immoral in character are treated more harshly than other defendants? Kalven and Zeisel's judges reported some instances where this appeared to be the case.[19] In a homicide case the judge would have found the defendant guilty of involuntary manslaughter instead of murder as the jury had. He explained: "The defendant was charged with beating his companion to death with his fists. The testimony showed that during a drunken orgy the defendant and the decedent [sic] engaged in perverted sexual intercourse. It is probable that this fact weighed heavily with the jury." In another case involving commercial vice the judge commented: "Certain elements of the prosecution were legally weak, but the jury was probably impressed by the loose morals of both defendants. Evidence of lewd and vicious language of the parties made an undeniable impression on the jury."

The defendant's demeanor at trial was also attributed as the cause of another guilty verdict. In a trial on vice charges where the defendant was convicted, the judge explained: "The defendant gave the picture of a pious old fraud. She took her seat in plain view of the jury with a big cross swinging from her neck and thereupon opened her bible in front of her. Then she brought out a bottle of smelling salts, preparing herself spiritually and mentally for any eventuality." And in a drunken driving trial, where the case revolved entirely around the believability of the witnesses, the judge observed that the jury became prejudiced because the "[d]efendant, a blowhard and smart aleck, sought to impress the jury with the weight of his influence and importance of social connections."

Research with simulated juries has yielded similar results to those reported by the judges in *The American Jury* study.[20] But as was the case with pro-defendant sympathies, these findings about anti-defendant sympathies have to be put in context. Kalven and Zeisel calculated that anti-defendant feelings accounted for only about 10% of the instances where the jury returned a verdict that was more harsh than the judge would have given. Some other analyses suggested that this 10% tended to occur when the evidence for and against guilt was pretty evenly balanced—that is, a verdict in either direction could be justified. And the moral character tended to blend in with the issues involving the defendant's testimony. They concluded that

> Although it is . . . clear that the jury is often alienated by the unattractiveness
> of the defendant, we find no cases in which the jury convicts a man, so to speak,
> for the crime of being unattractive. In the cases examined it is apparent that there
> is always a considerable link, in the eyes of the jury, between the unattractiveness
> of the defendant and his credibility.[21]

Thus, the defendant's moral character becomes an issue only under two

conditions: when evidence of guilt is near the reasonable doubt threshold, and when it reflects on the trustworthiness of the defendant's version of the events. Kalven and Zeisel referred to the strong influence of the reasonable doubt threshold on the impact of extralegal factors as the "liberation hypothesis." In their words, "The closeness of the evidence makes it possible for the jury to respond to sentiment *by liberating* it from the discipline of the evidence."[22]

Trustworthiness was also at the base of some instances where the defendant exaggerated some parts of his testimony. In a drunken driving case, for example, the defendant claimed that the arresting officer severely beat him without cause. He embellished upon the account so much that the story was not credible. The judge did not believe the story about the beatings, but did believe the rest of the defendant's testimony and would have acquitted. The jury, however, relied upon the old latin maxim, *falsus in uno, falsus in omnibus* (false in part, false in everything) and convicted.

The effects of a defendant having a prior criminal record have already been discussed in the previous chapter on jury competence, but they deserve a few more comments as this too may be considered a form of prejudice. Myers's study of Indiana juries found that they were more likely to convict if the defendant had numerous prior criminal convictions.[23] This relationship has also been found in many simulation studies.[24]

Whether the defendant chooses to testify on his or her own behalf is closely related to the criminal record issue. Although our legal system makes it clear that a defendant does not have to testify and give his or her version of events—the burden of proof is on the prosecution—many laypersons infer guilt when a defendant remains silent. In our own research, we have frequently asked people what they would think about a criminal defendant who does not testify. Here are a sample of common replies: "Probably means he's guilty"; "What does an innocent person have to hide?"; "Only criminals take the Fifth [Amendment]." Therefore, exercising the right against self-incrimination is not viewed favorably. "Taking the Fifth" is, to some, an apparently odious and self-incriminating act. Kalven and Zeisel also examined these problems in their study.[25] They combined cases where the defendant did not testify and cases where he or she did testify but the jury became aware of the criminal record. Juries tended to be harsher in such cases. They accounted for another 10% of the cases in which the jury was more severe than the judge.

*   *   *

A common belief among trial lawyers—Melvin Belli and F. Lee Bailey to name two[26]—is that serving on a jury creates prejudice. In criminal cases, for example, jurors with previous jury experience are believed to be more inclined to convict defendants than jurors with no experience. The reasons why have never been made very clear. Some state that presumptions of innocence and reasonable doubt will be more readily accepted by a new juror. Experienced jurors, having heard lawyers' oratorical "tricks" before, will be more callous and skeptical of defendants' rights. Also, an emotional summation should have greater impact on novice jurors than on experienced ones. Another argument is that experienced jurors attempt to apply, inappropriately, principles and ideas that they learned in their previous trials.

An important question, therefore, is whether juries which contain a number of experienced jurors are "conviction prone," that is, prejudiced in favor of the prosecution and against the defendant. There is not much evidence bearing on this question, but it does not appear to support the conviction proneness hypothesis.

As part of the University of Chicago jury project, Dale Broeder interviewed 225 jurors who had served in sixteen civil personal injury trials and seven criminal trials.[27] He found a few instances where a juror inappropriately tried to apply legal principles from a previous case. "Mrs. A" served in a personal injury trial. She had previously served in two criminal trials and a case of personal injury from an automobile accident. In the deliberations, Mrs. A pointed out that in a previous case the injuries suffered by the plaintiff had been very serious, the defendant had been very negligent, and the jury had awarded only $11,000. She argued that in the present case the plaintiff had received "nothing but a sprained finger" and by comparison the defendant's negligence was "very slight." Yet, the plaintiff's lawyer was asking for $75,000. However, the other jurors rejected her analogy with the previous trial as being wholly improper. Broeder found several other attempts by jurors to apply principles across cases, as Mrs. A had done, but in every one it was rejected by the other jurors: for example, "That case and what was done there has nothing to do with this case and you shouldn't even be mentioning it"; "You can't bring in other cases." Broeder concluded that jury experience may be a factor in jury trial decisions, but in fact his anecdotes contradict his conclusion. While the occasional juror may have attempted improperly to inject arguments about previous cases, the other jurors soundly rejected their use.

Psychologist Norbert Kerr attempted to study the effects of jury experience in 210 criminal trials in California in a more systematic way.[28] The juries varied from ones that had all novice jurors to ones that contained up

to eleven jurors with experience. Kerr concluded that there was a slight indication that experience led to a greater likelihood of conviction. Another study of Kentucky jurors yielded a similar conclusion.[29]

An alternative explanation to these conclusions attributes apparent conviction-proneness not to prior jury experience but rather to the fact that prosecutors attempt to select people who served on previous juries that convicted the defendant and to reject people who served on juries that acquitted. It is common practice in many jurisdictions for prosecutors to keep detailed lists of jurors and the verdicts of the juries on which they served. They routinely reject persons who served on a jury that acquitted. Thus, attorney selection strategies instead of juror experience may be the reason that experienced jurors appear conviction-prone.

Other research findings suggest that sometimes prior jury service may make jurors more skeptical of the prosecution. June Tapp, a social psychologist, interviewed jurors who served in the Wounded Knee trial of leaders of the American Indian Movement.[30] She found that their experience bolstered higher levels of moral–legal reasoning in regard to rights, fair rules, laws, and compliance. They were also more aware that the government can make mistakes. Professor Tapp's findings lead to the conclusion that, if anything, the jury experience may have made the jurors more prone to favor defendants than to favor the prosecution.

The most that can be said, therefore, is that there is no clear evidence that juries composed of experienced jurors are more prejudiced against defendants. Jury service may occasionally prejudice individual jurors, but on the other hand, it may also make some more sensitive to matters that are favorable to the defendant. Moreover, Broeder's anecdotal data suggest that improper attempts to apply past experience in jury deliberations are usually rejected by other jurors.

*   *   *

A final issue is whether the jurors put the lawyers rather than the defendant on trial. As we noted at the beginning of this chapter, Clarence Darrow and Percy Foreman, among others, claimed that this was so. If lawyers can get the jurors to like them, the case is as good as won; if the jurors take a dislike, the case is lost. In this view, the defendant's actions are almost irrelevant.

Kalven and Zeisel found some evidence that the defense attorney can make a difference.[31] The judges in their study commented that some acquittals were due largely to the personality or status of the defendant's lawyer. In a robbery case the judge commented:

> Defendant had not been in trouble before. He was defended by a young, honest, and sincere lawyer who had known defendant before and believed the fantastic tale told by the defendant. The honesty and decency of defense attorney rubbed off on the jurors who were hearing their first case.

In a trial involving a game law violation the judge put it this way:

> Defendant's attorney is one of the old timers and very colorful. He grunts and laughs and disparages witnesses' testimony on the other side by holding his hands to his ears. The court had to cut him down several times, But, everybody likes Mr. R., the defense attorney.

And in a few cases the judge suggested that the verdict was probably due to the fact that the jurors were obligated to the defense attorney. In a drunken driving case, for example, the judge observed:

> The defendant's lawyer has been practicing at the local bar about 35 years and has a tremendous number of clients, many of whom felt obligated to him in one way or another. Doubtless some of the jurors were under his influence.

Some evidence suggested that the character of the lawyer might have been a factor in some guilty verdicts as well. In a disorderly conduct trial the judge observed:

> The conduct of counsel for the defense became so argumentative and obnoxious that the court threatened to hold him in contempt. This conduct may have helped to influence the jury.

Reactions to the personal characteristics of lawyers, however, must be kept separate from the actual skills of the lawyers. Kalven and Zeisel did uncover a number of instances where skill—or the lack of it—on the part of one of the opposing attorneys may have influenced the outcome. As one judge observed about an acquittal in an incest case, "Defense attorney delivered a brilliant argument and in my opinion this argument meant the entire difference between a verdict of guilty and one of not guilty." In a fraud case the jury was moved to acquit because of a "[d]istinctive defense counsel who obfuscated the jury by bringing in extraneous testimony attacking [the] complaining witness's credibility." In another incest case the judge commented that "[d]efendant signed a confession verifying the girl's story. A skillful defense counsel demonstrated successfully that the two county detectives [involved in the case] should have been out digging ditches." And it worked the other way around. Unskilled defense counsel, for example, sometimes failed to call witnesses or to follow up the implications of potentially incriminating testimony.

To assess the impact of lawyers, we need to think about the relative abilities of attorneys for the two sides. If both are equally skilled or equally unskilled, the effects of the lawyers should be canceled out. Kalven and Zeisel asked the judges in their study to indicate whether the prosecutor was better,

the defense lawyer was better, or whether they were about equal. The sides were rated as balanced in 76% of the cases. While defense counsel was superior in 11%, the prosecutor was superior in the remaining 13%. Interestingly enough, the imbalance differed by the type of crime. In murder cases the two sides were on average evenly balanced. However, in trials involving income tax evasion, perjury, gambling, and kidnapping, the defense lawyer was frequently superior to the prosecutor. Tax evasion tends to be a rich person's crime, and the rich can afford to hire better lawyers. There was also some indication that black defendants and poor defendants were more likely to be represented by inferior defense counsel.

Some additional calculations led Kalven and Zeisel to the conclusion that in about 25% of the cases in which the defense counsel was superior, he or she had some effect on the jury that would possibly not have occurred if the case was tried before a judge. On the other hand, taking all cases, not just those where there was disagreement between the judge and jury, led them to the conclusion that defense counsel made a significant difference in slightly more than 1% of all trials.

Norbert Kerr also found some evidence that lawyers make a difference in the California juries that he studied.[32] Defense lawyers who displayed a good working knowledge of the evidence and made convincing arguments tended to win. Prosecutors who were unemotional and relentless in pressing their case also were more likely to win. However, overall these effects were small and accounted for differences that were of the magnitude estimated by Kalven and Zeisel.

On balance, then, lawyers sometimes make a difference. However, the difference is likely more often due to their skills and preparation, and arguments about the meaning of the evidence than through their ability to make pure appeals to the jurors' emotions. Maybe the Clarence Darrows and Percy Foremans do have the ability to move the jury—but maybe not. In any event, the Darrows and Foremans do not appear in the average trial. The evidence suggests that the jury is not often swayed to sympathies and prejudices by the charisma of the lawyers.

* * *

We must conclude that sometimes Mr. Prejudice and Miss Sympathy are sitting in the jury box. However, their presence is not nearly so frequent as Judge Frank would have us believe. We've even raised the possibility that in some circumstances jury verdicts may be more likely to be correct than verdicts that would be rendered by a judge. We need more research on some of these topics but even without it, it is clear that Mr. Prejudice and Miss Sympathy cannot account for most of the disagreement between judge and jury.

CHAPTER 10

The War with the Law

Having dispensed with incompetence and prejudice as primary determinants of jury verdicts, we are left with a final charge: Juries ignore or "nullify" the law and render verdicts based upon their own standards of justice. Critics of the jury system claim that juries are routinely at war with the law. Supporters acknowledge that the war takes place but argue that it occurs only when strict application of the letter of the law would result in an injustice.

We introduced the concept of "jury nullification" in the cases of William Penn and John Peter Zenger. Jury nullification refers to the refusal of juries to apply the law when they believe that to follow the letter of the law would mean an unjust verdict. Historically, the jury has often played this role. In England during the 18th and 19th centuries, the "Bloody Code" prescribed over two hundred offenses that were punishable by death. Many of the crimes were as minor as stealing bread and a number involved political dissent. Juries often acquitted guilty defendants rather than send them to their death. In 1819 English bankers requested that the death penalty for forgery be eliminated since juries refused to convict forgers because of the severity of the penalty. Historians maintain that the reluctance of juries to return verdicts of guilty during the period of the Bloody Code led to the decline of capital punishment in England.

In the United States, the jury proved to be an important tool for abolitionists before the Civil War. The Fugitive Slave Laws enacted in 1850 outlawed helping slaves to escape or impeding their capture and return. Northern juries frequently acquitted the abolitionists who assisted slaves, even though the evidence clearly indicated guilt.

And jury nullification still occurs. On May 17, 1985, a jury acquitted eight anti-apartheid demonstrators charged with trespassing at the South African Consulate in Chicago. Defense attorneys presented a "defense of necessity" to the jury, arguing that the activists' conduct was necessary to avoid greater public injury from the apartheid policies of the South African government. According to one juror's report, the jury was split initially. But after

149

jurors read the Illinois statute that excuses some criminal conduct by reason of necessity, they concluded that "the defendants had to do what they did." As one defendant rejoiced after the jury verdict: "A jury of our peers acquitted us but indicted the Government of South Africa."[1]

In Toronto, Dr. Henry Morgentaler was acquitted by a jury of his peers in November of 1984 on charges that he violated Canadian laws regulating abortions. It was his fourth trial. Since 1967, the laws of Canada have permitted abortions if continuation of pregnancy poses risks to a woman's life or health. But the law also requires a cumbersome and time-consuming review of each request for an abortion by specially selected boards of accredited hospitals. Furthermore, citizens opposed to abortion rights have taken control of some review boards, with the result that, in certain hospitals, no abortion requests have been granted for years. To alleviate what he saw as a pressing social problem, Dr. Morgentaler opened abortion clinics, first in Montreal and later in Toronto and Winnipeg. He openly admitted performing abortions, and his actions were in clear violation of Canadian law. His defense was also one of necessity—he claimed that it was justifiable to give an abortion to any woman who wanted one because such a woman is in desperate straits. In four separate trials, juries hearing the evidence acquitted the doctor of wrongdoing.[2]

In another Canadian case, Jane Stafford shot and killed her common-law husband on the night of March 11, 1982, after he had passed out drunk in his pickup truck. Stafford had been beaten and abused for five years. During the trial, the jury of ten men and two women heard that the victim was no ordinary bully. He weighed over 250 pounds. Local Royal Canadian Mounted Police officers had been instructed that if they were called to his home, they should go armed and ready to shoot. He had beaten and abused two previous wives, numerous children, and the defendant's father. He was also a sexual sadist who forced Stafford to have sex with a dog. Nevertheless, he had been killed while unarmed and unconscious, and Stafford admitted the deed. She stood trial on charges of first-degree murder. In closing arguments to the jury, her defense lawyer argued that under the circumstances, a verdict of manslaughter was appropriate. To the surprise of almost everyone, the jury returned a verdict of not guilty instead.[3]

It is doubtful whether the judges in any of these cases would have reached the same verdicts as the juries did. Were the decisions fair and just? An observer's assessment of whether justice was done in the first two cases may depend on whether he or she opposes apartheid or supports abortion rights. While polls show that the majority of citizens in the United States and Canada both oppose racial discrimination and support abortion, there are many who

take the opposite view. Stafford's case might achieve more consensus in favor of the jury's verdict, but it too raises important questions. There must be limits to self-defense. Some critics might argue that because she was in no immediate peril, she should have called the police rather than taking the law into her own hands. The jury acquittal could encourage others to take the same route. However, before we consider the moral issues, we should ask how widespread jury nullification is and when it occurs.

*   *   *

Again, we can turn to Kalven and Zeisel's study because it provides the most systematic information on jury deviations from the law.[4] Recall that in the one case in five where judge and jury disagreed, it was usually because the jury was more lenient. The judges' explanations of why juries behaved as they did yielded not one but a number of reasons. Four of them accounted for almost two-thirds of the disagreements.

Some laws courted rebellion because they were unpopular in the community. These were game laws, gambling, liquor violations, and drunken driving. In these cases, juries tended to acquit regardless of the evidence. Hunting animals out of season, playing a little poker, or making a little moonshine were seen as areas of morals rather than criminal activity, and in the eyes of the jury the government had no right to regulate this sort of victimless crime. The responses to drunken driving were more complex. Sometimes the juries appeared to object to the use of Breathalyzer tests, and other times to believe that the penalty upon conviction, mandatory loss of a driver's license for a year, was too severe. In other instances, the jury may have acquitted because they too had driven after taking one drink too many: "There but for the grace of God go I." These four types of cases were the only ones that seemed to evoke an outright war with the law.

A second set of cases involved self-defense. The jury often interpreted self-defense more liberally than the law specified. The judge would adhere to a legal rule that self-defense requires a situation where a threat of violence is immediate and there is no opportunity to escape. Jurors had a different view. In one case, for example, the defendant and his son-in-law got into a drinking bout that turned into a fight. The defendant was severely beaten, and went home. The son-in-law followed him, and was shot and killed as he entered the house. The judge would have found the defendant guilty of murder in the first degree, because he was armed and the victim was not. In the judge's view, the defendant could have held off his son-in-law by turning on the lights and holding him at gunpoint "rather than hiding in the dark and

shooting him." However, the jury took the prior beating of the defendant as a provocation and returned a verdict of second-degree murder.

Another case involved the defense of property. The victim, caught stealing gas from the defendant's truck at a lumber camp, was shot and killed. It turned out that the victim had been warned off twice earlier that same evening. The judge would have found the defendant guilty of murder but the jury acquitted. In the judge's view: "The jury evidently took into consideration the fact that there is much gas stealing in our logging operations." In other cases, the jury was affected by a victim's harassment, insults, or provocation even if these did not rise to the level of a substantial threat to the defendant. For instance, a man was charged with assault and battery for striking another man on the nose. The judge would have found the defendant guilty, but the jury, taking into account the fact that for days the victim had been doing all he could to irritate the assailant, returned a verdict of not guilty. Finally, there were many instances similar to Jane Stafford's case where the jury was influenced by a pattern of wife abuse in judging self-defense.

The third set of cases was similar to the self-defense cases. These involved the jury taking into consideration the victim's contribution to the events. In criminal law, there is no such thing as "contributory negligence." That is a concept in civil law only. But juries appeared to operate as if contributory negligence was part of criminal law as well. The jury acquitted a defendant whose automobile struck a pedestrian who was known to be an excessive drinker and who had staggered into the road. In a number of fraud cases, the jury seemed to endorse W. C. Fields's dictum that "you can't cheat an honest man." A defendant was acquitted of misrepresenting and selling poor-quality goods. The judge favored a guilty verdict but observed: "The victims actually received a poor grade of roof paint for their money; they were looking for a bargain and got beat at it." Rape, which we will consider separately in a later chapter, was another instance where the jury took into account the behavior of the victim. If she was perceived as a "loose woman," had voluntarily gone to the scene of the assault with the defendant, or had had prior sexual relations with him, the jury tended to acquit the defendant of rape.

A fourth set of reasons was based on what lawyers call the *de minimus* principle, namely that whatever harm was done was trivial. Judges adhered to the law but juries looked at the consequences. Thus, in one case the jury acquitted a defendant of robbery because only two dollars was taken. In an embezzlement case an employee was detected with the money before she left the building. The judge would have convicted her of embezzlement, but the

jury found her guilty only of petty larceny. In some other cases, the application of the *de minimus* principle was more controversial. In a manslaughter case where the jury acquitted the defendant, the judge observed: "The parties were both Indians and jurors can't get excited about the fact that one Indian kills another Indian."

The remaining sources of judge and jury disagreement occurred much less frequently but deserve mention. If the defendant suffered injury as a result of the criminal act, such as a drunk driver who was badly injured in an accident, the jury was lenient. In other instances, the threat of a severe penalty for the defendant caused the jury to acquit. Sometimes the jury took a lenient view when it appeared that a defendant's accomplice might escape punishment. There were also instances when juries acquitted when the police had employed improper methods to induce confessions, or had used entrapment as in the DeLorean case discussed earlier. When the crime was minor, the jury sometimes took a broader view than the judge of mitigating circumstances like intoxication.

Three decades later, some of Kalven and Zeisel's findings are dated, but others have a very contemporary ring. Attitudes toward drunken driving have radically changed in the past few years as people have come to recognize the harm caused by drunks on the highway. To our knowledge there have been no recent and scientifically controlled studies on jury responses to drunken driving, but newspapers and magazines report many instances of convictions and severe penalties for driving while intoxicated.[5] Jury behavior in rape cases may also be less tolerant as the public's attitudes toward women and knowledge of myths about rape have changed in the intervening years.

On the other hand, even back in the 1950s, juries responded sympathetically to victims of spouse abuse in a manner reminiscent of today's public concern with this major social problem. The juries translated their sympathy into liberal interpretations of self-defense. And the broadened view of self-defense for personal and property assaults that were documented in *The American Jury* have current analogues. Despite evidence that his actions may have been premeditated, one New York grand jury refused even to indict the "subway vigilante" Bernhardt Goetz for assault in the subway shooting of four black teenagers who asked him for five dollars. Instead, Goetz became a hero overnight and his actions garnered widespread public support. (A second grand jury, presented with additional information by the prosecutor, did ultimately indict him.)

In England, Oxford University's Penal Research Unit undertook several studies to determine if the jury was at war with the law.[6] Particular emphasis

was placed on jury acquittals. The Oxford researchers concluded after studying over 300 jury trials that it was "generally correct to say that the acquittal of a defendant was attributable to a single cause—the failure of the prosecution . . . to provide enough information, or to present it in court in a way that would convince both judge and jury of the defendant's guilt."

As part of the Oxford project, the judges allowed a series of "shadow" juries to participate in 30 different criminal trials. The shadow jurors were people who were eligible for jury duty who sat in the courtroom and listened to the evidence just as the real jury did. Afterwards, they deliberated and reached a verdict. The advantage of the shadow juries, of course, was that unlike real juries, their deliberations could be tape-recorded and later analyzed to determine how the verdicts were reached.

Most of the time the verdicts of the shadow juries were the same as those of the real juries. The tape recordings of the deliberations showed that the shadow jurors frequently expressed concern about the burden of proof and insisted that the evidence clearly implicate the defendant before they could return a guilty verdict. Similar to Kalven and Zeisel's findings, in a small percentage of cases the shadow jurors acquitted the defendant even though technically he or she was probably guilty. When the criminal activity appeared trivial, when jurors felt that the defendant should be given another chance, or when they believed that the notion of self-defense in some assault cases should be interpreted more liberally than the judge's instructions, they sometimes acquitted the defendant. However, the overall conclusion of the Oxford researchers was that there was little sign of perversity in the verdicts. Jurors looked at the evidence; and in those cases in which the evidence was equivocal, they applied their sense of equity to decide the case.

The findings of *The American Jury* are also echoed in more recent studies. Similarly, in her study of Indiana juries, sociologist Martha Myers found that when juries departed from the law, their deviations were limited and principled.[7] They were more likely to deviate from the judge's instructions when the circumstances involved a serious offense, a young victim, and an employed defendant, but the deviations were not excessive.

While juries do depart from the law, there is one final and important qualification first noted by Kalven and Zeisel and later confirmed by Myers and the Oxford researchers. Departures occurred predominantly in those cases where the evidence itself was ambiguous or contradictory. When the evidence was clear, the jury was inclined to follow the law, but when it was unclear, jurors felt liberated to give rein to their own sense of justice and equity. Thus, the facts do not support the claim that juries are lawless. Deviations are not widespread, nor routine. When they do occur, they are not invariably irrational

and capricious. Rather, in most cases the jury bends the law to comport with its own standards of justice and fairness.

*   *   *

Despite what the data tell us, the jury's right to ignore the law remains controversial, particularly because the issue of jury nullification has been central in a number of widely publicized trials that have political overtones to them. The trials of antiapartheid demonstrators and Dr. Morgenthaler are but two examples. In England civil servant Clive Ponting was put on trial for breach of the Official Secrets Act. He had supplied a Member of Parliament with classified information about the controversial sinking of the Argentine cruiser General Belgrano during the Falklands crisis. A jury completely exonerated him with an acquittal despite the judge's comment to the jurors that the facts and the law virtually required a conviction. In the United States the issue has arisen in the religiously based sanctuary movement. Members of religious groups have helped refugees from war-torn countries such as El Salvador illegally immigrate into the United States and have given them "sanctuary" in their churches. As the religious workers have stood trial, they and their attorneys have asked that juries be instructed about jury nullification.

Most people feel somewhat uneasy about giving any decision-making group in society the prerogative to disregard the law. However, the great legal scholar John Wigmore maintained that to assure justice it is essential that juries have this power. He noted that law and justice will on occasion be in conflict. While laws dictate general rules, justice is the fairness of the outcome in a particular case considering all the circumstances. Because lawmakers cannot anticipate every set of circumstances, it is up to the jury to adjust the general rule of law to the justice of the specific case. Sometimes, too, laws may be unjust and oppressive, either because they were intended to be so or because values have changed while the law has not. As we saw in earlier chapters, views such as those of Wigmore were not always accepted. Bushell's case arising from the trial of William Penn served as a turning point; afterwards jurors could not be punished for their verdicts. But the controversy over the power of the jury did not end with that case.

In the United States during the first century after the Revolution, it was widespread practice to allow juries to decide the law as well as the facts. Remember that in *Sparf and Hansen v. United States* (1896), the Supreme Court curtailed the right of juries to deliver a verdict that was at odds with the evidence. Sparf and Hansen, two sailors, were charged with murder for throwing a fellow sailor overboard. The defendants argued that they should

be found guilty only of manslaughter, and asked that the judge instruct the jurors that they could render a verdict either of murder or manslaughter. The judge refused on the grounds that there was no evidence to support a manslaughter verdict. The judge instructed the jury that:

> In a proper case, a verdict for manslaughter may be rendered, . . . and even in this case you have the physical power to do so; but as one of the tribunals of this country, a jury is expected to be governed by law, and the law it should receive from the court.[8]

Sparf and Hansen were convicted but appealed on grounds that the jury had been improperly instructed. The Supreme Court rejected the appeal and stated that juries should not be permitted to reduce penalties or nullify laws.

Jury nullification surfaced as an issue more recently at the time of the Vietnam War. There was widespread public disagreement over U.S. involvement in Vietnam, and many Americans engaged in acts of civil disobedience to illustrate their opposition and to call attention to moral issues concerning that war. As the defendants came to trial, their attorneys often attempted to argue that civil disobedience was justified on the basis of the questionable legality and morality of the war. But judges characteristically ruled that the defendants' motivation was irrelevant. Few judges allowed defense attorneys to tell the jury about its historic power to nullify the law by acquitting the defendants. The trial of Benjamin Spock and several others on charges that they conspired to encourage young men to burn their draft cards was typical. According to one account, jurors in that case were sympathetic to Spock and his codefendants. But in his charge to the jury, the judge told the jurors that they must use the law that he gave to them and not their own views of the law. The jury convicted Spock and several of his codefendants, though apparently not without some anguish. The following comments from some of the Spock jurors interviewed by Jessica Mitford are instructive:

> Of course you wonder if you made the right decision; but the way the judge charged us, there was no choice. People I've talked with since the verdict are sympathetic to the actions of Spock and Coffin—they seem to think the jury should have been there to decide if the law is right or wrong, but we weren't there to decide that. You can't have juries deciding whether *laws* are right—there are certain laws on the books.[9]

> I'm in agreement with what they're trying to accomplish—my friends were amazed I found them guilty; but they did break the law. . . . I don't have to stress where *my* sympathy lay . . . I think it's a senseless war. But my personal views don't count. . . . I'm convinced the Vietnam war is no good. But we've got a constitution to uphold. If we allow people to break the law, we're akin to anarchy.[10]

The dilemma of the jurors was acute: How could they simultaneously

uphold the rule of law and achieve justice in the Spock case? The power of the judge in leading the jurors to follow the rule of law and to ignore their personal sentiments is apparent in the following comment by a juror in that trial:

> I knew they were guilty when we were charged by the judge. I did not know prior to that time—I was in full agreement with the defendants until we were charged by the judge. That was the kiss of death![11]

Since *Sparf,* the Supreme Court has not directly discussed the propriety of jury nullification. However, perusal of Supreme Court opinions on the function of the jury over the last two decades reveals that the Court has often described the jury's chief function as political. In *Duncan v. Louisiana* (1968), the Court stated that the "right to jury trial is granted to criminal defendants in order to prevent oppression by the Government."[12] In *Taylor v. Louisiana* (1975), the Court described the jury's purpose: "to guard against the exercise of arbitrary power—to make available the commonsense judgment of the community as a hedge against the overzealous prosecutor and in preference to the professional or perhaps overconditioned or biased response of a judge."[13] Finally, in a long line of decisions the Court has consistently maintained that the jury cannot be the "organ of a special class" but must fairly represent the entire community. These decisions can be interpreted to mean that the Court supports the infusion of community sentiment in jury verdicts, and would sanction, under certain circumstances, jury verdicts at odds with unfair laws or oppressive prosecutorial practices.

In two states, Maryland and Indiana, juries have the constitutional authority to judge both the facts and the law. In line with the Maryland Rules of Procedure, the standard judge's instruction to the jury is as follows: "Anything which I say about the law, including any instructions which I may give you, is merely advisory and you are not in any way bound by it. You may feel free to reject my advice on the law and to arrive at your own independent conclusion." Because juries and not judges are the final arbiters of the law, counsel may argue differing interpretations of the law to the jury. Maryland and Indiana are the exceptions. The *Sparf* ruling is followed by most other states. However, while *Sparf* appears to have taken away the legal *right* of criminal juries to decide a case contrary to the law, later court decisions seem to recognize that juries nevertheless have the ability or *power* to do so. A principal question, then, is whether or not the jury should be told that it has this power.

*   *   *

Some legal scholars have argued that jurors should be specifically instructed that they can deviate from the law if it seems justified. They claim that the real role of the jury is to act as the conscience of the community; juries should be able to acquit defendants who are legally guilty but morally correct.[14] A wife abuse case such as that of Jane Stafford is one example. Euthanasia cases are another. In both of these the legal authorities feel compelled to bring charges, but they rely on the jury's sense of fairness to acquit the defendant.

There might also be public support for this view. In a Canadian survey, people were asked whether jurors should be instructed that they are entitled to follow their own conscience instead of strictly applying the law if it will produce a just result. Over three-quarters of the respondents said yes. Furthermore, people who had actually served on a jury were even more supportive; 93% of them endorsed the idea of giving these instructions. (On the other hand, Canadian judges were overwhelmingly opposed: Fewer than five percent agreed that jurors should receive such instructions.[15])

Opponents have argued that nullification instructions could bring chaos to the courts and even work against defendants. While juries might acquit some defendants on moral grounds, the instructions could be a two-edged sword: In cases where there is community prejudice, instead of following the law the jury might find people who are legally innocent to be guilty.

Similar concerns about the dangers of instructing jurors were expressed in 1972 in *United States v. Dougherty*.[16] A number of people, including some Catholic priests, ransacked offices of the Dow Chemical Company to protest the company's manufacture of napalm which was being used to bomb targets in Vietnam and other countries of Southeast Asia. The defendants argued that their actions were a moral imperative and requested that the jury be given instructions that they had the power to nullify the law. The trial judge refused, and the U.S. Court of Appeals upheld his decision. The Court acknowledged that historically the jury has had the power to nullify the law as it did in the John Peter Zenger and Fugitive Slave Law cases. However, it also asserted that jurors informally know about their ability to nullify the law and will do so when the circumstances warrant it, but specific instructions about nullifying powers would cause the jury to operate in a radically different way.

There seems to be merit in both sets of arguments. On the one hand, better justice might prevail if the jury is informed of its power to apply its own standards, but on the other hand, the outcome might be just the opposite. Political scientist Gary Jacobsohn attempted to shed light on the debate by asking Maryland judges about the impact of the jury nullification instruction in their state. Overall, the judges felt that the law had minimal impact on

verdicts, but when it did affect a case it was usually the defendant who benefited. Despite the instruction, the Maryland trial judges retained considerable power over the jury. One judge, for instance, mentioned, "When the jury is told that they are judges of the law, I doubt that they have any grasp of what is meant." The degree to which the judges emphasized the jury's right to decide the law varied from courtroom to courtroom and was related to the judges' attitudes toward the jury and the propriety of jury nullification.[17]

Psychologist Irwin Horowitz studied the issue in a more systematic way.[18] He asked whether the jury functioned differently if it was given nullification instructions; whether the impact of such instructions depended on the precise form in which they were given; and whether their impact also depended on the type of case in which they were given. The answer he got was yes to all three questions.

For his experiment, Horowitz recruited people who had previously served as jurors in an Ohio court. All of them underwent a *voir dire* examination by a prosecutor and a defense attorney before being seated as members of six-person juries. The juries heard an audiotaped trial performed by professional actors, then deliberated until reaching a unanimous verdict. Some of the juries heard a murder trial in which a grocery store owner was killed during a robbery. Others heard a drunk driving case in which a college student killed a pedestrian. Others heard a euthanasia case in which a nurse was tried for the "mercy" killing of a terminal cancer patient. Before deliberating, however, each jury received one of three types of instructions. Some received standard Ohio pattern instructions which made no reference to nullification. Other juries received the Maryland instructions which draw attention to the jury's power to decide the law. Finally, some juries received what Horowitz called "radical nullification" instructions in which the jurors were told that they had the final authority to apply the law to the facts, that it was appropriate for them to express community sentiment and their own feelings of conscience, and that despite their respect for the law nothing could bar them from acquitting the defendant if they felt the law in this particular case would produce an inequitable or unjust result. They also heard about the jury's historic power to ignore the law and decide cases in line with community sentiment.

The three types of instructions had no effect on verdicts in the murder case. However, the juries that had been given the radical nullification instructions were more likely to acquit the defendant in the euthanasia case, and they were more likely to convict the defendant in the drunk driving case. Juries instructed with the Ohio and the Maryland instructions judged the cases similarly. Horowitz also studied what the jurors discussed in their deliberations. He found that when jurors received radical nullification instructions,

they spent less time discussing the actual evidence, and spent more time discussing the nullification powers, the character of the defendant, and their own personal experiences as they applied to the case.

Professor Horowitz's study provides some grist for the debate about what the jury should be told. It suggests that the Maryland nullification instructions may not affect jury behavior, as the Maryland judges suspected. Even the radical instructions may have no effect with some kinds of cases, but with other types of cases jury verdicts may be more lenient or harsher, depending on the crime and the defendant. The findings, of course, do not answer the question of which verdicts were the correct or the best verdicts; that is a value judgment. Yet we do have grounds for believing that if juries were told very specifically that they have the right to ignore the law, their verdicts might differ in specific cases.

*   *   *

What about civil cases? The jury has been accused of being at war with noncriminal law as well. In 1933 a judge with long experience asserted that in case after civil case:

> . . . the jury has made the law . . . in . . . direct conflict with the law as laid
> down by the highest law-making authority of the state. The jury has substituted
> its own notion of law for that which the law-books say is law.[19]

In more recent years, newspapers have carried articles about enormous damage awards to plaintiffs in jury trials, awards that are often subsequently reduced by higher courts. Large corporations claim that today's juries pay little attention to the legal merits of the case; no matter how weak the plaintiff's evidence is, juries find in their favor and make the defendant corporations pay.[20] An executive of an insurance company that pays liability claims says that "misguided juries [base] their awards on sympathy for the plaintiff and on the assumed financial resources for the defendant."[21] A current handbook on personal injuries used by lawyers also suggests that whereas juries give large awards when the defendants have "deep pockets," that is, are perceived to have the ability to pay, they discriminate against black, poor, and uneducated plaintiffs.[22]

To assess the merits of these charges, we can begin once again by returning to the seminal work of the Chicago Jury Project.[23] In an earlier chapter, we described how the researchers compared jury verdicts with the hypothetical verdicts of the presiding judges in civil trials. A little over half the time, the jury's verdict was for the plaintiff and a little less than half the time the jury favored the defendant. These figures do not necessarily mean

that the jury is biased in favor of the plaintiff, because it could be that plaintiffs only take cases to a jury when the evidence is in their favor. Indeed, judges favored plaintiffs in a little over half the cases as well. Recall that in civil cases, judge and jury agreed in four trials out of five. In the fifth trial, about half of the time the jury favored the plaintiff when the judge would have decided in favor of the defendant, and in the other half the jury decided in favor of the defendant when the judge thought the plaintiff should have won. This even split tells us that the juries did not have a bias in favor of plaintiffs.

This is not the full story, because civil juries not only make decisions about who is at fault, they also decide the amount of the damages that the plaintiff should receive if he or she wins. The study revealed that there was substantial disagreement over money. Juries tended to give larger awards than judges in over half the cases. Overall, jury awards were 20% higher than those of judges.

There may be more than one reason why juries were more generous than judges. A major factor was that juries often considered how much the plaintiff would receive after the lawyer's costs were deducted. One of the peculiarities of American law is that legal fees are not considered part of damages. If you are hit by an automobile, you can sue for your doctor's bill, your lost wages, and your pain and suffering, but the cost of the lawyer to fight your case is not a legitimate claim. Yet, lawyers working on a contingency-fee basis may collect up to 30% of whatever you receive. Juries saw no impropriety in taking this fact into account. Anecdotal reports of their deliberations showed a straightforward kind of reasoning: Joe Plaintiff deserves $10,000 for the accident, but his lawyer will probably take about $3,300. So let's give an award of $13,500.

Further insights about the civil jury have come from some recent studies undertaken by the Rand Corporation's Institute for Civil Justice.[24] They have examined jury verdicts in personal injury cases in Cook County (Chicago), Illinois. Some of the findings contrast with those of the Chicago Jury Project. There is evidence that juries penalize large corporations, but closer inspection reveals that the anomalies are not as great as they first appear.

One interesting finding is that the average jury award in personal injury cases was modest, about $7,800. This seems to contradict the view that juries are out of control in the awards that they give. In fact, most of the trials involved a plaintiff who had suffered slight or moderate injuries such as cuts, bruises, or sprains to the head, neck, back, or torso. Damage awards in the 1970s were higher than in the 1960s, but after adjustments for inflation and for changes in the types of cases being brought to trial, the jury decisions were, on the whole, remarkably stable.

There is a major exception to this conclusion. Twenty-five percent of the trials were claims for serious injuries such as loss of hands, legs, or eyes, or for a wrongful death. Jury awards for some types of these major claims jumped 20% or more between the 1960s and the 1970s. Claims that involved wrongful death, medical malpractice, product liability, and street or sidewalk hazards—we'll arbitrarily call them Type A claims—were more likely to result in large awards than claims involving automobile accidents or injuries on someone else's property. We'll call these latter cases Type B claims.

The Rand Corporation researchers generated several hypotheses to attempt to explain the different behavior of juries hearing Type A and Type B cases. One explanation was that in Type A cases the injuries suffered by the plaintiff were more severe than in Type B cases. This turned out not to be true, however. Even when the seriousness of the injury was similar, someone hurt in an automobile accident was likely to receive only one-third of the money that someone hurt in a workplace accident received. Another hypothesis, which was partly supported, was that defendants in Type A cases were usually large corporations with "deep pockets" while defendants in Type B cases were usually individuals. Corporations, hospitals, and governments were more likely to be found liable and they usually had to pay larger damage awards. The more serious the injuries, the more the defendants had to pay. The third hypothesis was that lawyers used different legal strategies in Type A cases. This hypothesis too received some support. In comparison to the 1960s, Type A cases were more complex in the 1970s. In the 1960s, lawyers usually raised a single legal argument about why the defendant should be held liable, but in the 1970s, they tended to raise multiple theories of liability. This suggests that jury decision-making may not have changed; rather, the nature of the cases that juries were asked to decide had changed. If judges instead of juries had heard these more complex and sophisticated arguments about defendant liability, they too might have favored the plaintiffs more than in the past. Unfortunately, this is only speculation, because judges' opinions were not studied in the Rand research.

The picture that emerges from the Rand studies is complex and incomplete. There is an indication that for some types of cases, jury decisions may not be entirely equitable. Juries may have a moderate bias against corporations. Nevertheless, it should be apparent that the charge that juries are lawless in civil trials is not proven. Most jury awards are moderate and even the large awards might be explained by other factors. Finally, even if it proves to be true that juries do express some bias against certain kinds of defendants, it may be because community attitudes about the responsibility of hospitals (and doctors), corporations, and governments have changed. In the past they were

not seen as accountable, but today they are. Jury decisions may be reflecting those sentiments.

*   *   *

So now we have a better grasp of how the jury functions. Sometimes the jury is at war with the law, but for the most part it is, in Kalven and Zeisel's phrase, a "modest war." There are very few instances in which the jury rejects the law outright. Rather it sometimes bends the law to comport with its own sense of what is just, fair, and equitable. Some will argue that this is still wrong; the law should always be followed. Others will say that the jury is doing exactly what it was intended that it should do. Regardless, the hard facts indicate that on the whole the jury behaves responsibly and rationally.

CHAPTER 11

Six versus Twelve, All versus Some

For hundreds of years, in both English and American courts, the jury was a twelve-person group whose members were required to agree unanimously on a verdict. In recent decades, two significant changes have altered the jury's form. Some jurisdictions now employ juries of six rather than twelve; others allow juries to reach majority decisions rather than unanimous ones. To conclude our study of jury decision-making, we need to explore the impact of these two changes on the functioning of the contemporary jury.

*   *   *

In 1973, Claude Davis Ballew managed the Paris Adult Theatre on Peachtree Street in Atlanta, Georgia. The theater showed the sexually explicit movie *Behind the Green Door* in November of that year. On November 9, two investigators from the Fulton County Solicitor General's office joined the regular patrons of the Paris Adult Theatre. After viewing *Behind the Green Door,* the investigators left to obtain a warrant for its seizure on the grounds that the movie was obscene. They took the warrant back to the theater and seized the film. Investigators returned to the theater later that month, again viewed *Behind the Green Door,* obtained yet another warrant, and seized a second copy of the film. Ballew was subsequently charged with two counts of distributing obscene material. Under Georgia law, material was obscene if, applying community standards, its predominant appeal was to prurient interests, it had no redeeming social value, and it went substantially beyond "customary limits of candor."

The charges against Ballew were misdemeanors. In the Criminal Court of Fulton County, where Ballew was to be tried, misdemeanor trials were heard before juries of five members, as required by the Georgia Constitution. Ballew argued that the Court should empanel a twelve-person jury in his case. Ballew pointed to the fact that a central function of the jury in an obscenity trial is the application of community standards to decide whether the material

in question is obscene. Ballew maintained that a five-person jury would not adequately reflect the range of opinions of the community. The Court, however, denied his request. A five-person jury heard Ballew's case, and after 38 minutes of deliberation convicted him on both charges. The judge fined Ballew two thousand dollars and sentenced him to a year in prison, to be suspended upon payment of the fine.

Ballew then began the appeals process which would ultimately take his case to the U.S. Supreme Court. The Court of Appeals of the State of Georgia heard Ballew's claim that the five-member jury deprived him of his constitutional right to trial by jury, but they rejected his contention. The Supreme Court of Georgia refused to hear his case. Finally, in 1977, the U.S. Supreme Court agreed to consider his arguments, in part to review the issue of whether a five-person jury is unconstitutional.

*   *   *

Ballew's case was not the first time the Supreme Court had explored the constitutionality of juries of different sizes. In 1970, in *Williams v. Florida,* the Justices examined Florida's practice of using six-person juries in most criminal trials. The sole exception were death penalty cases, which were heard by twelve-member juries. Williams, charged with robbery, asked for a twelve-person jury instead of the usual six-person jury, but the judge denied the request. Williams was duly convicted and sentenced to life imprisonment. He appealed to the U.S. Supreme Court on several grounds, including the constitutionality of a six-person jury.

In their decision in *Williams,* the Supreme Court justices traced the history of the twelve-person jury and concluded that the number twelve appeared to be a "historical accident unrelated to the great purposes which gave rise to the jury in the first place."[1] The key constitutional issue for jury size, they judged, was whether different sizes affected the jury's functioning. They held that a six-person jury did not undermine the jury's essential functions:

> [Jury performance] is not a function of the particular number of the body that makes up the jury. To be sure, the number should probably be large enough to promote group deliberation, free from outside attempts at intimidation and to provide a fair possibility for obtaining a representative cross-section of the community. But we find little reason to think that these goals are in any meaningful sense less likely to be achieved when the jury numbers six, than when it numbers twelve.[2]

The Court cited several "studies" as support for its conclusion that there were no discernible differences between six- and twelve-person juries. Scholars, however, devastatingly criticized the studies upon which the Court relied.[3]

One critic was Hans Zeisel, a coauthor of *The American Jury*. He reviewed the six articles the Court cited and concluded that they provided "scant evidence by any standards." For instance, one study was really only a report by a judge who had presided over certain trials in Washington, D.C. that used five-person juries; he wrote that he found them satisfactory. In another, a judge summarized the economic advantages of smaller civil juries. Another article reported the impressions of the court clerk and three lawyers that six-member juries in 43 Massachusetts trials seemed to produce about the same verdicts as twelve-person juries.

Zeisel went on to show through statistical analyses that there should be important consequences of a decision to employ a six- as opposed to a twelve-person jury. A central purpose of trial by jury is to represent the divergent views of the community. Zeisel demonstrated that the twelve-person jury will be better able to represent these different views than the six-person jury. His example: Suppose that 90% of the community holds one view and 10% holds a minority viewpoint. Further suppose that we draw 100 twelve-member juries and 100 six-member juries from this population randomly. Seventy-two of the 100 twelve-person juries would have at least one person with a minority viewpoint on the jury, while only 47 of the 100 six-person juries would have a minority representative.[4]

Another important consequence of jury size is the variability of the decisions. The larger the sample of individuals from a community, the lower the margin of error is. Because six-person juries are smaller samples of the community, we can expect them to produce a wider variety of outcomes than twelve-person juries. Put another way, twelve-person juries are more likely to reach the same decision than are six-person juries. Zeisel showed how this principle would affect damage awards in personal injury cases. We know that jurors have very different ideas about how much injured claimants should be compensated, and that the ultimate award by the jury will be somewhere around the average of its individual jurors. Suppose that the community is divided into six groups of equal size with differing beliefs about how much money a particular plaintiff should be awarded, with an average award of $3,500. Again, let's randomly select 100 six-person juries and 100 twelve-person juries from this "community" and calculate their average awards. A statistical analysis reveals that over two-thirds of the twelve-person juries will have average damage awards close to the community average, compared to just half of the six-person juries. The six-person juries are four times as likely to have extremely low or extremely high average damage awards. Hence, the twelve-person jury should provide a more accurate and a more reliable reflection of the community's assessment.

A final way that six- and twelve-person juries should differ, according

to Zeisel, is in the number of deadlocked, or "hung," juries. Deadlocked juries should be *less* likely in six-person groups for several reasons. Almost inevitably, hung juries are found in groups which contain several dissenters at the beginning of the deliberation. Psychologically, jurors are able to hold out against a majority only when they have some initial support. There will be fewer minority jurors on six-person juries, and the likelihood that more than one dissenter will appear on a six-person jury is slimmer still. Zeisel compared the hung jury rate for twelve-person juries nationwide with the hung jury rate in Miami Circuit Court in which six-person juries were utilized. Hung juries were more than twice as frequent in the larger juries: 5.5% of the twelve-person juries hung while just 2.4% of the six-person juries hung. While the smaller size jury will thus be more economical, this reduction in hung juries, in Zeisel's words, "is but the combined result of less representative, more homogeneous juries and of a reduced ability to resist the pressure for unanimity."[5]

*   *   *

The Supreme Court's next opportunity to confront the issue of jury size came just two years after Professor Zeisel's article was published. In *Colgrove v. Battin*, the Court considered jury size in federal civil cases rather than criminal cases.[6] Justice Brennan, writing for the majority, sanctioned the use of the six-person jury in civil cases. Brennan wrote that the purpose of the jury trial in civil cases was to assure a fair and equitable resolution of factual issues. He stated that the key question, as in *Williams*, was whether jury size affected the jury's ability to do its job. Justice Brennan noted that much had been written about jury size since *Williams* had been decided. However, nothing persuaded the Justices to depart from their earlier conclusion that the reliability of the jury as a fact finder was unrelated to its size. Brennan cited Professor Zeisel's article, but countered it with another study showing that people in smaller juries discussed matters more openly. Brennan capped off his discussion of empirical work by stating, "In addition, four very recent studies have provided convincing empirical evidence of the correctness of the *Williams* conclusion that 'there is no discernible difference between the results reached by the two different-sized juries.' "[7] Thus, the Court upheld the use of the six-person jury in federal civil trials.

Justice Marshall harshly dissented in the Colgrove decision:

> . . . my Brethren mount a frontal assault on the very nature of the civil jury as that concept has been understood for some seven hundred years. No one need be fooled by reference to the six-man trier of fact . . . as a "jury.". . . We deal

> here not with some minor tinkering with the role of the civil jury, but with its
> wholesale abolition and replacement with a different institution which functions
> differently, produces different results, and was wholly unknown to the Framers
> of the Seventh Amendment.[8]

Marshall focused primarily on constitutional issues and said that he thought that research studies were irrelevant to the issues of concern to him about six-person juries. Nevertheless, he cited the article by Professor Zeisel as indicating that changes in jury size did seem to produce variations in jury functioning and verdicts.

The *Williams* and *Colgrove* decisions had far-reaching consequences. Before 1970, only a handful of American courts used six-person juries. But after these two decisions, many jurisdictions across the nation embraced them. In part, this widespread adoption was related to a movement already under way to modernize and streamline the increasingly overburdened courts. Legislators and court administrators saw the reduction to the six-person jury as a measure that would simultaneously increase efficiency and reduce costs. To them, six-person juries meant fewer people to organize and less money required to pay jurors.[9]

The response to the *Williams* and *Colgrove* decisions in the academic community was not nearly so favorable. The "convincing empirical evidence" that Brennan had cited so positively was evaluated and found wanting.[10] Boston College psychology professor Michael Saks reviewed the studies and discovered that they suffered from a variety of research problems. For instance, two studies compared outcomes between six- and twelve-person juries in states where the attorney could choose the jury size. One of the studies found that six- and twelve-member civil juries in New Jersey Superior Court were no more likely to favor the plaintiff. However, the types of cases tried before juries of six and twelve were not the same; these differences may have hidden any effects of jury size. For instance, attorneys tended to choose smaller juries when the case was less complex and less costly. The twelve-person juries heard cases in which the damage awards were roughly triple those of the smaller juries. Attorneys may have been unwilling to take a gamble with smaller juries when the dollar amount at issue was large.

Another study cited by Justice Brennan examined the impact of a legal change in Michigan that reduced the size of the civil jury beginning in July of 1970. This study compared the outcomes of trials before that date with twelve-person juries and after that date with six-person juries, and found no differences in verdicts. However, several other important changes in the trial court also occurred at that time, and may have masked any effects of the change in jury size. Finally, a laboratory study with simulated jurors found

no differences when jurors decided in groups of six or twelve. But the single case used in the simulation was an odd one. Not a single jury found for the plaintiff. The results, therefore, were essentially meaningless. Professor Saks and other scholars concluded that the four studies cited by Justice Brennan collectively were certainly not "convincing empirical evidence."

University of Michigan law professor Richard Lempert sounded another alarm.[4] He argued persuasively that typical research strategies would not reveal differences between six- and twelve-member juries even if jury size had a significant impact in certain cases. Drawing on past jury research, he pointed out that in the majority of cases, the evidence in favor of one side or the other is clear, and would be decided similarly by juries of six, juries of twelve, or even judges deciding the case alone. Lempert calculated that six- and twelve-member juries could disagree over the verdict in no more than 14% of all cases. Even if jury size had a strong and important impact in most of these cases, the effects would be overshadowed and masked by the larger number of cases that would show no differences.

Many researchers, worried that the Court had overgeneralized from scanty and methodologically poor research, began to conduct better research studies comparing the performance of groups of different sizes.[9] By the time that Claude Ballew's case was about to be heard by the U.S. Supreme Court, there was a considerable body of literature on differences between six- and twelve-person juries. Most of the literature supported the arguments of early critics that smaller juries provided poorer representation of community viewpoints and that the variability of six-person group decisions would be much greater than that of twelve-person groups. But recall that Ballew was not battling for a twelve-person jury over a six-person jury; rather, he was arguing that a *five*-person jury was unconstitutional.

*   *   *

The *Ballew* decision was in some ways gratifying and in other ways disturbing. Justice Blackmun wrote the majority opinion for the Supreme Court. After outlining Ballew's case and analyzing the constitutional issues, Blackmun wrote that the *Williams* and *Colgrove* decisions had generated a large quantity of research on the topic of jury size. He then carefully reviewed the myriad empirical studies, law review articles, and social science critiques, and concluded that the empirical data suggested that smaller juries were less likely to engage in effective group deliberation, to represent different views in the community, to counterbalance various biases, and to produce accurate verdicts. All but one of the studies Blackmun cited compared six- and twelve-

person groups, and after Blackmun was through reviewing these studies and the deleterious effects of the six-person jury, one might have expected Blackmun to overrule the earlier decisions in *Williams* and *Colgrove* and declare the six-member jury unconstitutional. He did nothing of the kind. Instead, the Court reaffirmed the earlier decisions, while using the empirical data to justify drawing the line at six. As Blackmun put it:

> While we adhere to, and reaffirm our holding in *Williams v. Florida*, these studies, most of which have been made since *Williams* was decided in 1970, lead us to conclude that the purpose and functioning of the jury in a criminal trial is seriously impaired, and to a constitutional degree, by a reduction in size to below six members. We readily admit that we do not pretend to discern a clear line between six members and five. But the assembled data raise substantial doubt about the reliability and appropriate representation of panels smaller than six.[11]

Ballew's five-person jury was thus declared unconstitutional. Why did the Court fail to overturn its earlier decisions, in light of the new empirical evidence? Scholars speculated that because juries had been reduced from twelve to six throughout the nation after the Court's prior decisions, to reverse the earlier ruling would be very disruptive and no doubt unpopular. The safest, although somewhat illogical, decision in *Ballew* was to get off the slippery slope: to halt further reductions in the size of the jury while leaving the six-member jury intact.[12] Thus, the line has been drawn; American juries must contain at least six persons.

In 1981, a Colorado man tested the limit. Charged with criminal mischief, he requested a jury of one person. A Colorado law stated that a criminal defendant may, with the approval of the judge, choose to be tried by a number of jurors less than the number to which he or she is otherwise entitled. The defendant's attorney reasoned that a lone juror would be very hesitant to convict. The trial judge granted the defendant's motion. But before the trial in front of a jury of one could proceed, an appellate court overruled the judge and said that six jurors was the lowest number a defendant could choose.[13]

*   *   *

Another aspect of trial by jury that has undergone change in recent years is the requirement that jurors must unanimously agree on the verdict. The origin of the unanimity requirement is unknown, although the first report of a case in which it was required dates back to 1367. One explanation traces the unanimity requirement back to an earlier form of the jury trial—trial by compurgation. As we discussed earlier, in trial by compurgators, jurors were added to an original panel of twelve until twelve people voted for one of the

parties. When the practice of adding jurors was discontinued, the requirement that the twelve jurors agree on a verdict was maintained. A second possibility is that jury unanimity developed to compensate the defendant for the inadequate legal and procedural rules which characterized trials in earlier times. Likewise, the penalties for offenses were extremely harsh in common law, and jury unanimity may have been viewed as some protection for the accused. Jury unanimity may also have developed because jurors originally were witnesses and had personal knowledge of the offense being tried. As noted earlier, in medieval times, it was presumed that there was only one correct view of the facts; if jurors did not agree, then they could be punished for perjury. This provided considerable incentive for unanimity.[14]

Like jury size, jury unanimity came under close scrutiny by those interested in streamlining the justice system. In 1967, Great Britain abolished the centuries-old unanimity requirement in the wake of a discovery that in trials of professional criminals, some jurors had been bribed and intimidated to vote not guilty. England passed a law that allowed the jury in a criminal trial to return a majority verdict of 11 : 1 or 10 : 2. However, the jury first had to deliberate at least two hours or whatever the judge thought was a reasonable amount of time. The Secretary of State for the Home Office, Roy Jenkins, justified the reform when he introduced the new law:

> [Majority verdicts] are not likely to result in different verdicts in many cases, but these few cases may well be crucial from the point of view of law enforcement and the breaking-up of big criminal conspiracies. . . . The disagreements undoubtedly occur in certain cases, not because one or two jurors are borderline—quite the reverse—but because one or two jurors have been persuaded, by bribery or intimidation, to hold out against the evidence. . . . [To] allow criminal interference with juries, which is very difficult to prove except where it fails, to enable big criminals to frustrate the process of justice, is to fight crime with our hands tied behind our backs.[15]

The move to majority verdicts was made with little prior study, and it set off a storm of protest in the British Houses of Parliament. Those against the change pointed out that there was little evidence on which to base the abandonment of the unanimity requirement; no one had any idea how frequently jurors were bribed and even whether eliminating the unanimity requirement would solve the problem. One opponent of the change, Lord Denning, simply asked: "What is the mischief?" Furthermore, many worried about the consequences of doing away with unanimity. Britain would, in effect, be taking a leap in the dark.

In the United States, just two years after the Supreme Court justices had decided that state criminal trial juries need not consist of twelve persons in

Williams, they concluded that unanimity was not constitutionally required for those juries either. In a pair of cases decided in 1972, *Johnson v. Louisiana* and *Apodaca v. Oregon,* the Court dealt a double blow to the unanimity requirement in state courts. However, it left intact the requirement that jurors agree unanimously in federal courts.[16]

On January 20, 1968, Frank Johnson was arrested at his home. The victim of an armed robbery had identified Johnson as the culprit from photographs. Johnson then proceeded to a lineup, at which he was identified by still another robbery victim. At his trial on the second robbery charge, he pleaded not guilty, but a twelve-person jury convicted him by a nine-to-three vote. For crimes of robbery, Louisiana law specified that defendants be tried by a jury of twelve; moreover, a minimum of nine jurors had to agree on the verdict. Johnson appealed the majority verdict, arguing that because three of the jurors did not agree to convict, the prosecution had not proved the case beyond a reasonable doubt.

But Justice White, writing for the majority of the U.S. Supreme Court, said that just because some jurors dissented did not necessarily imply that the reasonable doubt standard had been violated. Justice White revealed some of the Court's assumptions about jury behavior when he stated:

> We have no grounds for believing that majority jurors, aware of their responsibility and power over the liberty of the defendant, would simply refuse to listen to arguments presented to them in favor of acquittal, terminate discussion and render a verdict. On the contrary it is far more likely that a juror presenting reasoned argument in favor of acquittal would either have his arguments answered or would carry enough other jurors with him to prevent conviction. A majority will cease discussion and outvote a minority only after reasoned discussion has ceased to have persuasive effect or to serve any other purpose—when a minority, that is, continues to insist upon acquittal without having persuasive reasons in support of its position.

Justice White suggested that at this point a minority juror should probably question whether his or her own doubts are reasonable, since they have failed to make an impression on the rest of the jurors.

Several other Justices, disagreeing with the majority opinion, cited a long line of Supreme Court cases upholding the right of all citizens, regardless of race, color, or creed, to participate on the jury. But under a majority rule like Louisiana's, nine jurors could ignore their fellow jurors of a different race or class. The dissenting Justices lamented that "today's judgment approves the elimination of the one rule that can ensure that such participation will be meaningful—the rule requiring the assent of all jurors before a verdict of conviction or acquittal can be returned." To these Justices, unanimity and

impartial jury selection were complementary; they operated jointly to promote fairness and community confidence in the criminal justice system.

In the second case involving jury unanimity, *Apodaca v. Oregon,* three Oregon defendants convicted by less than unanimous juries challenged the constitutionality of the verdicts. The Court took the same approach to thinking about the importance of jury unanimity as it had taken when thinking about jury size in *Williams.* The Justices focused on the functions of the jury in contemporary society and inquired whether the requirement that jurors agree unanimously affected those functions. To fulfill its functions, the jury must interpose between the government and the accused the commonsense judgment of a group of laypeople. Justice White wrote for the majority that the exercise of this commonsense judgment was not significantly affected by jury unanimity, and he rejected the notion that jury unanimity was required to ensure meaningful participation of all segments of society.

Justice Douglas dissented strenuously. He maintained that eliminating jury unanimity would reduce the reliability of jury verdicts.

> The diminution of verdict reliability [in juries where unanimity is not required] flows from the fact that nonunanimous juries need not debate and deliberate as fully as must unanimous juries. . . . It is said that there is no evidence that majority jurors will refuse to listen to dissenters whose votes are unneeded for conviction. Yet human experience teaches that polite and academic conversation is no substitute for the earnest and robust argument necessary to reach unanimity.

Justice Douglas pointed out that jurors deliberated just 41 minutes in Robert Apodaca's trial before convicting him by a ten-to-two vote.

The Supreme Court's decisions about jury unanimity in the *Johnson* and *Apodaca* cases rested in part on the Justices' views about how unanimity would affect the quality and reliability of jury deliberation, and about equal participation in the jury room. Social scientists subsequently tested some of these assumptions in jury simulation experiments. For instance, one of us (V.P.H.) had six-person juries decide a case of robbery. At the beginning of the deliberation, all the groups had four members who favored a guilty verdict and two members who favored not guilty. Half of the groups deliberated knowing that they had to reach a unanimous decision. The other half were told instead that although it was desirable that they all agree, a majority verdict, involving just five out of six jurors, was acceptable. The group deliberations were videotaped. Later, law students scrutinized the videotapes and evaluated them. The law students agreed that, when there was a unanimity requirement, jurors trying to argue a minority position participated more actively and were more influential in the deliberations. Further analysis of

the videotaped deliberations confirmed that minority members took a more active role in groups deliberating under a unanimous decision rule.[17]

Psychologists Reid Hastie, Steven Penrod, and Nancy Pennington also conducted a jury simulation study to test the effects of the unanimity requirement.[18] With the cooperation of local officials, they recruited members of the Superior Court jury pools in three Massachusetts counties to serve as subjects in their experiment. They presented all subject-jurors with a videotaped reenactment of an actual murder trial. Groups of twelve jurors were randomly assigned to one of three conditions. One-third of the juries were required to come to a unanimous decision, one-third had to reach a majority decision in which ten of the twelve agreed, and the final third had to reach a majority decision in which eight of the twelve agreed.

Although the ultimate verdicts were similar, under unanimous and majority rules the juries deliberated quite differently. Those required to come to a unanimous verdict spent a longer time deliberating, but their deliberations were not simply longer versions of those of majority juries. Professor Hastie characterized the unanimity juries as "evidence-driven" in contrast to the majority juries who engaged in "verdict-driven" deliberations. Unanimity juries were more thorough in their evaluation of the evidence and the law; jurors in the minority participated more actively in the discussion; and jurors were more satisfied with the final verdict under a unanimous decision rule.

These studies, as well as others,[19] shed some doubt on assumptions underlying the majority opinions of the Supreme Court decisions in the jury unanimity cases. Jurors take a subtle message from the instruction that they need not be unanimous. They deliberate in a different manner, and the influence of jurors trying to argue a minority position is diluted, exactly as the dissenting Justices in *Apodaca* had feared. We will never know whether Ralph Johnson and Robert Apodaca would have been acquitted if their juries had been required to reach unanimous verdicts, but the research studies indicate that their juries would have deliberated more carefully and with greater attention to minority viewpoints.

*   *   *

As one pundit has noted, the Supreme Court is not last because it's supreme; rather, it's supreme because it is last. The Supreme Court has had, for the time being, the last word on the jury size and jury decision rule issues. In 1979, the Court decided *Burch v. Louisiana,* in which past jury size and jury unanimity decisions were combined to prohibit majority verdicts in six-

person juries. The Court reasoned that since six is the absolute minimum number of jurors necessary to preserve the great functions of trial by jury, then a rule that allows just five of the six jurors to agree on a verdict is unconstitutional. If juries consist of six persons, they must reach unanimous verdicts; but if they consist of twelve, majority verdicts are acceptable.

Time will tell whether the important decisions to allow six-person juries and majority verdicts in larger juries have so fundamentally affected the functioning of the jury that, in Justice Marshall's words, the jury as we have known it has been replaced by an entirely new institution which functions differently and produces different results.

PART IV

The Jury in the Eye of the Storm

Mad or Bad? Juries and the Defense of Insanity

One of the most controversial jury verdicts in recent history was delivered on June 21, 1982, for the trial of John Hinckley, Jr. On the gray, drizzly day of March 30, 1981, as President Ronald Reagan was leaving the Washington Hilton Hotel after giving a speech, Hinckley managed to shoot and wound the President, White House Press Secretary James Brady, District of Columbia police officer Thomas K. Delahanty, and U.S. Secret Service agent Timothy McCarthy. A camera operator covering Reagan's departure from the Hilton captured Hinckley's shooting spree on videotape. The graphic footage was played again and again on television broadcasts nationwide.

Police evidence suggested a bizarre motive for the crime: that Hinckley had tried to kill the President to win the attention and love of actress Jodie Foster. Jodie Foster had played a young prostitute in the movie *Taxi Driver,* a film that Hinckley had seen many times. Hinckley identified with the movie's fictional hero, Travis Bickle, a cab driver who befriended the prostitute. In the film, Bickle rescued the teenage prostitute during a murderous rampage after he stalked a presidential candidate in an unsuccessful attempt to assassinate him.

Hinckley apparently wrote a letter to Foster just before he went out to shoot the President. Hinckley claimed in the letter that she was the motivation for his assassination attempt: "Jodie, I would abandon this idea of getting Reagan in a second if I could only win your heart and live out the rest of my life with you, whether it be in total obscurity or whatever. . . . Jodie, I'm asking you now to please look into your heart and at least give me the chance, with this historic deed, to gain your respect and love." Police found the letter, along with an airplane hijack note Hinckley may have been planning to use, in Hinckley's hotel room after the shooting.

With Hinckley caught literally with the smoking gun, his defense lawyers decided to raise the insanity plea at his trial on thirteen charges relating to the incident. The prosecution began the eight-week trial by calling eyewit-

nesses and by presenting over 100 pieces of evidence related to the event. Jurors saw the videotape of the shooting. Dozens of Hinckley's poems were introduced, as were the airplane hijack note and letter to Foster.

While Hinckley himself did not take the stand, several psychiatric experts testified for the defense that Hinckley suffered from the serious mental illness of schizophrenia, which is often characterized by delusions, a severe break with reality, and depression. The experts stressed Hinckley's history of emotional and psychiatric problems. They pointed to his bizarre fantasies of kidnapping Foster, hijacking a plane, and moving into the White House with her, his morbid poetry, and his near-total social isolation. The parallels between Hinckley and his hero Travis Bickle were illustrated by a courtroom showing of *Taxi Driver*.

Hinckley's millionaire parents took the stand on behalf of their son. In heart-wrenching testimony, they described how they agreed to carry out a plan, fashioned by Hinckley's Denver psychiatrist, to force their son to become more independent by the end of March 1981, coincidentally the very time that he shot Reagan. They barred their son from their home weeks before the shooting, hoping their actions would force him to get a job and become self-sufficient. On the witness stand, John Hinckley, Sr. lamented to the jury that forcing his son out was the greatest mistake of his life.

The prosecution countered with its own psychiatric experts. These experts claimed that while Hinckley suffered from personality disorders, none was sufficient to prevent him from understanding that shooting the President was wrong or from controlling his behavior. Rather, the prosecution experts characterized the defendant as a narcissistic, manipulative parasite, who chose assassination as a method of "becoming famous without working."

The psychiatric testimony was often contradictory and complex. Many commentators wondered whether lay jurors would be capable of interpreting it. Even Judge Parker said, at the close of the psychiatric evidence, "Well, I think there is either enough to guide the jury or to confuse the jury."

When the trial began, few seriously thought that the Hinckley insanity plea would succeed. After all, no person had avoided conviction for assassinating or attempting to assassinate an acting president since 1835. In that year, a jury took five minutes flat to find Richard Lawrence not guilty by reason of insanity for his unsuccessful attempt on the life of President Andrew Jackson. But as Hinckley's troubled past, his history of psychiatric problems, and his delusions concerning Foster were paraded before the jury, some observers began to doubt Hinckley's ability to control his actions and to wonder what the jury would do.

Fueling these doubts was a growing awareness of the laws governing

insanity trials in the District of Columbia. In line with District of Columbia law, presiding Judge Barrington Parker instructed the jurors that, for them to find Hinckley guilty, the *prosecution* had to prove to them beyond a reasonable doubt that Hinckley was sane at the time of the shooting. If the defense raised in their minds a reasonable doubt about Hinckley's sanity, then they had to find him not guilty by reason of insanity. In contrast, many other jurisdictions instead require that, in insanity cases, the *defense* prove by a preponderance of the evidence that the defendant was insane.

The jurors, mostly blue-collar workers, all but one of whom was black, took a total of four days and approximately 25 hours to reach a verdict in the case. Judge Parker, speaking later with a reporter, described the moment that Hinckley's fate was decided. As evening approached on June 21, the jury continued to deliberate. Parker was sitting at his desk working. He glanced at his watch; it was close to dinnertime. "I was thinking of having them [the jurors] deliberate for another half-hour or so. That's when they sent a note saying they had a verdict. I asked the marshal to knock on the door and they gave it to him in a sealed envelope." Parker reconvened the court for the reading of the jury's verdict. The courtroom quickly filled with news reporters and interested onlookers, eager for the conclusion of the case. The jury filed in, looking somber and weary. Parker stated that "When I opened the envelope [containing the jury's verdict] in the courtroom I was surprised but I didn't show it." Although it is traditional for the jury leader to read the jury's verdict in open court, Parker decided to read the verdict himself "so nothing would go wrong." Thirteen times, for each of the thirteen charges against Hinckley, he repeated the verdict: "*Not Guilty by Reason of Insanity.*"

The verdict stunned spectators and trial participants alike. After a moment of silence, the crowd became so noisy that Judge Parker was forced to quiet it. While the prosecution team remained expressionless, the defendant's parents embraced each other in tears. John Hinckley, Jr., his hands shaking, wiped his eyes, shook his head, and sighed. U.S. marshals quickly led him out of the courtroom after the reading of the verdict.[1]

*   *   *

To say the verdict was unpopular would be an understatement. The uproar in the courtroom at the announcement of the verdict anticipated the popular response. An ABC News poll, taken just after the verdict, revealed that three out of every four Americans surveyed felt justice had not been done in the Hinckley case.[2] In another survey, the majority of respondents claimed that had they themselves been jurors in the trial, they'd have convicted the would-

bc assassin. Most believed that Hinckley was not insane and had little faith in the psychiatric testimony presented at the trial. They wanted to see Hinckley treated for his mental problems, but they also wanted him to be punished for his crimes.[3]

Judge Parker was deluged by a flood of some 1500 letters complaining about the jury's verdict. Many correspondents exhorted Judge Parker to keep Hinckley off the streets. One couple from Mobile, Alabama ominously charged that: "This jury and you and this trial with that verdict have let loose a monster in our country that will pursue us for eons to come. Our justice system in the country is the laughingstock of other countries, and now they can claim their right to laugh, where our President is shot in plain view of the public and Jim Brady's life is ruined. How much more proof is there that our justice system is sick when this crime proves that the victims lose, not the criminals." One (unsigned) letter stated, "Concerning the Hinckley case, I think you and the whole U.S. justice system stink. License to kill requirements. 1. pretend you're insane. 2. have lots of money. 3. hire Hinckley's attorney. 4. see Judge Parker."[4]

As these comments reveal, protest over the Hinckley verdict culminated in anger at the criminal justice system, the insanity plea, and trial by jury in insanity cases. Indeed, nine out of every ten respondents in one survey concluded that the insanity defense was a "loophole" that allowed too many guilty people to go free.[3] The tradition of psychiatric testimony in insanity cases was assailed. Social satirist Andy Rooney probably spoke for many people when he noted that "the only people who look worse than Hinckley at his trial are the psychiatrists who have testified."[5] Many people also questioned the ability of lay jurors to sift through the complex and often contradictory testimony of the psychiatric experts and to make reasonable decisions. Others criticized the judge and his legal instructions to the jury.[6]

In the wake of the Hinckley verdict, many American citizens called for the abolition of the insanity defense or insisted on radical reforms. Legislators and politicians were not deaf to their cries. In the three days following the Hinckley verdict, a dozen proposals to reform the insanity defense were introduced in Congress, nine in the House of Representatives and three in the Senate.[6] The White House responded by generating its own proposal for limiting the insanity plea.[7] State legislators also reacted swiftly to the verdict. For instance, the day after the Hinckley verdict was reached, the Delaware legislature passed a law providing a "guilty but mentally ill" verdict as an alternative in insanity cases.[3] To date, the federal government and over half the states have changed their insanity laws.[8] Indeed, the Hinckley trial promises to be a landmark case in the reform of the insanity defense.

*   *   *

In the face of widespread public criticism of their verdict in the Hinckley trial, a number of the jurors defended themselves. Some spoke to news media representatives after the conclusion of the case. And, in an unprecedented move, five of the jurors voluntarily agreed to give testimony about their views of the insanity defense and their reactions to the Hinckley case before a Senate subcommittee considering legislation to change the insanity defense.[9]

One juror, Nathalia Brown, a 31-year-old machine repairer, was one of the last two holdouts for conviction but ultimately voted to find Hinckley not guilty by reason of insanity. In the Senate hearing, she talked about the difficulties of serving on the Hinckley trial:

> They lay this in our laps. And the people are looking down on the jurors. They do not realize what it means to be a juror in this type of case. They do not know the different pressures of being away from your family. They sit and tell us: Hinckley, he's out here playing, he's locked up playing Ping-pong, what a good basketball player he is. Here we are incarcerated by justice trying to figure out what his outcome is going to be. Those pressures.
>
> I had all the opportunity to try to prove to the other jurors that he was sane. But the prosecution could not do it, how am I going to do it? I got 10 other people to try to prove that he is sane. We went through all the evidence. Here the evidence shows he had a mental disorder. But he contradicted himself so much and made fools of a lot of psychiatrists. How were we really to pinpoint what was his problem?
>
> And then for our own mental state we had to think about that, too. I felt that I was on the brink of insanity myself going through this, you know.[9]

Even though the jurors ultimately found Hinckley not guilty by reason of insanity, they were haunted by the same anger and doubts that characterized the public's response to the case. For instance, despite the fact that Ms. Brown finally voted with the majority to find Hinckley not guilty by reason of insanity, she nevertheless stated: "The issue is not whether he was a little off, or whether this poem or that one didn't make sense. He shot those people, he shot them on purpose, he planned the whole thing out. Ain't nothing wrong with him."[10] Her distrust of Hinckley's claim of insanity mirrored that of many Americans.

Indeed, in their Senate testimony, all five jurors agreed that they believed that Hinckley knew what he was doing at the time of the shooting.[11] But several stated that while Hinckley was aware of his actions, his mental illness made him unable to control himself. Therefore, according to the law, he had to be found not guilty by reason of insanity. The jurors said their decision would have been the same even if the President had been killed. Recall that

under the existing District of Columbia law, the prosecution had to prove beyond a reasonable doubt that Hinckley was sane. Right after the verdict, some commentators claimed that the fact that the burden of proof was on the prosecution led inevitably to Hinckley's insanity verdict. The Senators asked the Hinckley jurors whether they understood this burden of proof, and whether a different rule would have changed their verdict. It was clear from the Senate questioning session that at least some jurors understood the burden of proof requirement.[12] But jurors asserted that they would have reached the same verdict even if the burden of proof had been different.

The jurors revealed some impatience with the psychiatrists who testified at the Hinckley trial, a sentiment that mirrored public feeling. Several jurors stated that because both prosecution and defense witnesses had repeated the key points to them again and again, they felt they understood the psychiatric testimony. But Maryland T. Copelin, who joined Brown as a holdout for conviction, expressed frustration that the psychiatric testimony in the case was not more conclusive: "There were laymen on the jury and professionals giving evidence. The professionals couldn't prove him innocent or guilty; how did they expect us to?"[13] One senator asked Ms. Copelin if she thought a jury decision was the proper method of determining the guilt or innocence of an accused when insanity is involved. She replied: "Yes, I do because, even though we had the doctors and all the professors there, they did not prove anything either with all their knowledge and degrees. They did not prove anything. So, yes, I think the jury is qualified for that."[14] The jurors also rejected the idea that an "objective" panel of psychiatrists replace the current use of psychiatrists hired by the prosecution and the defense. Mr. Glynis T. Lassiter, a custodian at American University, stated: "I know that the defense had their psychiatrists; so did the prosecution. So, I know that both of them are going to try to influence us that they are right. So, I didn't pay it any mind. I just heard both sides [and thought about them.]"[15] Mr. Woodrow Johnson, a parking lot attendant, agreed. After Johnson listened to the psychiatrists for the two sides, it seemed to him that some of them were overstating Hinckley's mental problem and some of them were understating it. He felt nevertheless that the prosecution and defense should still have the right to hire their own psychiatrists.[15]

In other testimony before the Senate subcommittee, the Hinckley jurors said they wished the law would allow someone like Hinckley to be both treated for his mental illness *and* punished for his crimes. For instance, Mr. Coffey, a 22-year-old banquet worker who served as jury foreman, said: "I think [the law] should be changed in some way where the defendant gets mental help, gets help enough that where he is not harmful to himself and

society, and then be punished for what he has done wrong."[16] Ms. Copelin agreed: "If a person is mentally ill, have them get the correct treatment and then also have them punished for their crime."[17] As Ms. Brown put it: "If they go out here, shoot or commit a crime, they should not be excused for it. If there is something wrong with them, treat them but make them pay. We have too many people that are victims of these crimes, and people are just walking away from them. And I think you should pay for your crimes."[17] In line with their dual desires to punish and treat the mentally ill who commit crimes, three of the five asserted that if there had been an option to find Hinckley guilty but mentally ill, they would have selected it.[18]

Indeed, one sees that, far from being completely at odds with the American public's perceptions and reactions to the Hinckley case, the jury instead reflected much of the public's ambivalence. They felt Hinckley knew what he was doing; they thought he had mental problems; they wanted him both treated and punished; they had some grave doubts about the credibility of the psychiatric testimony. While people were angry at the Hinckley verdict and felt that justice was not done by finding him not guilty by reason of insanity, it is entirely possible that many juries of twelve other individuals, who actually heard the evidence and Judge Parker's legal instructions, would have reached the same verdict.

* * *

Some critics have questioned why our legal system includes such a controversial, almost universally hated provision like the insanity defense.[19] Defenders, however, point out that the insanity defense is an integral part of our legal system. The entire system is predicated on the assumption that we exercise free will in our actions and thus can be held accountable for them. In our criminal law, the assignment of criminal responsibility requires not only that we commit a criminal act but also that we *intend* to commit that act. Those without a guilty mind or criminal intent are thus usually not held accountable. For instance, we don't punish very young children in the same way as adults for committing serious crimes, since we judge that children can't tell what they are doing is wrong. If a woman robs a bank because a man with a gun pointed to her head tells her to, we don't hold her accountable for the robbery. We may absolve of legal guilt a careful driver who accidentally kills a child darting out in front of his car, whereas we convict a driver who purposefully runs over a child. Similarly, we often judge that the insane lack criminal intent. Mental illness may undermine the ability to tell whether what one is doing is wrong or may hamper the capability to control one's actions.

The insanity defense allows some mentally ill people absolution from criminal responsibility.

Many legal scholars maintain that none of the goals of the criminal justice system is served when insane defendants, who lack the ability to control their actions or cannot tell right from wrong, are convicted and imprisoned. They believe that such goals as individual rehabilitation, deterrence, protection of the public from dangerous persons, and retribution or punishment, are not served by punishing the insane. Judge Irving Kaufman, of the United States Court of Appeals for the Second Circuit, and a staunch advocate of the insanity defense, tells why:

> No rehabilitative function is served when the mentally incompetent are placed in prisons rather than in institutions specifically designed to treat them. No deterrence is achieved, since those who cannot restrain their conduct are, by definition, 'undeterrable,' and their imprisonment cannot serve as an example to other individuals who may contemplate committing a crime. Therefore, the only benefit that derives from placing a mentally incompetent individual in a prison, rather than in a hospital, is a punishment that seems not at all just.[20]

While the insanity defense holds a central place in the law, widespread animosity toward it exists. Recent research suggests that much of this negativity stems from lack of knowledge and outright misconceptions about the insanity plea. One study of 434 community residents conducted right after the Hinckley verdict discovered that, even though most people thought the Hinckley verdict was unfair, only *one* respondent was able to define accurately the legal test for insanity.[3]

Several other research projects have found that people drastically overestimate the use and success of the insanity plea. Experts judge that, nationally, less than 1% of felony defendants plead not guilty by reason of insanity. Studies of court records show different success rates for the insanity plea in different jurisdictions (from 1% to 25% of that 1%) but all confirm that only a tiny proportion of defendants avoid criminal responsibility with a plea of insanity. Yet in two studies, community residents from Wyoming and Delaware estimated that four out of every ten criminal defendants plead not guilty by reason of insanity, and that a third of them are successful.[21]

The public also has a mistaken notion about just what happens to defendants found not guilty by reason of insanity. These notions fuel their fears that the insanity defense allows dangerous people to go free. For instance, most Delawareans surveyed estimated that Hinckley would be out of the mental hospital in two years or less, a prediction that time has proven incorrect.[3] Those who thought many defendants succeeded at the insanity plea

or who thought that insanity acquittees were held only short periods of time had more negative attitudes toward the insanity defense.[22]

*   *   *

While the dangers of the insanity defense may be overestimated, trying to set up guidelines for determining who deserves to be found not guilty because of insanity has never been simple. The history behind the insanity plea demonstrates just how hard it has been. Early cases used fairly crude definitions of insanity. In 1582, the Englishman William Lambard advanced one criterion:

> If a madman or a natural fool, or a lunatic in the time of his lunacy, or a child that apparently hath no knowledge of good or evil do kill a man, this is no felonious act, nor anything forfeited by it . . . for they cannot be said to have any under-standing will. But if upon examination it fall out, that they knew what they did, and this it was ill, then seemeth it otherwise.[23]

Another standard developed in the 1724 trial of Edward Arnold, known to his neighbors as "Crazy Ned." He was accused of shooting and wounding Lord Onslow. The trial judge instructed the jury that to find the defendant not guilty by reason of insanity he must be "totally deprived of his under-standing and memory, and doth not know what he is doing, no more than an infant, than a brute, or a wild beast."[24] This came to be known as the "wild beast" test. Apparently, Crazy Ned failed it, for the jury found him guilty. These cases were among the earliest versions of what is labeled the right versus wrong test for legal insanity. If defendants did not know what they were doing or that it was wrong, then they could be absolved of criminal responsibility.

Legal scholars and judges in subsequent cases refined the concept of insanity. Changes in notions of legal insanity paralleled changes in ideas about the brain and human psychology.[20] For instance, one popular theory in the 1700s was the notion of the compartmentalized mind, with different mental functions allocated to different physical areas of the brain. The famous English judge, Sir Matthew Hale, drew on this theory to develop a differentiation between total insanity and partial insanity. Individuals afflicted with partial insanity were, he argued, insane in some ways but could function perfectly well in others. Some defendants relied on this theory to explain how they could have purchased a pistol, loaded it, and killed a person with it despite suffering all the while from insane delusions.

Take the case of James Hadfield, a 29-year-old soldier who had been

released from the army for insanity resulting from brain damage incurred in battle. In 1800 he was tried for attempted regicide. Though Hadfield shot at King George III, he missed him. During his trial, the defense argued that Hadfield was laboring under the delusion of being the savior of the world, who could preserve humanity by sacrificing his own life. Because suicide was morally repugnant to him, and the punishment for attempted regicide was death, he fired his pistol at the King. The prosecution pointed out that Hadfield had enough sense to buy a pistol and ammunition, and therefore could not be mad. The defense conceded that Hadfield knew right from wrong, and was able to plan out his act, but argued that the act was a direct consequence of his insane delusions. The jury agreed with the defense and found Hadfield not guilty by reason of insanity.

History provides an intriguing parallel to the case of John Hinckley. In 1843, a young Scotsman named Daniel McNaughtan[25] was found not guilty by reason of insanity in circumstances reminiscent of the Hinckley trial. McNaughtan attempted to assassinate the Tory Prime Minister Sir Robert Peel, but mistakenly shot and killed Peel's private secretary Edward Drummond instead. At McNaughtan's trial on murder charges in London's Old Bailey, the only issue in dispute was the defendant's mental state. The Crown prosecutor maintained that McNaughtan must be held responsible for his actions since he could distinguish right from wrong, but the defense argued that McNaughtan was suffering from partial insanity and should be relieved of criminal responsibility. Nine medical experts testified on behalf of the defense. According to these witnesses, McNaughtan's attempt on the life of the Tory Prime Minister was a direct consequence of his delusions that he was being persecuted by the Tories. The Crown presented no medical testimony to rebut the defense claims, and the trial judge virtually directed the jury to acquit. The members of the jury did not even retire to their chambers. Instead, they huddled in the jury box and in less than two minutes found McNaughtan not guilty by reason of insanity.[26]

Like Hinckley, McNaughtan attempted to assassinate his country's leader and failed. Like Hinckley, he was absolved of criminal responsibility by a jury's verdict. Just as Americans reacted strongly, swiftly, and negatively to the Hinckley verdict, so too did the Victorians react to the verdict in the McNaughtan case. While there were no public opinion polls in Victorian days, the following stanza of a poem by Thomas Campbell captured the popular sentiment. The poem was widely reprinted in British newspapers right after the McNaughtan verdict:

> Ye people of England: exult and be glad
> For ye're now at the will of the merciless mad.

> Why say ye that but three authorities reign—
> Crown, Commons, and Lords!—You omit the insane!
> They're a privileg'd class, whom no statute controls
> And their murderous charter exists in their souls.
> Do they wish to spill blood—they have only to play
> A few pranks—get asylum'd a month and a day—
> Then heigh! to escape from the mad-doctor's keys,
> And to pistol or stab whosoever they please.[27]

Campbell's poem provides a succinct and eloquent reflection of the public's response to the McNaughtan verdict: the view that the insanity defense is a loophole that puts the public at risk; the perception that the insane are dangerous; and the belief that those found not guilty by reason of insanity will be confined for only a brief while, "a month and a day." These perceptions, of course, are very similar to modern-day Americans' views of the insanity defense.

Such negativity was not limited to the masses. In a letter Queen Victoria wrote to Sir Robert Peel following McNaughtan's acquittal, she commented unfavorably about the insanity verdicts of McNaughtan and another defendant:

> Buckingham Palace, 12 March 1843. . . . The law may be perfect, but how is it that whenever a case for its application arises, it proves to be of no avail? We have seen the trials of Oxford and McNaughtan conducted by the ablest lawyers of the day . . . and they allow and advise the Jury to pronounce the verdict of Not Guilty on account of Insanity,—whilst everybody is morally convinced that both malefactors were perfectly conscious and aware of what they did![28]

With a few changes in wording, Queen Victoria's comment could easily have been made in the days following the Hinckley trial.

Just as the Hinckley trial has spawned a whole new era of reform of the insanity defense, so too did the McNaughtan verdict provoke attempts to change rules governing insanity trials in the 1800s. Britain's House of Lords engaged in lengthy debates over the McNaughtan case and the proper test for insanity trials. Ultimately, the highest judges of England reaffirmed the traditional right–wrong test for legal insanity. The McNaughtan Rule, as the right–wrong test came to be called, is employed to this day as the standard in many insanity trials in Britain and the United States. The Rule reads as follows: "At the time of committing the act, the party accused was laboring under such a defect of reason from disease of the mind as not to know the nature and quality of the act he was doing, or if he did know it, that he did not know what he was doing was wrong."

The Hinckley and McNaughtan verdicts, however, are the exceptions rather than the rule. Precisely because of the negative public sentiment sur-

rounding the insanity plea, juries have been noted for their lack of receptivity to the insanity defense. Several other individuals who have assassinated or attempted to assassinate public figures and mounted an insanity defense have failed. Consider the cases of Jack Ruby, who in 1963 killed Lee Harvey Oswald, the assassin of President Kennedy, and Arthur H. Bremer, who in 1972 shot Alabama Governor George C. Wallace, crippling him for life. Both Ruby and Bremer presented evidence of mental distrubance but both were convicted anyway.

Another case in point is the fascinating trial of Charles J. Guiteau, who in 1881 fatally wounded President James A. Garfield. Guiteau, whose life history revealed repeated patterns of extremely bizarre behavior, insisted on defending himself at the trial. Claiming that divine inspiration had been the source of his motivation to kill Garfield, Guiteau carried out his own defense in a theatrical and often erratic manner, much to the amusement of the packed courtroom. At the conclusion of the two and a half month trial, the jury took just one hour and five minutes to find Guiteau guilty as charged. Enthusiastic applause by courtroom spectators greeted the announcement of the jury's verdict. However, an autopsy done after Guiteau was hanged for his crime found syphilitic lesions on his brain. After Guiteau's death, medical opinion shifted to accept the likelihood that Guiteau's behavior was the product of organic disturbance.[29]

Although many jurisdictions continue to employ the McNaughtan Rule in cases involving the insanity defense, the Rule has its critics. Some have attacked the cognitive–moral emphasis of the Rule, which forces juries to rely only on a single aspect, the ability to determine right from wrong, in reaching a decision about criminal responsibility. Psychiatrists who have testified under the Rule claim that it unduly restricts what they can say on the witness stand. Other mental health professionals note that what they consider to be "insane" and the right-versus-wrong definition of legal insanity are just not congruent.[30]

A number of states, convinced that the right–wrong test was too narrow, added an "irresistible impulse" component to their insanity laws. In these states, if defendants could show that they were affected by sudden, immediate, irresistible impulses to engage in crime, then they could be found not guilty by reason of insanity. But according to some scholars, judges and juries were hostile to the irresistible impulse test. They found it hard to differentiate between the *irresistible* impulse and the *unresisted* impulse. As one Canadian judge cynically commented to a defendant: "If you cannot resist an impulse any other way, we will dangle a rope in front of your eyes and perhaps that will help."[31]

In 1954, in response to criticisms of the McNaughtan Rule, the Washington, D.C. appellate court proposed a new test for legal insanity in the case of Monte Durham. Durham was a man with a troubled history of mental disorder, mental hospital commitments, suicide attempts, and minor money-related criminal offenses. He was charged with housebreaking, but his defense attorney argued that he should be found not guilty by reason of insanity. Psychiatrists testifying on Durham's behalf stated that he was suffering from a psychopathic personality with psychosis, but they could not say whether he could tell right from wrong. The jury, instructed to use the McNaughtan Rule, convicted the defendant. The appeals court announced a new test for legal insanity, the Durham Rule, in its opinion, while it overturned Durham's conviction on other grounds. The Durham Rule states that: "An accused is not criminally responsible if his unlawful act was the product of mental disease or mental defect."

The Durham Rule, used in some jurisdictions, broadened the grounds for an insanity verdict, as did the irresistible impulse test. No longer did the defense have to prove the narrow right-versus-wrong criterion of the McNaughtan Rule. Now it was sufficient to establish merely that criminal conduct was produced by a mental disease. Psychiatrists and psychologists became in great demand, since their testimony was necessary to prove the existence of mental disease.[32]

As might be expected, the Durham Rule had its detractors too. Some argued that the concepts of mental disease and defect were difficult ones for lay jurors to apply consistently. Opponents maintained that mental disease was interpreted generously by some juries but very narrowly by others, which led to a great deal of variability in the decisions made by juries. Others claimed that the psychiatric evidence was too technical and confusing; hence, mere lay jurors could not possibly understand the concepts and apply them correctly.[33]

In a subsequent case, the problematic Durham Rule was discarded in favor of the American Law Institute's Model Penal Code definition of legal insanity. The ALI Rule stipulates: "A person is not responsible for criminal conduct if at the time of such conduct as a result of mental disease or defect he lacks substantial capacity to appreciate the wrongfulness of his conduct or to conform his conduct to the requirements of the law." This definition was employed in the case of Hinckley.

The ALI Rule essentially combined some of the previous legal tests for insanity. It is broader than McNaughtan, since it goes beyond the narrow right-versus-wrong definition of legal insanity. Yet it is not as expansive as Durham, since it requires that mental disease not merely produce an unlawful

act but rather significantly impair ability to control behavior. It too has its opponents, most of whom argue that the ALI Rule is still vague and confusing. After the Hinckley verdict, some maintained that it was too generous to defendants trying to claim legal insanity.

*   *   *

Clearly, legal scholars, judges, and juries have struggled with a proper definition of legal insanity over the centuries. Definitions of what ought to be excusable by reason of insanity have evolved, affected by celebrated court cases and shifting ideas about human psychology. Recommendations for further change are often predicated on beliefs about how jurors respond in insanity cases. To evaluate them, we need to explore two key topics: jurors' reactions to different legal definitions of insanity; and jurors' treatment of psychiatric testimony.

*   *   *

Rita James Simon conducted the landmark study on juries and insanity trials in the 1950s as part of the Chicago Jury Project.[34] At the time of the study, the Durham Rule had just been announced by the District of Columbia appellate court amid much discussion and debate. Professor Simon wanted to discover whether the substitution of the new Durham Rule with its product of mental disease test for the old McNaughtan Rule with its right–wrong test would affect jury decision-making. To answer this question, she decided to conduct a jury simulation study. Enlisting the cooperation of the courts, she asked jurors who were on jury duty to participate in her study as part of their regular duty. The study was in many ways very realistic, as it took place at the courthouse. The jurors listened to a recording of a reenacted, edited trial. Each jury heard only one case. A real judge gave them legal instructions. Jurors even broke for lunch about halfway through the presentation of evidence. The lunch break was an opportunity for the simulated jurors to interact with one another before they started their formal deliberation.

Simon used two different cases in her experiment. One was modeled after the housebreaking trial of Monte Durham, the man with a long history of mental disorder and petty crimes, whose case led ultimately to the formation of the Durham Rule. The other case was based on another real trial, *United States v. King*. In the King trial, jurors were to decide whether a father, charged with incest, who had no history of mental problems, should be found guilty or not guilty by reason of insanity.

To study the impact of different legal instructions, Simon arranged for the judge to tell a third of the jurors hearing each case that they should decide the case using the McNaughtan Rule, and tell another third instead that the Durham Rule should guide their deliberations. The final third received no specific legal instructions about the standard for finding the defendant not guilty by reason of insanity. Jurors met in groups of twelve to discuss the evidence and reach a verdict in the case before them.

One of the interesting findings of her study was that whether different legal instructions led to different jury verdicts depended on the case. In the incest case, in which the father was accused of having sexual intercourse with his two daughters, none of the juries deciding under the McNaughtan instructions found the father not guilty by reason of insanity, while 19% of the Durham-instructed juries did so. However, in the housebreaking case, over half of all the juries found the defendant not guilty by reason of insanity, and there was no significant difference in jury verdicts for the McNaughtan- and Durham-instructed juries.[35] The specific legal rule for insanity was not so important as to overwhelm the evidence in the case. Rather, the juries took both the rule and the specific facts of the case into account.

Another juror simulation study, this time done with college students, also found that the exact wording of the legal definition of insanity did not make much of a difference in jury decisions. Norman Finkel gave students five cases in which the defendant was described as suffering from different types of mental disease or defect: epilepsy, chronic alcoholism, split-brain disorder, paranoid schizophrenia, and stress. He compared six different tests of insanity, most of which we have discussed: the wild beast test, Mc-Naughtan, McNaughtan plus an irresistible impulse component, Durham, the ALI Model Penal Code test, and a novel test labeled the Disability of Mind (DOM). Students found defendants not guilty by reason of insanity at about the same rate regardless of the legal instructions.[36] Recall also that several of the Hinckley jurors claimed that legal changes in the burden of proof would not have affected their decision in the case.

Thus, the evidence, although it is not very extensive, suggests that the exact wording of legal instructions in insanity cases may not be as important to jurors' actual decision-making as many legal scholars and legislators would believe. There are several possible reasons why the specific form of the legal instructions may not make much of a difference. The first possibility is that jurors don't understand what the different legal instructions mean. Recall the research on jury instructions by Elwork, Sales, and Alfini we discussed earlier. They noted that legal instructions are typically written in turgid prose that makes the content of the instructions virtually inaccessible. In a study of

insanity defense instructions, Elwork and his colleagues found that simulated jurors had a very hard time understanding the original instructions. But once the researchers rewrote the instructions using principles from linguistics to make them more straightforward, the jurors' understanding increased dramatically. If legal instructions about the insanity test were written so that ordinary people could grasp their basic import, perhaps jurors would respond differently to variations in wording.

A second possibility is that jurors understand the instructions but ignore them. We know that jurors sometimes wage a modest war with the law. In insanity defense cases, instead of attending to the legal instructions, jurors may concentrate exclusively on the actions performed by the accused. Or they may use their own lay notions of what should constitute legal insanity in deciding their verdict. When community residents in one study were asked to define the legal test for insanity, they most frequently said that it was when defendants "didn't know what they were doing."[37] Perhaps juries use this lay criterion. If the defendants don't appear to appreciate what they are doing, jurors may find them not guilty by reason of insanity, but if defendants seem to understand what they are doing, juries may convict them. Or jurors may consider the nature of the crime and the dangerousness of the defendant in deciding on their verdict.

The final possibility is that jurors both understand and follow the instructions, yet the instructions may not matter anyway. People found not guilty by reason of insanity under one rule may well be largely the same people who will be found not guilty by reason of insanity under another rule. The number who receive different verdicts under different legal tests could be so small that we cannot detect it through statistical analysis.

Probably all of these factors play a role in minimizing the apparent differences in jurors' responses to legal tests for insanity. But the evidence is far from conclusive. Before legislators pass yet more changes in the legal definition of insanity, they should test beforehand, using simulated jury methodology, the likely impact of the changes in wording.

Another study of jurors' reactions to the insanity defense looked not at the impact of legal instructions but rather jurors' response to defendants with different types of mental problems. In this research project, conducted by psychologists Phoebe Ellsworth and William Thompson and attorneys Raymond Bukaty and Claudia Cowan, subjects read summaries of four different cases in which the defendant pleaded insanity to charges of homicide. The subjects were asked to reach a hypothetical verdict in each case. In two cases, the defendant suffered from schizophrenia, a "nonorganic" disorder. In the

other two cases, the defendant had "organic" problems—in one instance, mental retardation, and in the other, psychomotor epilepsy.

Furthermore, subjects were classified on the basis of their attitudes toward capital punishment. About one-half of the subjects were so opposed to capital punishment that they would not be allowed to serve as jurors in a death penalty case. The other half had varying attitudes toward capital punishment, but all would be able to serve as capital jurors. These were described as the "death-qualified" subjects.

Professor Ellsworth and her colleagues discovered that the subjects' reactions to the cases were a function both of their attitudes toward capital punishment and the type of disorder the defendant had. Subjects opposed to the death penalty rendered guilty verdicts at about the same rate in each of the four types of cases. For them, the origin or type of the defendant's mental disorder appeared to be unimportant. However, for the other subjects, the type of the defendant's disorder made a dramatic difference. They were much more likely to convict the defendants who had schizophrenia (the nonorganic disorder) than the defendants with mental retardation or epilepsy.

The researchers traced the greater doubt about the schizophrenic defendants on the part of the death-qualified subjects to other attitudes the subjects held. For instance, death-qualified subjects estimated that only 31% of defendants who plead insanity are "really" insane, while those subjects very opposed to capital punishment estimated that 56% of insanity defendants were really insane. Apparently, these death-qualified subjects were distrustful of the schizophrenic defendants and concerned that they might be making up their mental problems literally to get away with murder. In contrast, the other defendants suffering from organic problems could not have generated them merely as an excuse, and therefore did not engage the resentment or doubts of the death-qualified subjects. This study is important, for it suggests that personal views about responsibility for crime contribute to jurors' mistrust of the insanity plea in specific types of cases.[38]

*   *   *

One of the major concerns expressed about juries in insanity cases is their evaluation of psychiatric testimony. On the one hand, some critics argue that juries can't understand psychiatric testimony and therefore don't give it enough weight. On the other hand, other critics complain that juries are so impressed by the expert credentials of the psychiatrists that they give their testimony too much weight.

The research conducted by Rita James Simon provides some insights about how jurors deal with psychiatric testimony. From reviewing the tape-recorded jury deliberations, Simon judged that juries did not act as rubber stamps for the psychiatric experts who testifed in her experimental cases. In fact, jurors discussed the limitations of psychiatry and its status as an inexact science. One joked: "This is like the story of the two psychiatrists who passed one another on the street. One said good morning. The other psychiatrist walked about two steps past, then paused and said 'I wonder what he meant by that?' "[39]

One source of tension for jurors was wondering how much weight they should give to psychiatric testimony. It is probably impossible to estimate what the "proper" weight for expert testimony should be. We would say that jurors should consider psychiatric evidence, but their verdict should not be entirely determined by it. In Simon's experiment, the psychiatrists described the defendants' states of mind, but they did not conclude whether or not the defendants should, in their opinion, be found not guilty by reason of insanity. The jurors recognized the distinction between the role of the jury and the more limited function of the experts, but found it frustrating nevertheless. Their annoyance that the psychiatric testimony could not be more conclusive is captured in the following excerpt from their deliberations:

> Well, these doctors didn't say he was insane.
> They didn't say he was sane, either.
> No, that's why the doctors aren't helping us at all.
> They left us out on a limb.[40]

This is reminiscent of the impatience expressed by the Hinckley jurors, some of whom berated the psychiatrists for not being more conclusive.

Far from being a rubber stamp for psychiatric experts, the juries in Simon's study relied heavily on the trial record, especially the details and context of the defendant's behavior, to determine whether he should be found not guilty by reason of insanity. They also exchanged and considered their own knowledge and experiences with the mentally ill during deliberations. They expressed a good deal of skepticism about the insanity plea, and insisted that to be found not guilty by reason of insanity, a defendant's mental disturbance had to be considerable.

Simon concluded that juries understood the difference between clinical diagnosis and the moral–legal decision they themselves had to make. Lawyers and psychiatrists Simon surveyed shared her positive judgment of juries. Simon asked psychiatrists and lawyers what they thought was the usual effect of psychiatric testimony on a jury.[41] Most respondents thought jurors either

treated psychiatric testimony like any other testimony or listened carefully to the psychiatric experts but based their verdicts on all factors in the case. Only a minority said that juries ignored or conformed completely to the experts.

Despite these limited but generally positive findings, critics of the jury continue to insist that the jury is unfit to assess the mental state of the defendant. In one recommended change, a board of court-appointed psychiatrists would meet together and decide by consensus on a diagnosis and evaluation of the defendant. Then, the board would present its conclusions as a *fait accompli* to the jury. The American Medical Association has put forth a more radical proposal. Citing the widespread public derogation of psychiatrists who testify in insanity cases, the AMA has proposed that the insanity defense be abolished altogether.

Such moves are misguided on several counts. First and foremost, the not guilty by reason of insanity decision is a moral and legal decision about a defendant's responsibility for a criminal act. It is *not* a medical decision, best left to the medical–psychiatric profession. To be sure, psychiatrists may, by describing their examination and analysis of the accused, shed some light on the defendant's mental state at the time of the act. But the final judgment rests on the community's view, as represented by the jury, of the legal–moral responsibility of the defendant. Indeed, the American Psychiatric Association, in a *Statement on the Insanity Defense,* maintained that while psychiatrists should continue to play a role in insanity trials, they should not overwhelm the basic legal–moral decision to be reached by the jury.

Thus, whatever difficulties juries have in evaluating defendants' mental states, the decision should properly remain with them. It has not been demonstrated that juries' evaluation of psychiatric testimony is inappropriate. And the adversary system may well be the best possible forum for testing and exposing the strengths and weaknesses of expert testimony. Experts could hide behind their credentials; without adversarial questioning, the foundation of their confidently announced conclusions may never be examined. Furthermore, if there are honest differences of opinion within a discipline, the jury ought to have the benefit of exposure to such differences in weighing the testimony. A final and related issue: Who will appoint the court psychiatrists? Isn't there a danger that such psychiatrists might be predisposed to favor, in case after case, one side rather than another?

*   *   *

The tapestry woven from the strands of experience of the Hinckley jurors, the history of the insanity defense, and the research on juries in insanity cases

is a rich and complex one. There is a great deal of negative feeling toward the insanity defense. Much of this negativism appears to stem from misconceptions about the frequency, success, and consequences of the plea. This public negativism—particularly after the Hinckley trial—translates into juries that are, on the whole, suspicious of the insanity plea. As research on this topic suggests, there appears to be little support for public fears that juries are overly gullible to malingering defendants or to psychiatric experts. The insanity plea is not used all that often, and when it is used juries rarely accept it. They reserve it for severely disturbed defendants. We see no pressing need to abolish the insanity defense, as some have advocated. Yet some improvement is necessary in clarifying the legal instructions. Elwork and his colleagues have demonstrated that lucid prose in place of legal language can have dramatic results in getting its meaning across to the jury.

CHAPTER 13

Jurors' Views of Rape: Anger and Ambivalence

Initial press reports of the event shocked the nation.[1] According to the police, a woman had been raped by several men in a New Bedford, Massachusetts tavern, Big Dan's, while onlookers cheered. The woman, a 21-year-old mother of two, had reportedly gone into Big Dan's to buy cigarettes. After having a drink, the woman tried to leave, but instead, a number of men dragged her to the pool table, stripped her, and raped her or forced her to engage in other sexual acts, while others watched and shouted "go for it!"

The first response was horror, and extreme sympathy for the victim. Feminists held a candlelight march, attended by 3000 people, to express support for the victim and condemnation of the apparently callous acceptance of rape by the bar patrons. Columnists drew comparisons between the Big Dan rape and the case of Kitty Genovese, the New Yorker who was brutally murdered while observers failed to intervene or call police.[2] The initial reaction, then, was of support for the victim and anger at the rapists.

Yet as the trial approached, people began expressing doubts about the victim's role. Had she "asked for it" in some way? Was she actually to blame for the rapes? Many local residents rallied to support the six Portuguese defendants. Over half of New Bedford's population of 100,000 is Portuguese, and many of them felt that the criminal justice system was treating the accused men unfairly because of their ethnic background. One of the defendants, John Cordeiro, claimed that a police officer had pushed him around and called him a "punk" at the time of his arrest. Others pointed out that charges of rape were frequent in the United States and that the disproportionate attention to the Big Dan case smacked of racism. Many local residents decried the press coverage as sensationalistic. A Portuguese radio telethon raised $100,000 bail money for two of the defendants, indicating the breadth of community support for the accused men.

The nationally televised trial stemming from the incident at Big Dan's was unusual. The large number of defendants was atypical; so were the public

setting of the rape, the presence of observers, and television coverage of the trial testimony. Yet the furor surrounding this distinctive incident illustrates the public's profound ambivalence toward the crime of rape. The Big Dan trial serves as a premier example of the problems juries face in deciding cases of rape.

In all, a total of six men—Daniel Silva, Joseph Vieira, John Cordeiro, Victor Raposo, Jose Medeiros, and Virgilio Medeiros, who are not related—were charged with aggravated rape. There were two separate trials, with Silva and Vieira in one trial and the other four in a second trial. The separation was necessary since some of the men were expected to make statements implicating others. In a novel procedure, the presiding Judge William Young decided to conduct the two trials simultaneously, with one in the morning and the other in the afternoon. Judge Young was concerned that if the trials were conducted consecutively, the verdicts in the first trial would make it impossible to select a fair jury for the second.

Indeed, even though the trials were conducted at the same time, jury selection proved difficult. The trials were moved to nearby Fall River, Massachusetts, which had more commodious courtroom facilities. With extensive pretrial publicity, most prospective jurors in Fall River had heard about the event; many already had preconceptions about the guilt of the defendants. In the end, almost 600 people were screened and asked about their views of the case, how much prime-time television they watched, and whether they felt Portuguese people were more likely than others to commit crimes. After the initial screening, men outnumbered women 2 to 1 on the jury panel. Although the county has approximately even numbers of men and women, more women than men asked to be excused from the Big Dan case. Many women claimed childcare responsibilities, but in addition more women than men said that they had already formed an opinion about the case and thus could not be fair and impartial jurors.

The morning case, involving charges against Cordeiro, Raposo, and the two Medeiroses, was heard by a jury with an even representation of men and women, and with a number of people who were older or who held blue-collar jobs. For the afternoon case against Silva and Vieira, twelve men and four women were ultimately selected as jurors or alternates. The jury was disproportionately young, male, and professional. It included several technicians, engineers, a social worker, and an assistant manager of a local bar. This jury's composition reflected defense strategies to select younger men and prosecution preferences for younger women. Reflecting the community at large, about half the jurors in both trials had Portuguese surnames.

The Big Dan rape evoked strong emotions that went beyond the partic-

ipants themselves. It was no surprise, then, that there was intense interest as the case came up for jury trial. The interest was heightened when Cable News Network announced that it would broadcast substantial portions of the rape trials live. While Massachusetts does allow camera coverage of trial court proceedings, the extent of national coverage of the Big Dan rape trial was unprecedented.

Attention was riveted on the case as the victim took the stand at the start of the trial. Unlike most other courts, the Fall River courthouse has no chair for witnesses. They are expected to stand during their testimony. So the victim stood and described again and again the events at Big Dan's on the evening in question. According to the victim, she had gone to Big Dan's to buy cigarettes and had gotten into a conversation with a woman friend in the bar. They had a drink together and watched the men play pool. When the victim attempted to leave, someone grabbed her from behind; others tried to pick her up, pull her pants off, and put her on the pool table. Then, several men had intercourse or oral sex with her. Finally, she escaped and ran out of the bar, wearing only a sweater and a single sock. She flagged down a passerby, told him that she had been raped, and proceeded to the police station. She returned with the police later that evening so she could identify the men.

During grueling cross-examination by six defense attorneys, the woman denied that she had flirted with any of the men or that she had agreed to have sex with one or more of them. Defense attorneys attempted to shake her credibility by pointing out some discrepancies between her courtroom testimony and what she told police right after the attack. Prosecutors objected time and again that defense attorneys were firing questions one after another at the woman and were characterizing her answers as lies and rehearsed testimony.[3]

The cross-examination was broadcast over cable television, although the woman herself was not shown on camera. This was the first time many Americans had seen a cross-examination of a rape victim, and many were appalled at the tactics of the defense attorneys. The prosecutor and local rape crisis center counselors reported another apparent effect of the publicity— that the number of women willing to report their rapes to the police or to proceed with prosecution was down. Several victims had cited the Big Dan trial, and their fear of harsh and wide-ranging questioning and widespread media coverage, as reasons for not bringing formal charges against their attackers.[4]

Following the victim were other witnesses for the prosecution. Bartender Carlos Machados, who had been at Big Dan's on the evening in question, gave detailed testimony that confirmed the essence of the woman's story and

implicated all six defendants. But his version of the incident contradicted parts of the victim's testimony concerning how much she had to drink and whether she had "flirted" with the men prior to the rape. Machados said that he tried to leave the bar to call police but that one of the defendants, Virgilio Medeiros, prevented him from leaving. He also said that he gave a dime to a bar customer and asked him to call police but that the customer refused, saying that he was afraid to do so. Police officer Carol Sacramento testified about what participants had told police right after the event. Her testimony combined with that of others produced some confusion about just who had done what in the barroom. Finally, another bar patron, Sylvester Vutao, supported the prosecution case by saying that he had witnessed defendant Silva having intercourse with the victim while she cried and other men laughed. Another patron said he also saw the assault and that he tried to call police but got a wrong number and so did not try again.

Daniel Silva, tried in the afternoon case, was the first defendant to take the stand in his own behalf. He claimed that the woman had approached him to ask for drugs. After some conversation, the two had started embracing and kissing and she agreed to have sex with him on the pool table. However, he was unable to have sex because the other men were distracting him. One, for instance, tickled his buttocks with a straw while Silva was atop the woman on the pool table. Afterwards, according to Silva, the woman asked him to take her home, but he said that he could not since he lived with his mother. She then became angry and ran out of the bar, Silva said. Vieira, Silva's codefendant, did not take the stand.

Silva and Vieira's case was the first to go to the jury. Defense attorneys argued that parts of the woman's testimony were inconsistent with her original police report and testimony of other witnesses, and that she had gone to the pool table willingly with Silva. Prosecutors acknowledged that the victim may have exaggerated some of her testimony but that even if the woman had indeed flirted with some of the defendants, that did not give them the right to rape her. Just before the case went to the jury, Judge Young explained that to find the defendants guilty as charged of aggravated rape, they would have to be satisfied that the woman was raped as part of a joint venture. Even if a specific defendant had not had sex with the woman, he could be convicted if he had been an "ally" of an attacker.

The jury deliberated only four and a half hours before announcing that they had reached a verdict. Both defense and prosecuting attorneys thought that the short deliberation time boded well for the defense. Silva and Vieira gazed at the jurors as they filed in to report their verdict. No jurors returned the defendants' looks as the verdicts—guilty of aggravated rape for both accused men—were announced.

Vieira's attorney and relatives began crying; the district attorney put his head in his hands. The crowd began shouting and pushing. Vieira's father was subdued by police during a disturbance outside the courtroom as almost 500 people gathered there. As the jurors were led out, the crowd swore and booed the jurors and called them racists.[5]

Meanwhile, the second jury, which still had not finished hearing testimony in the morning trial, was kept isolated so that they would not hear the result of the afternoon trial. The measures taken to keep them free from knowledge were extraordinary. For instance, the day of the first jury's deliberations, members of the second jury were put on a bus and taken to western Massachusetts.[6] During the remainder of the second jury's trial, security was tightened. The windows of the bus that transported jurors between their hotel and the courtroom were covered with heavy curtains to prevent jurors from accidentally seeing signs or newspaper headlines about the guilty verdicts.[7]

Testimony continued in the second case as Cordeiro took the stand in his own behalf and said that the woman had willingly had oral sex with him while Silva was on top of her. Cordeiro added: "I didn't feel I did anything wrong that night. I didn't feel anybody did anything wrong."[8] His three codefendants declined to take the stand, and the defense rested its case.

The six-man, six-woman jury deliberated about seven hours before reaching verdicts for the four defendants. The result: Two men, Raposo and Cordeiro, both of whom, according to witnesses, had oral sex with the woman, were convicted of aggravated rape. The other two men, the Medeiroses, were acquitted of all charges. Some testimony had indicated that these two men had shouted encouragement at the other men, but the jury apparently did not believe it or decided to convict only the men who had direct contact with the victim. Jurors and defendants alike cried as they left the courtroom.

Reaction to the jury verdicts was strong and swift. A crowd estimated at 10,000 to 15,000 marched around the courthouse to protest the guilty verdicts. Sentiment against the victim ran high at the demonstration. For instance, a New Bedford priest stated, "The girl is to blame. She led them into sin." Another marcher stated: "She is the one who deserves the prison sentence."[9] After the trial, at least six of the jurors received threats at their homes.[10]

Judge Young followed the prosecutor's recommendations and imposed sentences ranging from six to twelve years for the defendants. Defense attorneys lost no time in appealing the verdicts, which they claimed were contrary to the evidence and rendered by prejudiced juries. But the heavily publicized jury trials stemming from the incident at Big Dan's were finally over.

Many people wondered how the juries reached their verdicts in the two

cases. At the conclusion of the trials, the jurors agreed not to talk to the media about their decisions. So, unlike the DeLorean and Hinckley trials, in which jurors described the factors affecting their decision-making, we have no direct information about jurors in the Big Dan cases. But by studying how juries decide other rape cases, we can infer what probably occurred in the Big Dan jury deliberations. To understand the jury's reaction to rape cases, we must first look at the public's attitudes toward rape.

*   *   *

Few crimes evoke such a powerful but ambivalent response. On the one hand, people regard rape with horror and the rapist as contemptible and deserving of the most severe punishment. On the other hand, people often see the rape victim as responsible for her own victimization. For instance, in a *London Times* opinion survey of 1056 British men and women, fully 85% of the respondents recommended that convicted rapists be incarcerated for seven years or more or even executed. Yet a third of the sample said they believed that rape victims are usually to blame for their rape in some way, and a fourth of the respondents believed that men are often convicted of rape that they did not commit.[11] Similarly, in the United States, people think convicted rapists should spend much more time in jail than they currently do, although many Americans say that rape victims are at fault.[12] For instance, over half the respondents in one study agreed that "A woman who goes to the home or apartment of a man on the first date implies she is willing to have sex" and "In the majority of rapes, the victim was promiscuous or had a bad reputation." A similar number thought that at least *50% of all reported rapes* are reported because the woman is angry and trying to get back at a man or because she is trying to account for an illegitimate pregnancy.[13] Since the jury reflects the attitudes and biases of the community, jurors deciding rape cases will represent the anger, ambivalence, and myths that characterize public views of rape. Inevitably, these attitudes affect their perspectives and ultimately their decisions in cases of rape.

*   *   *

Trial lore has it that jury decisions about rape are based largely on prejudice. This prejudice can cut both ways—against the victim and against the defendant. Prosecutors lament that juries will not convict a defendant charged with rape unless the event matches the stereotype of rape—an un-attractive man in an alley attacking an eighteen-year-old virgin on her way

home from church. Defense attorneys counter that the crime of rape horrifies people and that jurors' natural inclination is to believe the victim's testimony. As a result, they must be especially vigorous in cross-examination to uncover weaknesses in the victim's testimony.

Compounding these apparent prejudices are the evidentiary difficulties in rape cases. In the Big Dan trial, observers validated the essence of the victim's story by their testimony. But that is unusual. By its very nature, rape is typically a private crime. For instance, in one study of jury trials of sexual assault, the overwhelming majority (85%) had no eyewitnesses other than the victim.[14] The problems of proof can be enormous. Without observers to confirm the parties' stories, it often comes down to the defendant's word against the victim's.

As a result of widespread beliefs that jury judgments in rape trials are inflamed by biases, the courts have developed special procedures for these cases. The procedures have included judges' instructions about the victim's credibility, requirements that the victim's testimony be corroborated by independent evidence in the case, and wide-ranging cross-examination about the victim's prior sexual relationships, not only with the defendant if applicable but also with any other men. These special procedures have had considerable impact on juries.

One special procedure requires the judge to instruct jurors about the need to confirm, or corroborate, the victim's testimony with other independent evidence in the case. There are two parts to a typical instruction about the need for corroboration. First, the judge warns of the special dangers of convicting a defendant solely on the testimony of the victim. Second, the judge lists for the jury independent evidence in the case that tends to be consistent with the victim's story. This might for instance include torn clothing, bruises, the quickness with which the victim reported the rape, or other evidence that supports the victim's statement that she was raped.

This special procedure developed to counteract what were at one time widespread beliefs that victims of sexual assault were very likely to make false claims of rape. It was thought that women would falsely claim rape to get back at their lovers, to deal with guilt or consequences of having sexual intercourse, or because rape fantasies led them to confuse voluntary sexual intercourse with rape.[15] The testimony of the victim in a rape case was perceived as unreliable. Interestingly, corroboration instructions are also used when children and accomplices to a crime testify. The reasoning is similar: Their testimony is assumed to be inherently suspect.

A second assumption underlying the corroboration requirement was that the jury was likely to be misled by the victim's testimony. Jurors, it was

believed, were unfamiliar with the range of reasons that might lead a woman to accuse a man falsely of rape, and thus jurors might have difficulty evaluating the credibility of her testimony without special help from the judge. Finally, it was assumed that special instructions from the judge could lessen the danger of juries deciding rape verdicts on the basis of prejudice rather than evidence. These instructions warned of the danger of convicting on the basis of the victim's testimony alone, and drew attention to evidence in the case that was consistent with the victim's testimony.

Judges' corroboration instructions were common in many jurisdictions up to the 1970s. In some jurisdictions such as New York, the danger of jurors' being duped by false rape charges was believed to be so great that juries were actually *forbidden* to find a rape defendant guilty unless the victim's testimony was corroborated by external evidence. This extraordinary measure, now repealed, made it extremely difficult to obtain rape convictions. It led one journalist writing a feature story on rape to entitle the piece: "Q: If you rape a woman and steal her TV, what can they get you for in New York? A: Stealing the TV."[16]

The assumptions underlying the corroboration instruction requirement in rape trials have been undermined by research into rape complaints and jury decision-making. First, the danger of false rape complaints has been vastly overrated. Police find the number of false rape charges to be comparable to the level of false charges brought in other types of crimes. There are rare occasions where individuals falsely accuse others of crimes, but evidence suggests that the episodes are no more frequent in rape cases than in other serious cases.

Fears that women often charge men falsely with rape were fanned recently by Cathleen Crowell Webb, who in 1985 claimed that she had falsely accused a stranger, Gary Dotson, of raping her in 1977.[17] Dotson was convicted of the crime and spent six years behind bars before Webb's recantation. But subsequent reviews of the evidence and testimony by some of the original witnesses cast doubt not on Webb's original claim that she was raped but rather on her recantation. According to Webb, who was sixteen at the time, she was afraid that she might have gotten pregnant with her boyfriend, and decided to claim she had been raped. Webb said that she bruised and cut herself with broken glass, and went to the police. She picked Dotson's photo out of a lineup. Although originally in 1977 she claimed Dotson was her rapist, in the recantation Webb said that she had never seen Dotson before she looked at his photograph in the lineup. However, Webb's boyfriend of the time contradicted parts of her recantation testimony. Dotson's alibi witnesses also gave conflicting testimony during the recantation hearing. Con-

sequently, the judge who heard the original case refused to accept Webb's recantation. So did Illinois Governor James Thompson, who presided over Dotson's 1985 clemency hearing. Although Governor Thompson did not believe the recantation story, he nevertheless commuted Dotson's sentence and freed him. In this light, the jury's original conviction of Dotson does not seem at all unreasonable.

Whatever the truth of the recantation, the case has worried rape law reformers. For instance, Harvard law Professor Susan Estrich commented: "The whole effort at reforming rape laws has been an attack on the premise that women who bring complaints are suspect. There's no proof whatsoever that rape complaints are more unfounded than those of any other crimes. Now Webb will be used to lend credence to all the fundamentally sexist assumptions about women."[18]

Other assumptions underlying the corroboration requirement have been found wanting. For instance, there is little evidence that juries are so overcome by sympathy for a rape victim that they cannot rationally evaluate her testimony. Indeed, as we reported above, many people are all too willing to believe that women bring false charges of rape. And as we shall see, juries if anything are more reluctant than judges to convict men of rape.

Finally, there is some evidence that the corroboration instructions don't work the way they ought to. In a jury simulation study one of us (V.P.H.) conducted, simulated jurors were presented with a rape case containing the same evidence but various corroboration instructions. Some jurors decided the case with no corroboration instructions, while others had different forms of instructions. The results were surprising. Juries with corroboration instructions tended to be less likely to convict the accused man of rape. But analysis of the tape-recorded jury deliberations revealed that, contrary to expectations, when jurors were given corroboration instructions, they were no more likely to scrutinize the victim's credibility or the potentially corroborative evidence. The judge's admonition to attend to the evidence did not produce a more evidence-oriented discussion. The juries did not seem to be affected by the corroboration instructions in the manner the courts intended. Instead, jurors appeared to develop a generally more favorable view of the defendant (and a less positive view of the victim) when they received corroboration instructions.[15]

Taken together—evidence that false rape charges are rare, juries are unlikely to be overly sympathetic to victims, and that corroboration instructions don't work as they are intended—suggests that corroboration instructions are unnecessary and could be positively harmful in a rape case. As a result of the struggle of feminists and legal reformers to do away with these in-

structions, in the middle to late 1970s many jurisdictions abolished the corroboration instruction or requirement entirely or left it up to individual judges
to give corroboration instructions if they wanted to.

A second procedure in cases of rape has been the defense attorney's
wide-ranging examination of the victim's past and present sexual behavior.
There have been some changes in recent years putting limits on what kinds
of questions attorneys may ask. But for many generations unfettered questioning about the victim's sexuality was the rule. The presumption was that
if a victim engaged in consensual sexual intercourse with other men she was
more likely to have agreed to sex with the defendant. An example of this
reasoning is found in an old case, *Camp v. State* (1847):

> Who is more likely to consent to the approaches of a man, the unsullied virgin
> and the revered, loved and virtuous mother of a family, or the lewd and loose
> prostitute, whose arms are open to the embraces of every coarse brute who has
> enough money to pay for the privilege?[19]

Almost a hundred years later, the Court continued to hold the same view:
". . . common experience teaches us that the woman who had once departed
from the paths of virtue is far more apt to consent to another lapse than is
one who had never stepped aside from that path."[20] The sexual behavior of
a woman was also thought to shed light on her credibility as a witness.

The practice of questioning rape victims about their sexual life was widely
supported by members of the Bar. Commitment to the adversary ethic and the
exploitation of a victim's sexual behavior is illustrated by the story of a 1966
Federal Bar Association meeting held in Washington, D.C. Lawyers were
asked to consider the following hypothetical case. Suppose you were a defense
attorney and your client told you that he had indeed raped the victim. The
victim was the daughter of the local bank president and engaged to be married
to a minister. However, there was a man she had jilted who was willing to
testify truthfully that he had sexual intercourse with the victim and that she
behaved "scandalously" with strange men. If this information became known
to the jury, it might well lead them to conclude incorrectly that the victim
had not been raped as she claimed but rather had consented to sexual intercourse with your client. Should you, the defense attorney, call that witness?
Commentators were unanimous: They would call the jilted lover, even though
the "truth may be dimmed in the doing." As one of the panelists stated: "The
function of an advocate, and particularly the defense advocate in the adversarial system, is to use all the legitimate tools available to test the truth of
the prosecution's case [and] the testimony of bad repute of the complaining
witness, being recent and not remote in point of time, is relevant to her

credibility."[21] The author of this missive? The current Chief Justice of the U.S. Supreme Court, Warren Burger.

Many reformers and feminists have argued that allowing wide-ranging information about the sexual behavior of the rape victim with people other than the defendant serves no useful purpose and is in fact detrimental. These critics say that even if it once were true that people could not trust the credibility of women who consented to sexual intercourse, changing patterns of sexual behavior today make information about third-party sexual relations irrelevant. In addition, the specter of harsh and potentially embarrassing cross-examination discourages women from reporting rape, which is already a grossly underreported crime.[18] Finally, critics say that such information is highly prejudicial to the jury.

That information about the victim's sexual behavior can be harmful to the prosecution's case is persuasively demonstrated by the results of a study conducted by Professor Eugene Borgida of the University of Minnesota. He wanted to test the effects of "rape shield" laws recently enacted in many jurisdictions. These laws vary but, in general, they limit the once-routine questioning about a victim's sexual behavior with people other than the defendant. Thus, they "shield" the jury from this information. In some jurisdictions, such evidence is completely excluded, while in others, the judge decides whether questioning about the victim's sexual behavior is relevant or not. Of course, any prior relationship between the victim and the defendant may still be explored by the defense attorney.

Borgida conducted jury simulation studies in which prospective jurors from the Minneapolis–St. Paul area saw a videotape of a mock rape trial, condensed into about two hours. In the case, the victim stated that she had been raped against her will, but the defendant maintained that she had consented to sexual intercourse. Borgida presented different versions of the trial to different groups of subjects. Some versions included information about the victim's prior sexual behavior with other men, while other versions did not. The results confirmed fears that juries would find the sexual behavior information prejudicial. Borgida discovered that when the subject-jurors learned about third-party sexual relations of the victim, they inferred that the victim had consented to intercourse with the defendant. They also more carefully and more unfavorably evaluated the victim's character compared to the defendant's character, and they attributed more responsibility to the victim for the event. Even in the situations where it was very likely that rape had occurred, when jurors learned of the victim's sexual history they became reluctant to convict the accused.[22]

*   *   *

Kalven and Zeisel's study of the American jury provided interesting information about how actual juries decide cases of rape. It examined the extent to which judges agreed with the verdicts reached by juries in two types of rape trials: aggravated rape and simple rape. Kalven and Zeisel labeled as "aggravated rape" those cases in which the act of rape was combined with other violence, where there were several assailants, or when the defendant and the victim were complete strangers. In these cases, the likelihood of victim consent or contributory behavior on the part of the victim was low. In the aggravated rape trials, the jury acquitted the defendant when the judge would have convicted on the same evidence just 12% of the time. But in cases of simple rape, in which no aggravating circumstances were present, judge–jury disagreements jumped dramatically. The jury acquitted rape defendants whom the judge would have convicted fully 60% of the time! Furthermore, in all but one of the ten cases in which the judge and jury agreed to convict, the jury convicted the defendant not on the major charge of rape but on a *lesser charge* only. If no aggravating circumstances were present, if the victim knew the defendant, or if the victim contributed in any way to her own demise, the jury simply would not convict of rape. In these cases, juries were saying that although the defendant may have done something wrong, the misbehavior did not deserve the disgrace of a rape conviction.

In Kalven and Zeisel's study, the reasons judges gave for the judge–jury disagreements in rape cases often included the victim's behavior and the presumption on the part of jurors that women engaging in certain behaviors deserved whatever outcomes they received. For instance, one judge described a case in which the jury acquitted a young defendant of raping a 17-year-old: "A group of young people on a beer drinking party. The jury probably figured the girl asked for what she got."[23] The jury's unwillingness to convict rape defendants when they learn of a victim's sexual behavior is sadly apparent in another case described by one judge. Three men kidnapped a woman from the street at 1:30 A.M., took her to an apartment, and brutally raped her. During the trial, however, it developed that the young woman was unmarried and had two illegitimate children. The defendant asserted that she was a prostitute although he presented no evidence to support his claim. The jury acquitted; the judge labeled the verdict "a travesty of justice."[24]

Kalven and Zeisel conducted their research on juries in the mid-1950s. Attitudes toward women and knowledge about the crime of rape have changed in the intervening decades. Yet research studies show that even today juries are still more reluctant to convict defendants of rape than of other crimes.

This may be due in part to the unique and difficult evidentiary problems associated with rape cases. There is proof of some change, however. A greater proportion of rape cases brought to trial now end in conviction. Professor James Levine of Brooklyn College of the City University of New York obtained data for federal jury conviction rates for most of the years between 1961 and 1980. The overall rape conviction rate over the 20-year period was 61.4%, much lower than the average conviction rate for other serious crimes. However, there was a steady upward progression of the jury conviction rate over that time period. In the early 1960s, juries were much more lenient toward rape defendants than they were in the late 1970s. Levine offers several explanations for the trend, including the impact of the women's movement, increased public support for women's rights, more sympathetic handling of rape complaints by police and court personnel, and changes in procedures of instruction and of questioning victims about their sexual lives.[25]

Another reason why jury conviction rates may be going up is that women are finally being represented on juries in proportion to their numbers in the population. In earlier times, you will recall, women were routinely under-represented on juries. Studies have shown that men and women have decidedly different perspectives on the crime of rape that translate into differential willingness to convict rape defendants. In general, women tend to have greater empathy for rape victims while men are more likely to see the defendant's point of view.[26] Women are also less likely to believe many of the rape myths we described.[13] In a number of studies, given the same evidence, women have been somewhat more likely than men to convict a rape defendant. However, they do not seem to have remarkably greater punitive attitudes toward convicted rapists. For instance, when asked to assign sentences to hypothetical defendants found guilty of rape, men and women often recommend similar punishment.[27]

Thus, women's greater likelihood to convict is not explained by consistent differences between men and women in punitiveness toward rapists. Rather, it can be accounted for by differences in the way men and women view the strength of the evidence in rape cases. It is therefore critical that both male and female perspectives are represented on juries, as they usually are today. Conviction rates for rape may be rising in part because of this better balance of perspective on the jury.

Although rape conviction rates have been going up, numerous studies show jurors still focus heavily on the victim's behavior in deciding whether to convict defendants of rape. Researcher Hubert Feild conducted one such study. In his research project, a sample of 896 white adults responded to a six-page summary of a rape case. Feild presented different versions of the

case to subjects in order to explore the impact of various features of rape cases, including the behavior of the victim, the type of rape, the strength of evidence, and race of the victim and the defendant. Professor Feild asked subject-jurors after reading the summary of the rape case to recommend a prison sentence for the defendant. Then Feild compared the prison sentences recommended by subjects who received different versions of the case. The results show the same pattern that Kalven and Zeisel found in the 1950s. Subjects who read that the victim "contributed" to her own demise by allowing into her apartment a stranger who later raped her gave the rapist a lighter sentence than subjects who learned that the defendant forced his way into the apartment. Subject-jurors responded to differences in the strength of evidence in their cases; those whose version of the case included strong evidence that corroborated the victim's story (torn clothing and scratches) were more likely to give the defendant a long prison sentence than subjects without that evidence.

Feild also discovered that the racial makeup of the crime affected his subject-jurors. When the victim was black, the offenders were treated no differently. But black offenders who assaulted white women were given much more severe sentences. This jury simulation result in the 1970s evokes the terrible history of extremely severe penalties for interracial rape common in the earlier part of this century in the United States. Black men have historically received more severe sentences than white men for rape.[28] Indeed, from 1930 until the U.S. Supreme Court declared the death penalty for rape unconstitutional in 1979, nine out of every ten men executed for rape were black.[29] Interestingly, in a similar jury simulation study with black subject-jurors, Feild found that the black subjects recommended comparable sentences regardless of the race of the defendant and the victim. Thus, the strong negative reaction to black men who rape white women appears to be limited to whites. Recall that until relatively recently, the jury was a white male bastion. The nonrepresentative character of juries was no doubt a contributory factor in harsh penalties for black men who were found guilty of rape.[30]

Feild also examined the extent to which the subjects' personal characteristics and attitudes toward rape affected their decisions in the jury simulation. Background characteristics were largely irrelevant. For instance, men and women sentenced the rape defendant similarly. But people's attitudes toward rape did affect their decisions. Beliefs that women should be responsible for preventing their own rapes, that women provoke rape by their appearance or behavior, that women should do everything they can to resist a rape, that rapists are normal men, and that rapists should not be treated harshly all led to more lenient recommended sentences for rape defendants.[31]

Another research project, this time with real jurors, confirms the strong influence of the victim's behavior on contemporary jurors. Gary LaFree, Barbara Reskin, and Christy Visher interviewed 331 jurors who heard cases of forcible sexual assault in Marion County (Indianapolis), Indiana, between July 1978 and September 1980.[14] After their trial was over, jurors told researchers whether they had believed that the defendant was guilty or innocent prior to their participating in the jury deliberation. Jurors also provided background characteristics and described their attitudes toward rape, crime, and sex roles. For each trial, observers noted the evidence presented in the case as well as both the defendant's and the victim's characteristics and behavior before and during the assault.

The researchers divided the cases into two groups for analysis. In the first group of cases, the defendant contested the victim's claim that the defendant had sexual contact with her or he said that she had agreed to have sexual contact. Surprisingly, in these cases, none of the measures of evidence, including eyewitnesses, the number of prosecution witnesses and exhibits, the use of a weapon, or injury to the victim, affected jurors' beliefs about the defendant's guilt or innocence prior to deliberation. However, jurors *were* affected by the characteristics of the victim and defendant. When the victim held a blue-collar job, when she reportedly had sexual intercourse outside marriage, or when she drank or used drugs, jurors were more likely to believe that the defendant was innocent. In contrast, defendants who had few social ties, a negative courtroom appearance, or a criminal record were more likely to be perceived as guilty by jurors. Thus, the "life-style" of both the victim and the defendant were important determinants of the jurors' initial perceptions of the case. Jurors who had conservative attitudes about sex roles were especially likely to believe the defendant was not guilty of rape when they learned that the victim used drugs or alcohol. Thus, in cases where the victim's word was a primary issue, jurors were influenced more by the character of the victim than by hard evidence, even corroborative evidence, in the case.

In the second set of cases, the defense either contested the defendant's identification as the rapist or argued for diminished responsibility due to insanity or drug use. Evidence of identification and the behavior of the defendant should be very important in determining the jury decision. Indeed, in contrast to the trials where the victim's consent was the key issue, the evidence of eyewitnesses and testimony about a weapon had marked effects on jurors' beliefs that the defendant was guilty. Jurors told the researchers in the interviews that evidence about weapons made them particularly anxious to get the defendant off the streets. Moreover, the defendant's character also played a role. Jurors were more likely to see as guilty those defendants who

had no stable work or family ties, and who made an overall bad impression in court. In the identification cases, the jurors apparently made judgments about whether the defendant was the "sort of man" who would commit a rape. Jurors often commented to interviewers that the defendant "seemed like" or "did not seem like" a rapist. Unattractive defendants with unstable family and work histories fit jurors' stereotypes of "the rapist" and thus increased the chances for conviction.

In these identification and diminished responsibility cases, the victim's behavior was not legally relevant to the issues in dispute. Thus, the victim's character and even her behavior should have had little or no bearing on the jury decision. Nevertheless, when jurors heard testimony suggesting that the victim was sexually active outside of marriage, they were less likely to believe that the defendant was guilty. Regardless of whether the sexual behavior of the victim is at all relevant to the legal issues, then, jurors take it into account in assessing the guilt of the defendant.

The results of these studies on jury decisions in rape cases, taken together, are troubling in some respects. Widespread adherence to rape stereotypes and myths make it difficult not only for victims who fail to match the pristine picture of the ideal victim, but also for defendants whose courtroom appearance and life-style make him "seem like a rapist." The problem, of course, is not exclusively that of the jury system. Indeed, according to some researchers, prosecutors' and judges' decisions also reflect beliefs in rape myths.[32] Legal reformers must fashion procedures in rape cases that take into account these preexisting sentiments.

*   *   *

One ubiquitous finding with implications for reform is the prejudicial effect of sexual behavior of the victim on jury decisions. We have seen that it biases the case regardless of whether it is in any way pertinent to the legal issues. In light of this, the rape shield laws now in place in many jurisdictions constitute a critical reform that should reduce prejudice in rape trials. By excluding information about a victim's sexual behavior, we can ensure that at least one potentially prejudical factor in rape cases does no harm.

There are some hints, though, that rape shield laws may constitute a change more in form than in substance. In the Indiana study, for instance, although the rape shield law was invoked in many cases, information often came out in testimony anyway. Victims openly admitted living with their boyfriends, or questioning revealed that a victim and her boyfriend shared the same address. Jurors mentioned this testimony to the researchers who

interviewed them after the trial. For example, one juror stated: "We weren't supposed to judge her as to her past relations, [but] it came out in testimony that she was living with her boyfriend of one week. It was hard not to judge her."[33] Despite the fact that the victim's sexual behavior may sometimes come out at trial, the range and content of defense attorney questioning is typically restricted under the rape shield laws.

Other major changes in rape laws have been aimed at the jury. For instance, in some jurisdictions, penalties for rape have been reduced in the expectation that juries will be more likely to convict defendants of rape. Another common reform involves change in the wording of rape statutes, so that what was once called "rape" is now called "sexual assault." Reformers hope that avoiding the word "rape" in court cases will minimize the impact of myths and stereotypes surrounding the crime of rape. In still other jurisdictions, to capture the differences among sexual assaults of varying severity and aggravating circumstances, the crime of sexual assault is categorized into degrees of criminal sexual conduct. While there has been a tremendous effort to change rape laws to ease the victim's plight and to make it easier for juries to convict, very little work has been done evaluating the impact of the legal changes.

According to one researcher, the division of sexual assault into degrees of criminal misconduct has had at least a symbolic effect. He compared samples of criminal cases from the state of Washington processed before and after a change in the criminal code that divided rape and other sexual assaults into three degrees of severity. The percentage of cases resulting in a conviction of rape increased substantially, from 37% before the reform to 56% after it. But the increase was offset by a decrease in convictions on lesser offenses. Before the reform, 35% of cases initially filed as rape resulted in convictions on lesser charges such as assault. (Recall Kalven and Zeisel's discovery that juries were much more likely than judges to convict defendants of lesser offenses in cases of nonaggravated rape.) After the reform in Washington, however, just 15% of cases initially filed as rape charges resulted in convictions on other charges. Judges and juries were more likely to convict of rape when they had the option of different degrees of sexual assault. Thus, the overall conviction rate was the same but more men were being labeled as rapists. The researcher dubbed the effect "truth in criminal labelling."[34]

A more thorough investigation of the impact of rape reform was conducted in Michigan.[35] That state passed a model rape reform law in 1974. Among other modifications, the law divided sexual assault into four degrees of seriousness and prohibited questioning about the victim's past sexual behavior with men other than the defendant. Both arrests and convictions in-

creased as a result of the legal changes. Just as in the state of Washington, after the reform, convictions on the initial charge increased while convictions on lesser charges decreased.

To obtain information about the law's effect on juries, the researchers interviewed judges about the impact of the law reform. Sixty percent of the Michigan judges in the survey thought jury behavior had changed after the new law, with most of these judges believing that juries were now more likely to convict. Yet surprisingly many judges stated their belief that it was not the law itself that had changed juries' willingness to convict. Rather, they saw jurors reflecting societal changes in attitudes toward sexual behavior and increased awareness about the crime of rape, due in part to the women's movement. One judge stated:

> Jurors are more liberal in their sexual attitudes than they were three years ago, but they do not reflect the same attitude as that in [the Michigan sexual conduct statute]—they are still fairly conservative regarding women and sexuality. For example, you can get a conviction for a hitchhiking rape, but you still cannot get a conviction in cases involving a pregnant complainant or a prostitute.[36]

Another judge's comment was a reminder that there are still barriers to fairness and equity in rape trials:

> Education is the essential factor. There is some reason [why] people don't want to convict on rape complaints, but I don't have an explanation for it. Down deep, people feel there is some reason why women are raped. Men believe women *can't* be raped. And I don't find women sympathetic or understanding toward victims. There seems to be a general social feeling against victims of rape.[37]

Rape reform efforts, then, have only partly addressed the problems the criminal justice system faces in rape trials.

*   *   *

With such widespread negativity toward victims of rape, how did the juries hearing the Big Dan cases ever agree to convict? The review of factors affecting jury decisions in rape cases allows us to speculate about how the jurors in these trials reached their decisions. Prior to the case, legal procedures in rape trials had undergone significant change in Massachusetts. A rape shield law was in place that restricted questioning about the victim's past sexual behavior. If such information existed and had been introduced as evidence, jurors might well have acquitted the accused men, judging from the strong prejudicial impact of such information shown time and again in jury studies. The Big Dan case, because of its multiple assailants, would be categorized

as an "aggravated rape" by Kalven and Zeisel. Recall that in their study judges and juries most often decided similarly in cases of aggravated rape. Another unusual and key aspect of the Big Dan trials was the existence of eyewitnesses. The bartender and bar patrons confirmed the essence of the woman's story, although they also highlighted some inconsistencies. There was considerable corroborating evidence that rape had occurred, even though the victim had spoken to and possibly flirted with some of the men. Jurors probably concluded on the basis of all the evidence that despite some questions they may have had about the victim's behavior, she did not "deserve" what she got. If there had been no observers to corroborate the victim's story and compensate for some weaknesses in her credibility, we doubt that the jurors would have convicted the accused men of rape. While evidence was likely the main factor in their decision, characteristics of the jurors themselves may have played a subsidiary role. Both juries adequately represented male, female, and minority perspectives from the community. The *voir dire* in which they were extensively questioned about their knowledge of pretrial publicity about the events in question and their attitudes toward minorities and rape probably sensitized them to potential prejudices. The television coverage may also have heightened their determination to reach a fair verdict. All these factors doubtless contributed to the jury decisions in the Big Dan trials.

The Jury and the Executioner

On the morning of May 25, 1979, John Spinkellink was strapped immobile in the state of Florida's three-legged chair named "Old Sparky." His head was covered by a leather hood and a heavy strap bound his chin, which effectively gagged him. The curtain to the death chamber was raised at 10 A.M., making him visible to the thirty-two witnesses. "He looked terrified and helpless," said one of the witnesses. Then a flap on the hood was lowered in front of his eyes.

At 10:12 A.M. the prison superintendent gave a signal; behind the wall a hooded executioner threw the switch. A charge of 2300 volts of electricity shot through Spinkellink, from his shaved head to a wire strapped to his leg. The hands of the 32-year-old drifter curled and blackened. His legs twitched. Smoke began to fill the execution chamber. A second and third surge of electricity went through his body. "And if you leaned forward and looked close you could see that he sizzled and sizzled again . . ." said official witness Andy Johnson, a Democratic state representative. When the smoke cleared, a prison doctor checked Spinkellink's heart three times and lifted the hood to look at his eyes before declaring him dead at 10:18 A.M.[1]

Spinkellink was the second person to be executed in the United States since 1967—the first was Gary Gilmore in 1977—and the first to be executed against his will. By mid-1985, forty-seven convicted men and one woman had been sent to their deaths. The United States, like Libya, China, South Africa, Pakistan, Angola, the Soviet Union, Iran, Guatemala, and Chile, among other countries, employs the death penalty. To the contrary, most of the major Western democracies—Great Britain, Canada, Portugal, France, Italy, Belguim, West Germany, Spain, Holland, Denmark, Sweden, Israel, Switzerland, Norway—have abolished capital punishment by law or by practice; they have judged it to be inappropriate and unnecessary to their legal systems.[2]

The death penalty is the great moral issue of the legal system in the

United States. And here the jury plays a crucial role, because in most states no person can be put to death unless the jury, through its verdict, says that he or she deserves to die. A few states such as Arizona and Nebraska give the responsibility for sentencing in capital cases to the judge. In other states such as Florida, the judge may overturn a jury's recommendation for mercy.[3]

An evaluation of the jury's role cannot be conducted independently of knowledge about the moral and legal background of capital punishment. Yet a number of studies of public attitudes that we and some of our colleagues have conducted indicate that the average citizen, even the average law student, knows almost nothing about the history of capital punishment or other facts that are essential to understanding the issues.[4] For this reason it is important to present an introduction on capital punishment before we examine specific issues relating to the jury and the death sentence. Two things should be noted. First, capital punishment is a complex subject involving many issues. Literally thousands of pages are written about it each year; thus, we can only sketch some of the major issues and encourage the reader to consult other sources for a more complete picture.[5] Second, if it is not already obvious, both of the present authors are opposed to capital punishment.

*   *   *

In 1972 the U.S. Supreme Court ruled that the death penalty, as it was then administered, violated the Constitution's Eighth Amendment proscription of "cruel and unusual punishment." It was the high water mark for an abolitionist movement against the death penalty that had begun with Dr. Benjamin Rush, one of the signers of the Declaration of Independence. Dr. Rush was an energetic advocate of penal reform and a follower of the influential Italian jurist Cesare Beccaria. In 1787 Dr. Rush lectured about penal reform in the home of Benjamin Franklin and a year later he published an essay entitled "Inquiry into the Justice and Policy of Punishing Murder by Death." In it he argued that there was no biblical support for capital punishment, that it did not deter but in fact increased crime, and that by putting someone to death the state exceeds the powers that the people entrust to it. In 1794, as a result of Dr. Rush's efforts, Pennsylvania passed a law that compromised between abolition and retention by recognizing degrees of murder and reserving the death penalty only for first-degree homicide. The other states did not immediately follow Pennsylvania's example, however, and the death penalty remained mandatory for murder and a number of other crimes.

In the 1830s the abolitionist movement took more definite shape through a series of antigallows societies. Abolition bills were constantly before the

legislatures in New York, Massachusetts, and Pennsylvania. Finally, in 1846 Michigan voted to abolish hanging for all crimes except treason; in 1852 Rhode Island abolished it for all crimes, and Wisconsin followed a year later. In other states the death penalty was eliminated for many lesser crimes. Then, the abolitionist movement lost its momentum as the antislavery movement claimed the energies of many reform-minded citizens.

After the Civil War a number of states abolished the death penalty but then restored it. Nevertheless, clear trends emerged almost everywhere to limit it and reform the laws. Late in the 19th century the electric chair and the gas chamber replaced hanging because these new methods were believed to be more humane. The list of capital crimes was shortened, then shortened again. Special legal rules further reduced the number of death sentences in many states. And very significantly, discretionary sentencing replaced mandatory death sentences. Previously, if defendants were convicted of certain crimes, they automatically received the death penalty. Juries, however, often refused to convict a guilty person because an automatic sentence of death was judged as too severe for the crime. Discretionary sentencing, it was believed, allowed the jury to decide the matter of guilt without being hampered by the burden of deciding on the punishment. Sometimes the sentencing decision was left entirely to the trial judge. However, more and more states either allowed the jury to make a recommendation to the judge or required that it actually make the decision about whether a convicted person should live or die. Death penalty cases, therefore, became the major exception to the rule that juries seldom play a part in the sentencing process. Indeed, in this instance their role has increased over the years. As we shall see shortly, in 1976 the Supreme Court formalized this trend by making the jury's role in the sentencing process central.

Attempts to keep statistics on executions did not begin until around 1900. One estimate is that between 1900 and 1966 there were 7,226 legal executions in the United States. The vast majority of these were carried out before 1950. In the 1950s, executions began to decline. In that decade the number of executions dropped to half that of the 1940s, while in the 1960s the number of executions plummeted still further. Public opinion polls paralleled the declining use of the death penalty. In 1936, for example, 62% of Americans favored capital punishment but by 1966 only 42% favored it. No one was strongly advocating executions. Juries' verdicts reflected the declining popular support, and the courts and public officials responded to this trend.

There was another reason, however. In what Michael Meltsner[6] called a "rare conjunction of vigorous men and ripe ideas," a group of lawyers, many associated with the NAACP's Legal Defense Fund (LDF), decided to

challenge the legality of capital punishment itself. The "ripe ideas" took several forms. One set of ideas flowed from the landmark school desegregation cases that led to proscriptions against racial discrimination in almost every area of public life. While public facilities, employment, and transportation were being opened to blacks and other minority groups, blacks were still being sentenced to death with much greater frequency than whites. Another set of ideas came from new notions about "due process." Supreme Court decisions of the 1960s recognized that people accused of a crime had a right to a court-appointed lawyer if they couldn't afford one; police were limited in their powers to conduct searches and "stop-and-frisk" operations; suspects had to be warned of their right to remain silent. This emphasis on due process led the lawyers to question whether legal procedures in capital punishment cases were fair. Finally, some legal scholars began to raise the question of whether the death penalty violated the Constitution's prohibition of "cruel and unusual punishment."

Taking advantage of the indifferent public climate of the 1960s, the LDF lawyers coordinated a strategy against the death penalty. Their first goal was to block all executions by raising due process obstacles in each and every case. The LDF prepared what was dubbed a "Last Aid Kit" to help defense lawyers devise procedural roadblocks. Their second goal was to raise constitutional objections to the death penalty. They enlisted the aid of social scientists whose studies indicated that capital punishment had no deterrent effect on murder, and moreover, that death sentences were applied disproportionately to blacks. The lawyers also pointed to the fact that executions were arbitrary and capricious; those persons sentenced to die were often not different from persons who committed equally bad crimes but who received other sentences instead.

The legal strategy was successful. Between 1965 and 1967 only ten executions were carried out and, after that, none. Meanwhile, the number of prisoners on Death Row in the nation's prisons began to pile up. Eventually, more than 500 people were awaiting execution. This backlog too was important to the LDF strategy. If the Supreme Court began turning down appeals against death sentences, it was faced with the prospect that a bloodbath of executions might begin. The LDF speculated that public opinion would not tolerate large numbers of executions. Finally responding to these pressures, in the early 1970s the Supreme Court agreed to consider whether the death penalty was "cruel and unusual."

William Henry Furman, a black man, was sentenced to die in Georgia's electric chair. Furman had broken into a home intent on burglary. At about 2 A.M. the occupant, a 29-year-old father of five, heard a noise and went

downstairs to investigate. Furman fled, but as he left the house he tripped over the cord of a washing machine that was on the back porch. His gun discharged; the bullet pierced through a closed, solid plywood door, fatally wounding the owner. Although the killing was unintentional, Georgia law authorized the death penalty when a killing occurred during the commission of a felony. State psychiatrists found Furman mentally competent to stand trial, although they discovered that he had a subnormal IQ and was prone to psychotic episodes.

Furman's appeal against the death sentence was heard along with three other cases. Earnest Aikens, also black, had been sentenced to die in California for the rape-murder of a pregnant mother of two small children. Lucius Jackson Jr., also black and an escapee from a prison work gang, had raped a 21-year-old white woman. He threatened his victim with a pair of scissors and she suffered bruises and abrasions. The Georgia court sentenced Jackson to die in the electric chair. In Texas, Elmer Branch, a black with an IQ of 67, robbed and raped a 65-year-old white woman. Branch left his victim after speaking briefly to her about her feelings toward black people. After conviction, Branch too was sentenced to die. These were all very serious crimes. The question was whether or not each merited the death penalty.

In 1972 the Court rendered its landmark decision in *Furman v. Georgia*.[7] By a bare majority of five-to-four, it declared that the death sentences of Furman and the other three convicted men were unconstitutional. The decision was anything but clear-cut. All nine members of the court wrote separate opinions. Justices Brennan and Marshall would have banned capital punishment outright, but the opinions of the other three members of the majority were less sweeping, and the minority members of the court offered vigorous dissenting opinions.

Justice Marshall voiced the strongest condemnation of the death penalty. He argued that while it may have been an acceptable punishment in the past, it must now be judged in terms of "the evolving standards of decency that mark the progress of a maturing society." He observed that over the years it was used for fewer and fewer crimes, and with much less frequency. He also argued that it did not deter crime, that it was cruel, and that it was unfairly applied. He conceded that public opinion polls showed that a majority of Americans favored capital punishment, but while this fact appeared to contradict his view that capital punishment was against contemporary moral values, he suggested that the polls were misleading. He asserted that most Americans knew almost nothing about the death penalty. If they actually learned the facts, he believed that the polls would show most of them opposed to it.

*   *   *

The facts Justice Marshall referred to merit a digression. One of the facts is the evidence that the death penalty is not a more effective deterrent to murder than long prison sentences. A large number of empirical studies have been conducted on the deterrence issue.[8] Some, for example, have compared murder rates in adjoining states, such as Nebraska versus Kansas or Michigan versus Indiana, one of which had the death penalty while the other did not. Others have compared murder rates within a single state both before and after abolition. Other research has studied the effects of well-publicized executions on murder rates. Seldom has there been even a glimmer of support for the view that capital punishment deters murder. Of course, it is impossible to demonstrate with absolute certainty that the death penalty, as applied in the United States in this century, has no deterrent effect on murder. Yet criminologists have provided many compelling explanations as to why it does not deter. In fact, today many proponents of the death penalty downplay the deterrence argument or abandon it altogether and focus on the argument that murderers deserve to die.

Another fact, attested to by John Spinkellink's execution, is that executions are not pleasant events. Most people—including abolitionists—would agree that some murderers are dangerous, vicious people who committed horrible crimes, but few proponents of capital punishment would argue that they should be tortured. The truth is, however, that executions are frequently not swift and painless. Persons who were hanged often strangled slowly and painfully rather than experiencing instantaneous death from a broken neck. A prison doctor who officiated at a number of hangings before Canada abolished the death penalty and who, incidentally, favored capital punishment, asserted that the hangman frequently bungled the job.[9] The neck often did not break and the executioner had to resort to pulling on the condemned person's legs to speed the strangulation process, or alternatively, to raise the rope and make a second or a third drop so that the neck would break. Spinkellink's last moments tell us much about the electric chair. The hope is that the condemned person will be knocked unconscious by the first jolt of electricity, but this is not always so. In 1946 a black convict named Willie Francis survived a first attempt at electrocution when the apparatus failed.[8] Francis described the event as "plumb miserable." He said that he "saw little blue and pink and green speckles" and that his mouth tasted like cold peanut butter. He added, "I felt a burning in my head and my left leg, and I jumped against the straps." The Supreme Court later turned down Francis's appeal that a further attempt to electrocute him would be cruel and unusual punishment.

A year later the state of Louisiana was more successful in its second try. Other methods of execution have their problems too. The gas chamber depends on cyanide gas which is caustic and can lead to a painful and slow death. Even execution by the injection of lethal drugs has its problems. There is the ethical issue of whether the attending physician is violating the Hippocratic oath by inserting the needle in the veins or in even advising the technician when to administer the drugs. Indeed, the American Medical Association has held that it is a violation of the oath for a doctor to cause death even in state-sanctioned executions. Hence, the doctor's role is largely limited to pronouncing the person dead. Moreover, pharmaceutical experts have testified that if the drugs are not administered precisely, death may be horribly painful.[10]

Aside from the execution itself, confinement of condemned people prior to execution triggers intense psychological stress. Guards place them in a segregated area of the prison, usually with the death chamber only a couple of steps away. They are given few privileges accorded to other prisoners and are watched constantly to ensure that they do not escape or "cheat the executioner" by committing suicide. Often, they remain under these conditions for years while their legal appeals are heard. On Death Row, the inmates' sanity often deteriorates. One issue is whether or not the state has the duty to restore the inmate's sanity before executing him or her. The confinement even leads some Death Row inmates to give up legitimate appeals and to instruct their attorneys to cease trying to overturn their death sentences. In effect, the inmates are "volunteering for death." This happened in the case of Gary Gilmore, the first person to be executed after the *Furman* decision.

Inequities plague the administration of capital punishment and they take a number of forms. In 1970 a group of teenagers killed an Arkansas farmer. They were arrested and Joey Newton Kagebein was the first to be tried.[11] The prosecution did not contend that Kagebein shot the farmer. The testimony strongly indicated that someone else fired the shot and that in fact Kagebein was asleep in the car during most of the arguing and scuffling. Nevertheless, he was present at the murder scene and was found guilty of aiding and abetting the murder and eventually sentenced to die. Perhaps he was guilty of something, but the death sentence seems out of proportion here.

In other instances, the state has executed innocent people. Great Britain's abolition of the death penalty was, in part, prompted by the fact that an innocent man was hanged. Such mistakes are not just a thing of the past. Charles Brooks, the first person to be killed by a lethal injection, in Texas in 1982, may not have been guilty.[12] Prior to his execution, another man submitted a sworn statement that he, and not Brooks, had shot an automobile mechanic to death in 1976, the crime for which Brooks was condemned.

Even the Texas prosecutor who convicted Brooks joined with civil liberties lawyers in a futile attempt to save his life. Afterwards the prosecutor said, "It may well be, horrible as it is to contemplate, that the State of Texas executed the wrong man." Or consider Spinkellink's case. Spinkellink had an accomplice, Frank Brumm, who held a gun on the victim and who also assisted by hitting the victim across the temple with the back side of a hatchet. Brumm was charged along with Spinkellink but did not testify at the trial, as Spinkellink did. The jury that condemned Spinkellink found Brumm not guilty. Brumm cannot be tried again for the crime because of the Constitution's prohibition of double jeopardy, and he has now openly confessed his part in the murder. Spinkellink is dead; Brumm is alive and a free man.[13] Another inequity arises from the fact that those sentenced to die are only a small percentage of those who are eligible for a death sentence. Of this number only a very small percentage are executed.

Finally, there is the problem of racial discrimination. Blacks (and other minorities) are more likely to be sentenced to die than whites. Criminologists Marvin Wolfgang and Marc Reidel, for example, studied how death sentences for rape were meted out between 1945 and 1965. Nearly seven times as many blacks as whites were given the death sentence. The figure rose to eighteen to one if the rapist was black and the victim white. Other studies showed similar racial discrimination with respect to the death sentence for murder.[14] These, then, are some of the facts to which Justice Marshall referred.

*   *   *

While the other justices in the *Furman* case were aware of these facts, they did not condemn capital punishment outright. Instead they condemned the way that it was applied. Justice Douglas objected to it because of the apparent racial discrimination. Justice Stewart said that it was "wantonly and freakishly applied." Finally, Justice Byron White voted against the death penalty because ". . . the death penalty is exacted with greater infrequency even for the most atrocious crimes and . . . there is no meaningful basis for distinguishing the few cases in which it is imposed from the many cases in which it is not." Justice White's opinion helps us to return to the subject of this book, the jury.

For all five of the majority justices in *Furman,* the jury appeared to be a central cause of the arbitrariness, caprice, and discrimination of the death penalty. They knew that over the years the jury had been given more and more responsibility in capital cases. Justice White asserted that this was the problem:

> The short of it is that the policy of vesting sentencing authority primarily in juries—a decision largely motivated by the desire to mitigate the harshness of the law and to bring community judgment to bear upon the sentence as well as the guilt or innocence—has so effectively achieved its aims that capital punishment within the confines of the statutes now before us has for all practical purposes run its course.[7]

The key problem with existing statutes was that the jury was given no adequate guidance from the law; in each case it had to make up its own guidelines for recommending death. Different juries came up with different rules. Another problem for the jury was that in some states it was asked to decide on the defendant's guilt and sentence all at once. In a "single-phase" trial, the jury would hear the evidence bearing on guilt and then be instructed by the judge that if they found the defendant guilty they should also determine if a death sentence was deserved. They were not told what standards they should use in deciding if execution was appropriate. What is more, they often had little information about the defendant, particularly mitigating factors, that might render their judgment on sentencing less harsh. In fact, the jury was sometimes provided with less information about the defendant than would be available in any other crime where the potential penalty was less severe. This was because the "single-phase" deliberation made capital murder trials different from all other types of trials.

For any other crime, there are usually two distinct phases to a trial. In the first stage the judge or jury decides whether the defendant is guilty or not. If the verdict is guilty, a second phase begins. The convicted person is allowed to submit additional evidence to the judge who decides on the penalty. During this second phase he or she may explain any mitigating circumstances. The defendant can, for example, produce evidence about good behavior in the past, or produce evidence that the crime was committed under emotional stress or drunkenness, or even suggest that a disturbed childhood helped to cause the criminal behavior. The defendant can submit evidence of remorse for the committed act. These submissions are allowed even when the defendant denies committing the crime or if he or she exercised the Fifth Amendment right not to testify at trial during the guilt phase. While the evidence may have little impact—and researchers have documented that judicial sentencing can sometimes be pro forma and routine—most defendants nevertheless have at least the opportunity to present their side.

In contrast to these other trials, the single-phase capital murder trial put the defendant in a difficult dilemma. If the accused person decided to exercise the right not to testify, a privilege guaranteed by the Bill of Rights, there was no opportunity to provide information to the jury about mitigating factors that

might cause the jury to temper the punishment. Even in instances where the defendant admitted the killing but claimed that a verdict of manslaughter or self-defense was the appropriate verdict, the court still conferred little opportunity to plead extenuating conditions. In short, defendants in capital murder trials were not given the same opportunity to plead for mercy as defendants on trial for much less serious crimes.

Thus, the existing statutes considered by the *Furman* court had major "due process" flaws. They compromised the rights of defendants and led to arbitrariness, caprice, and discrimination. This does not necessarily suggest that capital punishment is unconstitutional *per se,* only that the process by which it was applied was unconstitutional. That in fact was the thrust of the opinions of Justices Douglas, Stewart, and White. Theoretically, the flawed process could have been corrected by statutes that provided more opportunities for the defendant to make his or her case for mercy, and that provided the jury with guidelines to help them decide when a death sentence was appropriate and when it was not.

The *Furman* decision set aside the death sentences of the almost 500 persons on Death Row in 1972, but it did not end capital punishment. It left the door open. If state legislatures could devise laws that would ensure better due process, capital punishment might be acceptable. The invitation was there, and it was swiftly accepted. Within months many states passed new laws intended to ease the *Furman* Court's concern with the jury's "unbridled discretion."

The new law passed by Georgia serves as an example.[15] Under it, capital murder trials are divided into two stages, a guilt phase and a penalty phase. In the guilt phase the jury determines the defendant's guilt just as it would in any other kind of trial and reports its verdict to the judge. If the verdict is guilty, the second phase begins. The Georgia jury is provided with a list of ten possible aggravating conditions that make the crime more serious: for example, if the murder was committed against a police officer; if it was committed while the defendant was engaged in another serious crime; if the murder was committed for money; if the killing was "outrageously or wantonly vile, horrible, or inhuman"; or if the defendant has a prior conviction for a capital felony or a substantial history of serious assaultive criminal convictions. The prosecuting attorney can present evidence bearing on these aggravating conditions, and the defense can attempt to refute the evidence and make other submissions to the jury for mercy. The judge then instructs the jury that it should weigh the aggravating and mitigating circumstances. If it finds one or more of the aggravating conditions are present, and they are not outweighed by mitigating factors, the jury may return a recommendation for

death. The law also provides that the Georgia Supreme Court is to review each death sentence and compare it to other cases. This judicial review is an attempt to ensure that there are not major inequities in jury decisions, that one person receives a death sentence while another, equally deserving, does not.

Other states have passed slightly different laws. The Florida law, for example, contains a list of eight aggravating and seven mitigating conditions. The latter include absence of a significant criminal record, the influence of extreme mental or emotional disturbance, and the defendant's age at the time of the crime. The Texas law lists five forms of aggravated murder and three additional aggravating conditions that merit death.

In 1976 the Supreme Court was once again asked to rule whether capital punishment as provided in the new statutes violated the Constitution. This time in *Gregg v. Georgia*[15] it ruled by a vote of seven-to-two that death penalty laws that provided specific guidelines for the jury were acceptable. It singled out the Georgia law for praise because its guidelines direct the jury's attention to the specific circumstances of the crime and the characteristics of the person who committed the crime. The members of the Court concluded that "while some jury discretion still exists the discretion to be exercised is controlled by clear and objective standards so as to produce nondiscriminatory application." Moreover, Georgia Supreme Court review would correct any remaining problems.

*   *   *

Was the conclusion correct? It appears the answer is "no," even though the Court has not yet been forced to face this fact. Social scientists have conducted a number of careful studies on the effects of the post-*Furman* death penalty statutes. Criminologists William Bowers and Glenn Pierce, for example, studied how the death penalty was applied in Florida, Georgia, Texas, and Ohio between December 1972 and the end of 1977.[16] They found a clear pattern of racial discrimination in each of the states. Blacks were more likely to receive the death sentence than whites, particularly if the victim was white. In Florida, for example, if a black person killed a white person the chances of receiving a death sentence were about 1 in 5; if a white killed a white the chances were about 1 in 20; if a black killed a black the chances were about 1 in 167; and if a white killed a black the probability of a death sentence was zero. This basic pattern and even the levels of probability were closely approximated in the other three states. Even when Bowers and Pierce controlled for a large number of other factors (such as crime severity, past criminal

record, and the number of charges) that might have explained the differences in sentences, the basic pattern of discrimination remained.

Lawyer David Baldus and colleagues have conducted even more extensive research centering on the effects of the Georgia statute that was so highly praised by the Court in the *Gregg* decision.[17] Among other findings, they discovered that there was a strong influence of arbitrary and capricious factors in sentencing. The death sentence is applied more frequently if the victim is white than if the victim is black. Trials held in some regions of the state are more likely to result in death sentences than those held in other regions. Even after equity review by the Georgia Supreme Court, the death sentences remain excessive and disproportionate. Baldus suggested that the initial source of the bias can be attributed to the prosecutor's exercise of discretion. Prosecutors can decide to ask for the death penalty or not. They tend to ask for the death sentence more if a murder victim is white than if the victim is black. One explanation is simple racism; a white life is worth more than a black life. But another explanation is compelling. Whites are much more supportive of the death penalty than blacks, and the white community therefore may pressure the prosecutor to ask for the death penalty when a white victim is killed. In addition to the difference in the prosecutor's request for the death penalty, other biases can be traced to the jury.

Despite the new statutes, arbitrariness, caprice, and discrimination still persist in the application of capital punishment. While the research suggests that prosecutors and others share some responsibility for this outcome, experts from law and the social sciences also blame the jury, or at least the conditions under which the jury operates in capital cases. The criticisms fall on several fronts.

*   *   *

One explanation for nonequitable verdicts may lie in the fact that the death penalty jury is not composed like other juries—it is "death qualified." In the process of death qualification, as it is called, prospective jurors are eliminated from the jury based on their opposition to the death penalty. This procedure excludes a significant portion of the population, and may also bias the remaining jurors. The problems resulting from death qualification first came to public attention in the case of *Witherspoon v. Illinois* in 1968.

William Witherspoon was convicted for murder and sentenced to die in Cook County, Illinois, in 1960. He appealed his conviction to the Supreme Court.[18] He argued that the jury that convicted him was unrepresentative of

the population, consisted only of jurors highly supportive of the death penalty, and furthermore was stacked with jurors who were "conviction-prone." That is, rather than being neutral, they favored the prosecution. The Illinois statute, similar to those in most other states, provided that anyone who opposed the death penalty for any reason could be excluded from serving on the jury. The reasoning behind the statute was that jurors who were against capital punishment might not vote to convict an obviously guilty person if they believed that person would be sentenced to death. Such jurors would be able to thwart the intent of the law and the will of the majority of people. Witherspoon, however, pointed out that a large number of potential jurors were eliminated from jury service. Even people who expressed mild opposition or hesitancy about the application of the death penalty were excused. The resulting jury was composed only of people who staunchly advocated capital punishment. Thus, the jury was *more* likely than the general public to render the death penalty, regardless of the circumstances of the crime. He also contended that such a jury was more likely to return a verdict of guilty. His lawyer argued that people who favored the death penalty tended to hold attitudes that could be characterized as "tough" on law-and-order issues. They were inherently biased in favor of the prosecution. Three social science studies purporting to support Witherspoon's contention were cited in the arguments, but the studies were flawed or incomplete and their conclusions could only be considered tentative.

In its decision in *Witherspoon v. Illinois,* the Court distinguished between the verdict of guilty and the punishment. Witherspoon's conviction for the murder was affirmed but his death sentence was reduced to life imprisonment. The Court reasoned that it was "obvious" that the members of the jury had been selected for their harsh attitudes favoring punishment and therefore were uncommonly willing to let a man die. Constitutionally, it agreed with Witherspoon that the scales could not be tipped toward death this way. However, it concluded that there was not sufficient evidence to show that the jurors' attitudes toward punishment influenced their impartiality on the issue of guilt. The *Witherspoon* decision had two important consequences. First, it restricted the kinds of jurors that could be excluded. The Court said that people who have reservations about capital punishment, but who nevertheless state that they can follow the law and consider the death penalty, cannot automatically be excluded from jury service in capital murder trials, as had been the practice. However, two types of jurors could still be excluded: those who would never consider voting to impose the death penalty, and those who would vote not guilty just to keep the defendant from being in jeopardy of a death sentence.

Second, it acknowledged that Witherspoon's "conviction-proneness" argument might have some merit; and it left the door open for lawyers and social scientists to produce more evidence bearing on its validity.

The 1972 *Furman* decision striking down all death penalty statutes temporarily made the unresolved questions about *Witherspoon* unimportant, but the 1976 *Gregg* decision affirming the Georgia death penalty law brought them back to prominence. Indeed, in trial after trial in state after state, defense attorneys continue to challenge the validity of death qualification procedures. Their arguments are bolstered by a substantial body of research—nearly two dozen studies—that consistently shows that the arguments that were raised in the case do have validity. The studies show that even with the new guidelines for exclusion that were enunciated in *Witherspoon,* the death-qualified jury is unrepresentative of the population and is "conviction-prone."

Phoebe Ellsworth, a Stanford psychology professor, and her collaborators have conducted some of the best-known research on the issue.[19] Her research helps us to understand what death qualification does to the nature of the jury. In one study 811 randomly selected residents of California were interviewed in detail about capital punishment. About 21% said that they would never vote guilty in a capital murder trial; these people would be excluded under the new rules set forth in *Witherspoon.* Another 17% said that though they were opposed to the death penalty and could never vote to impose it, they could nevertheless vote on the defendant's guilt or innocence with an open mind. But these people, too, would be excluded from jury service because the *Witherspoon* rules require willingness to do both tasks, consider guilt *and* consider voting for a death sentence. These figures tell us that a significant number of otherwise eligible jurors will be automatically excluded from capital murder juries. But this is not all of the story because these death penalty attitudes are related to other characteristics. Women and blacks are more likely to be in both of these groups. So are Jews, atheists, and agnostics. So are poor people and Democrats. To put it the other way around, the typical juror in a capital murder trial is more likely to be wealthier, a Protestant or Catholic, a Republican, a male, and white. In short, juries in death penalty cases are not representative of the population, or similar to other juries.

Unrepresentativeness is not the only issue, however. Death penalty attitudes are correlated with other attitudes. Ellsworth's study showed that the remaining persons who were eligible to serve were less concerned with issues of due process. For example, they were more likely to say that an accused person who exercises his or her Fifth Amendment right to remain silent is probably guilty, or that if the police obtain evidence illegally, it should still be admitted in court.

The relationship of these attitudes to support for capital punishment suggested to the researchers that death-qualified jurors could be more disposed to convict defendants than are other jurors. A second study tested this hypothesis. Simulated jurors observed a two-and-a-half-hour videotape of a murder trial and then indicated what verdict they would give. Professor Ellsworth divided the subjects into two groups based on their attitudes toward the death penalty. The first group, the death-qualified jurors, would be allowed to serve on a capital murder jury. The other group was composed of people who would be excluded from jury service; they said that although they could never give the death penalty, they could be fair and impartial in deciding whether the defendant was guilty or innocent. Those people whose death penalty position would allow them to serve on a capital murder jury were more likely to vote guilty than the subjects who would be excluded under the *Witherspoon* rules.

After giving their individual verdicts, some of the jurors were assigned to juries composed of people who would meet the death qualification standards while others were assigned to mixed juries which included some members who would ordinarily not be allowed to serve. They were then tested after their deliberations. The persons who served on mixed juries were more critical of trial witnesses and better able to remember details of the evidence. Thus, consistent with some of the notions that we discussed in earlier chapters, the diversity of opinions that resulted from the mixed juries improved the vigor, thoroughness, and accuracy of the deliberations. The death-qualified juries appeared to be less competent. Other research showed that death-qualified jurors have a lower threshold for conviction. For them, less certainty was needed to prove "guilt beyond a reasonable doubt."

A study of real jurors showed that these differences in attitude surveys and behavior in jury simulations carry over into the courtroom. In 1954–1955, Professor Hans Zeisel interviewed jurors who had served on felony trials in Chicago and New York. He asked all the jurors two questions: whether they had conscientious scruples against the death penalty, and how they voted on the first ballot taken during their jury deliberation. Of course, jurors' votes are strongly related to the strength of evidence in the case. To control for this, Zeisel grouped the cases according to the proportion of jurors who voted to convict on the first ballot. He had eleven different constellations of first-ballot jury splits, from the weakest cases with eleven-to-one for acquittal, to the strongest cases with eleven-to-one for conviction. Zeisel discovered that in 10 of the 11 constellations, jurors with scruples against the death penalty voted to acquit more frequently than the other jurors.[20]

The accumulated evidence, then, suggests that from the outset, capital

murder juries are not the same as other juries. They are not likely to be representative of the population, and they are likely to be predisposed toward conviction.

Professor Craig Haney, who holds a law degree as well as a Ph.D. in psychology, speculated that death qualification has other implications.[21] To determine who is qualified to serve and who is not, prospective jurors are usually exposed to a lengthy *voir dire* questioning process that centers on the death penalty. Haney observed this process in real trials, and noted that it involves an extended discussion about the death sentence with each juror even before any evidence about guilt is presented. The judge and the prosecuting attorney ask the jurors to reflect about and predict whether or not they would be able to give someone a death sentence. They are questioned repeatedly about their attitudes. Frequently, they observe other jurors being questioned as well and discover that some who do not express the "right attitude" are dismissed by the judge.

The tone of the discussions with the jurors often appears to assume that the death penalty phase of the trial *will* occur rather than it *might* occur. There is a not-so-subtle implication that the jury will find the defendant guilty. In New Jersey, for example, the judge's instruction manual suggests that even before the questioning of individual jurors begins, the judge should address the whole panel of jurors with the following words:

> When I instruct the jury at the close of this trial I will outline in detail the factors to be weighed in deciding whether to impose a death penalty. Let me give you a general idea of what I will say so that you understand what we need to know about your views.

The expectation that the jury will find the defendant guilty is furthered by the questioning of the prosecutor. Consider an example that Haney provided from an interchange between a prosecutor and a prospective juror in a Maryland murder trial:

> The Prosecutor: All right. Mrs. Marshall, you know all that you are going to have to go through with the second phase?
> Prospective Juror: Yes.
> The Prosecutor: To determine the death penalty. Do you feel that this would have any bearing on your deliberation with regard to the guilt or innocence of it, knowing that you are going to have to—
> Prospective Juror: Let me get this straight now.
> The Prosecutor: There's two.
> Prospective Juror: Which, how I decide that, it was guilty of the crime, or not guilty, would this have anything to do with me deciding; no.
> The Prosecutor: No. Even though that you are going to have to go through and consider this the second phase?[22]

Even the defense attorney may begin to act as if a guilty verdict is inevitable and that the penalty phase will take place. In an Ohio trial the following exchange took place:

> Defense Counsel: And if there is this second trial that we are talking about and we put on evidence which tends to mitigate, would you be able to consider that evidence?
> Prospective Juror: Yes.
> Defense Counsel: What we are worried about, since you are on the jury that already made a determination as it comes to pass of guilty, that some of the jurors might close their minds to this mitigation, but I take it you wouldn't have any problem keeping your mind open during the second trial?
> Prospective Juror: No.[22]

From observations such as these, Haney hypothesized that the questioning process may psychologically induce conviction-proneness in the jurors. This could happen in a number of ways. By asking the juror to imagine in advance how he or she might behave in a penalty phase of the trial, the juror may estimate that the defendant will be found guilty. The questioning also desensitizes the juror to the penalty phase by implying that it is routine and matter-of-fact. It may make the penalty phase appear to be the central purpose of the *voir dire*. Jurors may develop the impression that the crime is especially heinous. Additionally, during the *voir dire* questioning, jurors must virtually commit themselves in advance to giving the death sentence under certain circumstances. For example, in one case the prosecutor asked the jurors the following question:

> In an appropriate case, based upon the information that will be given to you, and the law that his Honor, Judge Matia, will give you, if you come to the conclusion that the imposition of capital punishment is the appropriate verdict at the second trial, *do you feel that you could join with your fellow jurors and sign a verdict form indicating that?* [Italics added]

Finally, the whole process of selecting and rejecting jurors on the basis of their attitudes may create the impression that the judge considers some people "fit for service" while others are "unfit." A message is conveyed—the legally appropriate thing for jurors to do is vote for conviction and then vote for death.

Haney tested these propositions in an experiment. A sample of people were asked to observe a two-hour videotape of jury selection for a murder trial. They were asked to imagine that they were prospective jurors in "this very case." Half of them were randomly assigned to a "death qualification" condition where they saw jurors being asked not only standard jury questions that would be asked in any trial but also questions about death qualification.

The other half of the participants in the experiment served in a control condition; they saw exactly the same videotape but with the death qualification questions carefully edited out. After they had seen the videotape, both groups of people answered a series of questions about the case and the defendant. In comparison to the people in the control condition, those people who had been exposed to the death qualification questions were more likely to indicate that they believed the defendant was guilty and that he would be convicted of first-degree murder. They were also more likely to believe that the judge personally thought the defendant was guilty and that he probably favored the death penalty. In addition, people in the death qualification condition were more likely to believe that the law disapproved of people who opposed capital punishment. In short, Haney's hypothesis was confirmed. The process of death qualification itself predisposes jurors toward conviction. The California Supreme Court relied on Haney's research to order in 1980 that all pretrial questioning of jurors in capital cases be done individually and outside the presence of other jurors. The Court reasoned that group questioning of prospective capital jurors would exacerbate the problems that Haney documented, and that individual questioning might provide a partial remedy.[23]

There are some other research findings that bear on death-qualified juries. In some courts the prospective jurors are questioned individually and in others the questions are put to the jurors as a group. Michael Nietzel and Ronald Dillehay studied the effects of these two approaches in a number of Kentucky murder trials.[24] Their research indicates that group questioning is more likely to produce a jury less favorable to the defendant. Other studies suggest that the adversary system also plays a role. For those jurors who clear the hurdles of death qualification, prosecutors still have their peremptory challenges to eliminate blacks and other minority group members in a disproportionate way. The end result is a jury that is even more unrepresentative of the population. Still other research shows that people who meet the *Witherspoon* criteria are more likely to hold attitudes of prejudice toward blacks and other minority group members.

The evidence suggests, therefore, that the end result of death qualification is a jury that is not like other juries. It is not a body of peers. Psychologically, it is disposed toward conviction and its members are less sympathetic toward blacks and other racial minorities. This is not to say that death penalty juries will invariably vote guilty or will always act with prejudice—but they are inclined in that direction.

These studies on the impact of death qualification have formed the basis of recent and conflicting court decisions about the constitutionality of the death penalty. In July of 1981, a number of social scientists presented these

and other research findings before Judge G. Thomas Eisele in federal district court in Little Rock, Arkansas, on behalf of a man charged with capital murder. The evidentiary hearing took seven court days, and included thorough presentation and cross-examination on the findings. In addition, some other social scientists testified for the prosecution and criticized some of the studies in court. Judge Eisele was persuaded that the studies, taken together, provided strong support for the defendant's claim that death-qualified juries were unrepresentative and conviction-prone. He therefore declared the practice of death qualification unconstitutional. In January of 1985 the Eighth Circuit Court of Appeal upheld his decision in the case of *Grigsby v. Mabry*.[25] In the Eighth Circuit, death qualification procedures are thus now unconstitutional. Yet in the Fourth Circuit, the appeals court that considered the same evidence found it unpersuasive, and held that death qualification was not unconstitutional.[26]

Meanwhile, the U.S. Supreme Court has altered somewhat the standards that judges may use in deciding whether a person should be excluded from a capital jury. Recall that in *Witherspoon* the Court said that to be excused, jurors must make it unmistakably clear that they cannot be impartial or cannot render a death sentence. In January of 1985, the Court decided the case of *Wainwright v. Witt*.[27] Johnny Witt was convicted of murder and sentenced to die by a Florida jury. Witt argued that during the death qualification of his jury, three prospective jurors were improperly excluded. They had expressed some opposition to the death penalty, but hadn't made it clear that it would interfere with their duties as jurors. The Supreme Court, however, said that the jurors were properly excluded. They relaxed the strict standard that has governed jury selection in capital cases since *Witherspoon*. In theory, the *Witt* standard should increase the number of people who can be excluded from capital juries because of their feelings against the death penalty. The implications of this decision, and whether it will worsen the problems we have documented regarding death-qualified juries, remain to be seen.

*   *   *

The penalty phase of the trial also presents problems that reflect on the competence and fairness of jury decisions. Recall that in the 1976 *Gregg* decision, the Supreme Court majority believed that the new statutes would solve the problem of arbitrariness and discrimination. The separate penalty phase of the trial would allow both prosecution and defense attorneys the opportunity to present the jury with additional evidence about the defendant's crime and character. The aggravating or mitigating conditions presented to

the jury would provide standards to aid its deliberations. Emerging evidence suggests that the Court was optimistic in its predictions. It did not anticipate what types of evidence might be presented in the penalty phase, how prosecutors might shape their arguments, and how the jury might respond.

One unanticipated development is the calling of psychiatric witnesses by the prosecutor. In the death penalty laws of several states, one aggravating factor is whether the defendant is likely to continue to be a danger to society. In *Jurek v. Texas*, a case decided along with *Gregg*, the Court said this was a legitimate thing for the jury to consider, even though it acknowledged that predicting future behavior was a difficult task.

In the *Jurek* case, the jury deliberated on the defendant's dangerousness without any professional help. However, in many subsequent cases, the prosecution has called psychiatrists and psychologists to testify before the jury regarding the defendant's dangerousness.

In 1978, Thomas Barefoot was convicted in the killing of a police officer in Texas. He was found guilty, and the sentencing phase of the trial began. One of the issues that the jury was asked to decide was whether "there is a probability that the defendant would commit criminal acts of violence that would constitute a continuing threat to society." In addition to presenting evidence about Barefoot's prior convictions and his reputation for lawlessness, the prosecutor also called two psychiatrists. Neither had ever interviewed Barefoot, nor had either even requested the opportunity to interview him. Instead, on the witness stand they simply answered hypothetical questions about whether a defendant with Barefoot's background would be likely to represent a threat to society. Both psychiatrists said yes. Their testimony accounted for about half of the penalty phase. The defense did not call psychiatric witnesses. The jury verdict was death.

There are some extremely important issues raised by the *Barefoot* case.[28] The first rides on the fact that psychiatric predictions about future dangerousness are highly unreliable. Estimates are that two out of every three such predictions are inaccurate. Psychologist John Monahan, who has written the leading text on this matter, points out that predictions of dangerousness are unreliable under most circumstances, but particularly so with respect to the type of diagnosis that was made in Barefoot's case. The prediction of dangerousness was closer to speculation than diagnosis. Few people would put faith in a diagnosis that radical surgery was required if the doctor had never examined the patient. Yet the psychiatrists who testified in Barefoot's trial performed a similar feat. When Barefoot's case was appealed, the American Psychiatric Association submitted a brief to the Court opposing such testi-

mony. The Association's position is that because psychiatric diagnosis of dangerousness in cases like Barefoot's are unreliable, they ought not to be used in decisions about the death penalty.

In an earlier case, the California Supreme Court ruled that psychiatric predictions were too unreliable to be used in the penalty phase, and that such evidence would be likely to be uncritically accepted by the jury. However, in Barefoot's case, the U.S. Supreme Court decided that such testimony was admissible. It said that the diagnosis might be unreliable, but cross-examination of the psychiatrist should uncover any unreliability and that in any event the jury would weigh the testimony with a critical eye. Justice Blackmun strongly dissented from the majority. He observed that the "American Bar Association has warned repeatedly that sentencing juries are particularly incapable of dealing with information relating to the 'likelihood that the defendant will commit other crimes.' " In Blackmun's view, the jury might give undue weight to the testimony about dangerousness simply because the experts are psychiatrists.

At present, we have no satisfactory data bearing on the issue that Blackmun raised. It is unlikely that jurors disregard psychiatric testimony entirely, but whether they view it with appropriate skepticism or heavily rely on it is a question for which we have no answer. We do know that juries are sometimes incapable of separating knowledge about a defendant's prior criminal record from the question of guilt as they are asked to do, and that sometimes they accept expert evidence uncritically. Yet research about psychiatric testimony regarding the insanity defense shows that psychiatric opinions can be disregarded.[29] The problem is that none of this other research speaks directly to how jurors—and death-qualified jurors at that—handle such testimony in the penalty phase after they have already decided on the defendant's guilt. We hope that social scientists will soon be able to provide us with at least a tentative answer to this question.

*   *   *

Lawyer Robert Weisberg has raised another issue about the jury's behavior in the penalty phase.[30] He suggests that, psychologically, the jury may not feel that it has responsibility for the death sentence. He argues that prosecutors often attempt to convince the jury that the determination of death or life imprisonment is really a matter of applying a simple formula. Some suggestive examples from two California murder trials seem to bolster Weisberg's hypothesis.

Example 1.

The Prosecutor: It is never easy for someone to ask for another man's life. But your burden is lightened in this case because of the law.

The way the law is set up, as I'll explain it to you, the weighing process that you go through and the fact that if the aggravating circumstances outweigh the mitigating circumstances, you shall return a verdict of death.

It's just that simple. The law lightened your burden in that regard, in the analysis that you go through. . . .

The way the criminal justice system is set up, it's set up that every individual's rights are protected, and this defendant's rights have been protected.

You have no worry there. . . .

Example 2.

The Prosecutor: All you are going to hear is you are to consider these factors and you are then to return a verdict of death, a verdict of life without parole. That is all you decide. You decide what the verdicts are. You don't gas anybody.[30]

Of course, the defense counsel can attempt to offer arguments to counter the prosecutor's rhetoric by appealing to the consequences of the jury's task. In one case the defense counsel said:

Ladies and Gentlemen, when I was preparing for final argument, I thought how woefully inadequate my legal training has been, because I was never in anyplace in law school or anyplace else to argue life versus death.[30]

The question, then, is whether the prosecutor and defense counsel offset one another, or whether the prosecutors are more compelling. Since we have evidence that death-qualified juries are inclined toward the prosecution in the first place, it may be that the prosecutors are more compelling to them. Until researchers conduct interviews with jurors about their reactions to this rhetoric or gather other supportive data, we will not know the answer to this question.

Professor Weisberg has raised another argument, namely that contrary to what the Supreme Court assumed, the standards provided to the jury are often unclear. The jurors become confused by the legal jargon, and in the end the instructions are either not used or are used in a way that is contrary to what was intended under the law. Weisberg reports that in 1982, a California jury was deliberating on death versus life without parole for a defendant named Neely. The jury returned to the courtroom to ask the judge for help and was given some additional instructions. After further deliberation, the jury returned for still more instructions. The judge responded as follows:

Good morning, ladies and gentlemen. I have a note from Mr. Crill [the jury foreman].

Now, we have a note that reads as follows: "On this page the instructions state, 'If you conclude that the aggravating circumstances, et cetera you shall impose a sentence of death.' Does this mean we have to, or see page 22."

The note attached to that, "May we show mercy and give life without possibility even though we feel aggravating outweighs mitigating?"

I will answer that question as follows: I am going to now direct your attention to page 17 of those instructions, which has been previously read to you, which you now have with you in the jury room.

That page reads as follows: It is now your duty to determine which of the two penalties, death or confinement in the State Prison for life without possibility of parole, shall be imposed upon defendant.

After having heard all of the evidence, and after having heard and considered the arguments of counsel, you shall consider, take into account, and be guided by the applicable factors of aggravating and mitigating circumstances upon which you have been instructed.

If you conclude that the aggravating circumstances outweigh the mitigating circumstances, you shall impose a sentence of death. However, if you determine that the mitigating circumstances outweigh the aggravating circumstances, you shall impose a sentence of confinement in the State Prison for life without possibility of parole.

Before you may consider a particular aggravating circumstance to be true, you must be satisfied of the existence of that aggravating circumstance beyond a reasonable doubt.

Page 22 of the jury instructions, which you sent me, allows the jury to consider pity, sympathy, and mercy as those factors may constitute a mitigating circumstance within the Defendant's background. The language should not be interpreted as providing anything contrary to Page 17 of your instructions.

I will return the instructions with the Bailiff so you may take them into the jury room with you.[30]

Looking at his statements, we can see that the judge did little more than repeat the initial instructions. And the instructions simultaneously seem to encourage the jury to exercise compassion and to forbid compassion. Two hours after this exchange, Neely was sentenced to death.

While no good data yet exist to verify these hypotheses about the penalty phase of the trial, they appear plausible in the light of trial transcripts and comments of the critics. They also point to one of the possible explanations for juries' unfair application of the death penalty.

*   *   *

This chapter must end on an incomplete and sober note. Some of us believe that capital punishment should be abolished under all, or almost all, conditions. But even those people who favor capital punishment must reflect on the fact that appointments with the executioner are still made with arbitrariness and discrimination. This moral issue will not go away. The jury system has been placed in a central role in the determination of death, and the social

science evidence suggests that it contributes to this basic unfairness. We cannot yet say why this is so. Perhaps more research will indicate that changes in the laws and the procedures under which the jury operates can be made to perform better. On the other hand, it is perhaps expecting too much from juries that otherwise appear to serve our justice system so well. It may also be expecting too much from prosecutors, judges, and others in the criminal justice system. Some years ago, law professor Charles Black argued that unfairness in the administration of capital punishment was inevitable under any system. Eventually, the Supreme Court and the American public may also come to this conclusion. In the meantime, the jury will continue its controversial role in sending men and women to the executioner.

Conclusion

CHAPTER 15

Today and Tomorrow:
A Summary View and Judgment

We began this book by observing that the jury is a unique and fascinating institution that has evoked both praise and condemnation throughout its long history. Our working assumption has been that many key issues in the controversy surrounding the contemporary jury are subject to systematic examination by the methods of social science. It is time to take stock. What do we know? What else should be considered? What does the future hold?

* * *

Critics have charged that the jury falls short on three main grounds: it is incompetent, it is prejudiced, and it wages war with the law. However, when hard facts rather than anecdote and opinion are considered, the charges do not appear warranted. Juries are generally competent fact finders. Our best evidence suggests that in four cases out of five, juries reach the same verdict that the judge would have reached. In the remaining case, the verdict can usually be ascribed not to a failure to understand the evidence but rather to a different sense of justice.

The claim that jury verdicts are based on sympathies and prejudice cannot be absolutely dismissed, but such occurrences are infrequent. Jurors take their responsibilities seriously, and the prime determinant of verdicts is the weight of evidence. As was typified in the DeLorean trial, jurors can put initial assumptions aside and listen with an open mind. At the same time, community sentiment about a particular type of defense or crime can on occasion detrimentally affect jurors' perceptions. We saw in the discussions of the insanity defense, rape, and capital punishment that jurors' preconceptions about some issues may be so strong that they cloud views of the evidence and the ability to render a fair verdict. The assertion that juries engage in a war with the law also has a kernel of truth, but the battle is a very modest one. The jury

at times reflects the community's sense of justice in applying a standard different from the one that a judge would have used. Yet verdicts are affected by these "extralegal" sentiments predominantly in cases where the evidence is so close that either verdict could be defended.

While trial by jury is not perfect, calls for abolition of the jury seem draconian in light of the fact that it displays competence and fairmindedness in the overwhelming majority of criminal and civil cases. In instances where the jury falls short, jury performance could be improved by modification of existing legal procedures: through developing more coherent legal instructions, allowing jurors to take notes or to ask questions, or providing some directions at the beginning of the trial.

Another line of attack against incompetence and prejudice lies in the process of jury selection. One major advance has already been accomplished: making the jury much more representative of the entire community. In the past, a jury composed of white, middle-class, middle-minded jurors might well have reached verdicts that discriminated against the poor or minorities, but today middle-class jury members have to contend with other segments of society in the jury room. The increased representativeness of the jury is a critical factor in limiting the impact of bias in jury verdicts.

Another factor is the care that is now being taken in some courtrooms in highly publicized cases over questioning prospective jurors about their personal opinions on the case being tried. Though far from a perfect solution, in-depth, careful examination of prospective jurors that focuses on jurors' preconceptions or reactions to the specific case can help to minimize bias and incompetence.

We have also examined the controversy about jury experts in the courtroom. Some have claimed that recent developments involving utilization of the knowledge and techniques of social science corrupt the adversary process and damage the integrity of the jury system. The evaluation sheet yields both pluses and minuses. On the positive side, the tools of social science have helped lawyers argue for, and obtain, pools of jurors that are truly representative of the community. In some instances they have been used to demonstrate that a fair trial could not be held in a particular community. Social science has also been used to challenge some antiquated notions of the legal system and has helped to educate judges about contemporary notions of impartiality and prejudice. On the negative side, jury experts may be adding to an imbalance in the system of justice that already exists, especially in civil cases. The richer, more powerful adversary often begins with better lawyers and more resources to fight the case. If the advantaged party hires jury experts but the other side cannot afford them, the scales of justice tip even further

into imbalance. Simultaneously, and at least partly in contradiction to the above view, jury experts have been oversold. The label "scientific" jury selection is misleading; it creates an aura of predictive accuracy that has not been backed up by evidence. Used indiscriminantly, jury experts may unjustifiably add to the cost of the parties, increase the administrative burdens of the court, and cause judges and legislators to attempt to curtail *voir dire* rights and privileges. They may also create a public perception that the trial process is not fair.

On balance, social science methods can probably be helpful in advancing the cause of justice in some cases. While it is doubtful that jury experts can rig juries to produce a favorable verdict, they can sometimes help to eliminate the most prejudiced persons, and thereby create more impartial juries. The use of mock juries can help lawyers devise more effective trial strategies. In the long run, however, the legal system may be better served by social science studies that shed light on issues such as jury size, jury competence, and methods of improving the performance of jurors.

*   *   *

In judging the jury there are some other issues to consider. The first concerns the alternatives to the jury. In France, West Germany, and some other European countries, mixed tribunals composed of a judge and prominent laypersons decide legal cases. In Britain, minor crimes are tried in magistrate's courts by tribunals of laypersons. However, in most instances those who advocate abolition of the jury propose that the jury's work should be done by a judge. The question then becomes, are judges really superior to juries? Unfortunately, we have little data about the competence of judges, though, to reverse the logic of findings from *The American Jury,* we know that the jury would agree with their decisions in four cases out of five. To be sure, judges have training in law, and perhaps, as Judge Frank claimed, they attempt to be more scientific in their approach to the evidence. On the other hand, many knowledgeable legal commentators have argued that judges are not necessarily better triers of fact.[1] A jury which contains one or more persons proficient in automobile repair might be far better at assessing evidence in a products liability case involving a car manufacturer than a judge whose experience with things mechanical is limited to changing a spare tire. Even if one argues that the average judge is smarter in discerning legal facts than the average juror, is the judge as smart as twelve jurors?

We must also consider the fact that trials are about justice as well as law. The inescapable fact is that despite attempts in recent years to recruit

minority group members and women into the judiciary, the overwhelming majority of judges are still white males who come from a priviledged sector of our society. Often their views of the world reflect their backgrounds. Some rather rigidly adhere to a narrow perspective of justice and fairness that is not consistent with that of the general community. The outcomes in the cases of John Peter Zenger, John DeLorean, Dr. Morgentaler, or Jane Stafford, the abused housewife, might well have been different if decided by a judge, but an argument could be made that 12 citizens better reflected the community's sense of justice.

In 1835, Alexis de Tocqueville published his classic study, *Democracy in America,* which provided so many insights about the democratic process. He observed that the jury was even more a political institution than a judicial one:

> The jury is pre-eminently a political institution; it must be regarded as one form of the sovereignty of the people; when that sovereignty is repudiated, it must be rejected; or it must be adapted to the laws by which that sovereignty is established. The jury is that portion of the nation to which the execution of the laws is intrusted, as the houses of parliament constitute that part of the nation which makes the laws.[2]

Over a century later, Britain's Lord Justice Devlin made a similar observation in his often-quoted statement that

> Each jury is a little parliament. The jury sense is the parliamentary sense. I cannot see the one dying and the other surviving. The first object of any tyrant in Whitehall would be to make Parliament utterly subservient to his will; and the next to overthrow or diminish trial by jury, for no tyrant could afford to leave a subject's freedom in the hands of twelve of his countrymen. So that trial by jury is more than an instrument of justice and more than one wheel of the Constitution: it is the lamp that shows that freedom lives.[3]

There are two other aspects to the political side of the jury. One is its "legitimating" function. In a democracy the average citizen obeys the law not so much because of its threat but because he or she grants it legitimacy, that is, accepts it as a body of rules to be followed. It may be true that democracy can survive without juries. Many Western democracies do not have juries and seem to function quite well. Yet, in the United States, Canada, and Great Britain, the jury is an important symbol that helps to confer legitimacy to law. The importance of legitimacy is best illustrated by its absence. Recall the Miami riots that followed the acquittal by an all-white jury of the four policemen accused of killing a black salesman. Even if the verdict had been the same, the riots might not have occurred if blacks had been represented on the jury. Or to take some other hypothetical examples, would the acquittal

of John Hinckley, Jr., on grounds of insanity or the convictions of the defendants in the Big Dan rape cases have caused even more protest and controversy if the verdicts had been rendered by a judge?

The remaining political aspect of the jury concerns its socializing functions. Not only does the jury allow the people to contribute to the legal system, but the legal system, through the jury, contributes to the education of the people. De Tocqueville saw this very clearly. He was especially enamored of the effects of the civil jury:

> The jury, and more especially the civil jury, serves to communicate the spirit of the judges to the minds of all citizens; and this spirit with the habits which attend it is the soundest preparation for free institutions. It imbues all classes with a respect for the thing judged, and with the notion of right. . . . It teaches men to practice equity; every man learns to judge his neighbor as he would himself be judged.
>
> The jury contributes most powerfully to form the judgment, and to increase the natural intelligence of a people; and this is, in my opinion, its greatest advantage. It may be regarded as a gratuitous public school ever open, in which every juror learns to exercise his rights . . . and becomes practically acquainted with the laws of this country, which are brought within the reach of his capacity by the efforts of the bar, the advice of the judge, and even by the passions of the parties. I think that the practical intelligence and political good sense of the Americans are mainly attributable to the long use which they have made of the jury in civil causes.[4]

We know of no study that has attempted to assess the impact of civil jury experience on people's attitudes, but Professor Tapp's research on the effects of serving on the Wounded Knee criminal jury is in line with de Tocqueville's observations. Those jurors came away from the trial with higher levels of moral reasoning—and insights about the fallibilities of legal authorities—than they had before the trial. Jurors in other trials have reported similar educational experiences.[5]

In brief, political functions of the jury are not to be ignored.[6] They coexist with the fact-finding functions and should be considered in judging the jury's role in society.

*   *   *

In concluding a book about the jury, we feel compelled to speculate about its future. Will it survive? If so, what will tomorrow's jury look like? As we have described, the jury is a continuously changing institution, and one that is often in the center of controversy. Those who defend trial by jury have been dismayed by the changes in centuries-old traditions that have occurred within the space of a few decades. Changes in the size of the jury

and its decision rule, limits on the availability of jury trials, and restriction of the scope of *voir dire* are but a few examples. The civil jury trial has all but disappeared in Great Britain and is infrequently used in Canada. In the United States, Chief Justice Warren Burger for the past fifteen years has stated that the civil jury system has serious flaws and is an inordinately expensive and time-consuming drain on the legal system.[7]

In the end the criminal jury will probably survive. Not only is it firmly entrenched in the legal systems of the countries who use it, their people revere it. Survey research in the United States and Canada indicates that judges themselves have a strong respect for it. The U.S. Supreme Court has singled out the jury's importance in death penalty cases; other appeals courts have ruled that special verdicts that potentially restrict its exercise of power are unacceptable. Despite these favorable signs, some of the jury's power may be eroded. Courts and legislatures have always attempted to control the jury through rules and procedures that determine what the jury hears and how it operates. What might appear to be relatively insignificant changes can chip away at the jury's powers and over time have the same effect as more obvious curtailments of the right to trial by jury. Indeed, except in a few scholarly circles, the switch from unanimity to majority verdicts evoked little outcry because the average citizen did not realize the potential consequences of the change.

The future of the civil jury is more questionable. There are some indications that it is in peril in the United States. While the Seventh Amendment to the Constitution guarantees the right to a jury trial in civil disputes, in several recent cases the litigants have argued that there should be an exception to this constitutional right when the facts of the case are too complex for jurors to understand. One federal appeals court has supported this position. It ruled that while an antitrust case would ordinarily have been eligible for a jury trial under the Constitution, the case was too complex for the jurors because of the overall size of the suit, conceptual difficulties with the evidence, and problems of segregating various aspects of the case. Although such reasoning was rejected in a second antitrust case heard by a different appeals court, legal scholars find the first decision very threatening to the whole concept of the civil jury. The Supreme Court has not yet ruled on which appeals court is correct, but given Chief Justice Burger's public statements about the civil jury, there are fears that the Court will rule that there is a "complexity exception" to the Seventh Amendment. Trial judges could then have great discretion in deciding whether a case is too complex. Many exceptions might be found, the process might snowball, and the civil jury might be on the path to extinction.

Proponents of the civil jury have pointed out that there is no evidence that juries are incompetent in complex cases, at least no more incompetent than judges. Moreover, there are less drastic alternatives to abolishing the jury. For example, in some complicated cases, neutral experts are used to interpret and explain data to judges; such experts could be used to assist the jury about difficult evidence. In addition, some extremely complex factual issues could be decided by the judge, while leaving the central issues to the jury. Others argue against a complexity exception on the basis of the political function of the jury. Some civil matters involving giant corporations could have greater effects on society than criminal matters, and, thus, the people should have a say in them. A complexity exception would also ignore the important symbolic and legitimating functions of the jury. Additionally, it is argued that there are no Constitutional precedents for restricting Seventh Amendment rights.[8]

On the other hand, systematic examination might show that indeed juries do not funtion well in certain kinds of complex cases. Justice, as guaranteed under the Fifth Amendment's "due process" clause, should then take precedence over the right to a civil trial by jury. Research that assesses the competence of juries in complex cases is badly needed.[9]

*   *   *

Our final judgment on the jury system is a positive one. Despite some flaws, it serves the cause of justice very well. For over 700 years it has weathered criticism and attack, always to survive and to be cherished by the peoples who own it. Adaptability has been the key to its survival. It should remain open to experimentation and modification, but those who would wish to curtail its powers or abolish it should bear the burden of proof. Defenders of the jury clearly have the weight of the evidence on their side.

Notes

Chapter 1

[1] Steven Brill, who inteviewed 11 of the 12 DeLorean jurors and some of the other participants, reported the results of his research in "Inside the DeLorean Jury Room," in the December 1984 issue of *American Lawyer*, pp. 1, 94–105. Our description of the DeLorean trial is based on his excellent account of the case, the jury deliberation process, and jurors' perceptions of the trial. All direct quotes from the jurors are taken from his article. We only touch on some of the findings here. The reader is referred to the Brill article for more in-depth presentation of the reactions of the DeLorean jurors.

In addition, a number of key points made in the Brill article were corroborated by others. For instance, the defense strategy, the problem of pretrial publicity, and the judge's perspective were discussed in a symposium presented at the meeting of the American Psychological Association in Los Angeles, August 1985, entitled *Psychology and Law in the John DeLorean Trial*, which included Judge Robert Takasugi, defense attorney Donald Re, and three psychologists (cited as "Symposium"). The facts of the case and the multiple reasons by which jurors reached their decision to acquit DeLorean were laid out in a number of newspaper articles, including Lindsey, R. (1984, August 17). Jurors cite entrapment and failure to prove case. *The New York Times*, pp. A1, B6; Cummings, J. (1984, August 17). DeLorean is freed of cocaine charge by a federal jury. *The New York Times*, pp. A1, B6; and Mathews, J. (1984, August 17). DeLorean acquitted of all eight charges in drug-scheme trial. *The Washington Post*, pp. A1, A12. Reactions to the verdict were provided in MacDonald, K. (1984, August 17). Not guilty: Verdict's affect (sic) on 'stings' eyed. *The Washington Post*, pp. A1, A12; and Margolick, D. (1984, August 17). A case for DeLorean. *The New York Times*, p. B6.

[2] Brill (1984), p. 96; Cummings (1984); Mathews (1984).

[3] Brill (1984), p. 94; Symposium (1985).

[4] Brill (1984), p. 94; Symposium (1985)

[5] Both quotes are from Brill (1984), p. 95.

[6] Brill (1984), p. 95.

[7] Brill (1984), p. 96.

[8] Brill (1984), p. 97.

[9] Both quotes are from Brill (1984), p. 98.

[10] Brill (1984), p. 100; Cummings (1984).

[11] Brill (1984), p. 98.

[12] Brill (1984), p. 101.

[13] Brill (1984), p. 94.

[14] Brill (1984), p. 102.

[15] Mathews (1984), p. A12; Brill (1984), p. 103.

[16] Brill (1984), pp. 103–104.

[17] Brill (1984), p. 104.

[18] Brill (1984), p. 105.

[19] Brill (1984), p. 1.

[20] Burger, W. A. (1971). The state of the federal judiciary. *American Bar Association Journal*, *57*, 855–861; Burger, W.A. (1981, February). Is our jury system working? *Readers Digest*, *118*, 126–130.

Chapter 2

[1] Forsyth, W. (1971). *History of Trial by Jury* (2nd ed.). New York: Burt Franklin (reprinted; original: 1878), pp. 337–338. See also 6 State Trial 951–969. For a general account of trial by jury in England from 1200–1800, see Green, T. A. (1985). *Verdict According to Conscience*. Chicago: University of Chicago Press.

[2] See Forsyth (1971), pp. 330–337.

[3] See Forsyth (1971), pp. 59–60.

[4] Pluncknett, T. F. T. (1956). *A Concise History of the Common Law* (5th ed.). London: Butterworths & Co. See p. 108.

[5] Forsyth (1971), pp. 66–67.

[6] See Forsyth (1971), pp. 67–68; see also Kiralfy, A. K. R. (1958). *Potters Historical Introduction to English Law and Its Institutions* (4th ed.). London: Sweet & Maxwell, Ltd., pp. 240–241; Holdsworth, W. (1922). *History of English Law*. Boston: Little, Brown.

[7] Pluncknett (1956), pp. 111–112.

[8] Pluncknett (1956), pp. 115–116; Forsyth (1971), pp. 61–70.

[9] Hallam, as cited in Forsyth (1971), p. 69.

[10] See Pluncknett (1956), pp. 121–123.

[11] Pluncknett (1956), pp. 126–127.

[12] Pluncknett (1956), pp. 125–126; Kiralfy (1958), pp. 246–247.

[13] As quoted in Pluncknett (1956), p. 129.

[14] Pluncknett (1956), p. 128.

[15] See Vidmar, N., and Judson, J. (1981). The use of social science in a change of venue application. *Canadian Bar Review*, *59*, 76–102. See Chapters 3 and 4 for more discussion on change of venue.

[16] Cited in Forsyth (1971), p. 191 note 1.

[17] See Hans, V. P. (1982). Jury selection in two countries: A psychological perspective. *Current Psychological Reviews*, *2*, 283–300.

[18] See Forsyth (1971), pp. 282–288; Bloomstein, M. J. (1968). *Verdict: The Jury System*. New York: Dodd, Mead & Co., pp. 113–114.

[19] See Forsyth (1971), pp. 295–330; Bloomstein (1968), pp. 108–117.

Chapter 3

[1] There are exceptions to these rights. In fact, the ink was hardly dry on the newly ratified U.S. Constitution when U.S. courts decided that certain types of cases were really equity rather

than law cases, and therefore not eligible for jury trial. Some state constitutions do not provide for jury trials in any number of civil matters. Additionally, a number of state statutes have prescribed nonjury remedies such as bench trials or even nonjudicial remedies like arbitration for certain kinds of civil disputes. Often, either of the parties may subsequently request a jury trial if they are not happy with the result of these alternative remedies, but there are many pressures against applying for a jury trial. Nevertheless, the general statement regarding the right to a jury trial remains valid. For discussion of these issues, see Lempert, R. (1981). Civil juries and complex cases: Let's not rush to judgment. *Michigan Law Review, 80*, 68–132.

[2] See Lempert (1981); Gutman, S. M. (1972–1973). The attorney conducted voir dire of jurors: A constitutional right. *Brooklyn Law Review, 39*, 290–329; Moore, L. E. (1973). *The Jury: Tool of Kings, Palladium of Liberty.* Cincinnati, Ohio: W. H. Anderson.

[3] Recent evidence, nevertheless, suggests that this view is probably misleading. Zenger and his colleagues were not radical legal reformers but rather a narrow-minded political group seeking short-term political gain. Moreover, in actuality the eventual outcome of the case did not have much impact on the laws concerning freedom of the press. [See editor Stanley Katz's introduction to James Alexander's (1972, original date circa 1736) *A Brief Narrative of the Case of John Peter Zenger.* Cambridge, Mass.: Harvard University Press. Most of the remainder of the discussion of the Zenger trial is derived from this source.] However, it did help to establish unique American views on the jury and its place between law and those governed by it.

[4] See Gutman (1972–1973), pp. 293–294.

[5] See Gutman (1972–1973); Moore, R. D. (1928a). Voir dire examination of jurors. I. The English practice. *Georgetown Law Journal, 16*, 438–453; and Moore, R. D. (1928b). Voir dire examination of jurors. II. The Federal practice. *Georgetown Law Journal, 17*, 13–38. The law in England has changed somewhat, but challenges on grounds of nonspecific biases are rare in England [see Hans, V. P. (1982). Jury selection in two countries: A psychological perspective. *Current Psychological Reviews, 2*, 283–300]. Canadian law is also restrictive as to the type of questions that can be put to jurors (see *Regina v. Hubbert, Criminal Reports, N.S.*, 1975, *31*, 27–47).

[6] Gutman (1972–1973), pp. 294–295.

[7] *The Works of Thomas Jefferson* as cited in Howe, M. D. (1939). Juries as judges of the criminal law. *Harvard Law Review, 52*, 582–616.

[8] Gutman (1972–1973), pp. 295–297; Howe (1939); Note: The changing role of the jury in the nineteenth century. (1964). *Yale Law Journal, 74*, 170–192.

[9] Howe (1939), pp. 590–591.

[10] Gutman (1972–1973).

[11] See Note: *Yale Law Journal* (1964), pp. 175–176.

[12] See Howe (1939); Note: *Yale Law Journal* (1964).

[13] Today, however, in Maryland and Indiana, juries in state courts still have the legal right to decide the law.

[14] See Moore (1928a,b).

[15] Neubauer, D. W. (1984). *America's Courts and the Criminal Justice System* (2nd ed.). Monterey, Calif.: Brooks/Cole.

[16] See Note. (1938). Should the jury fix the punishment for crimes? *Virginia Law Review, 24*, 462–466; Note. (1967). Jury sentencing in Virginia. *Virginia Law Review, 43*, 968–1001.

[17] Note: *Virginia Law Review* (1938).

[18] Stubbs, R. S., II. (1969). Jury sentencing in Georgia: Time for a change. *Georgia State Bar Journal, 5*, 421–430; Morris, L. W. (1958). Criminal procedure—What agency should fix the sentence? *Kentucky Law Journal, 46*, 260–270.

[19] *U.S. v. Spock*. Federal Reporter, 2nd Series, 1969, *416*, 165–194. See also Kadish, M. R., and Kadish, S. H. (1971). The institutionalization of conflict: Jury acquittals. *Journal of Social Issues, 27*, 199–217.

[20] One intriguing aspect of the Spock trial had to do with the composition of the jury panel. The jury pool from which the Spock jurors were drawn contained a significantly lower percentage of women compared to the population. Of 100 prospective jurors, just four were female. The clerk who assembled the list sent out jury notices to many fewer women than men, although the motive, if there was one, was unclear. Was it merely to save time, since more women excused themselves than men? Could it have had anything to do with the possibility that women might have been more favorable than men to Spock? The one woman of the four on the jury panel who was randomly selected to serve on the Spock jury was eliminated by the prosecutor with a peremptory challenge, leaving Dr. Spock and his codefendants with an all-male jury. The gender composition could have played a role in the verdict, since according to a Gallup poll conducted at the time women were more likely than men to favor reduction in the Vietnam War. See the fascinating account of this problem in Zeisel, H. (1969). Dr. Spock and the case of the vanishing women jurors. *University of Chicago Law Review, 37*, 1–18.

[21] Lempert (1981); Kirst, R. W. (1982). The jury's historic domain in complex cases. *Washington Law Review, 58*, 1–38.

[22] Babcock, B. A. (1975). Voir dire: Preserving "its wonderful power." *Stanford Law Review, 27*, 545–565; Bermant, G. and Shapard, J. (1981). The voir dire examination, juror challenges, and adversary advocacy. In B. D. Sales (Ed.) *The Trial Process*. New York: Plenum Press.

[23] For general discussion of the role of the jury versus the role of the prosecutor, see: McDonald, W. (Ed.) (1979). *The Prosecutor*. Beverly Hills, Calif.: Sage; Jacoby, J. (1980). *The American Prosecutor: A Search for Identity*. Lexington, Mass.: D. C. Heath; Neubauer (1984).

Chapter 4

[1] Belli, M. M. (1976). *My Life on Trial*. Toronto: Popular Library.

[2] Ibid., p. 300.

[3] Ibid., p. 319.

[4] Kairys, D., Schulman, J., and Harring, S. (Eds.) (1975). *The Jury System: New Methods for Reducing Prejudice*. Cambridge, Mass.: National Jury Project and National Lawyers Guild.

[5] Cartwright, R. E. (1977). Jury selection. *Trial, 13*, 28–31.

[6] Hans, V. P. (1982a). Jury selection in two countries: A psychological perspective. *Current Psychological Reviews, 2*, 283–300. Hans, V. P. (1983). Unpublished data.

[7] Hans (1983), unpublished data.

[8] Hans, V. P., and Vidmar, N. (1982). Jury selection. In N. L. Kerr and R. M. Bray (Eds.) *The Psychology of the Courtroom*. New York: Academic Press.

[9] *Strauder v. West Virginia* 100 U.S. 303 (1880); *Carter v. Texas* 177 U.S. 442 (1900); *Norris v. Alabama* 294 U.S. 587 (1935); *Thiel v. Southern Pacific Company* 328 U.S. 217 (1946); *Patton v. Mississippi* 332 U.S. 463 (1947); *Hernandez v. Texas* 347 U.S. 475 (1954); *Whitus v. Georgia* 385 U.S. 545 (1967); *Carter v. Jury Comm. of Greene County* 396 U.S. 320 (1970); *Taylor v. Louisiana* 419 U.S. 522 (1975).

[10] Cloward's testimony is excerpted from the Seale–Huggins hearing, October 15, 1970, New Haven, Conn. (pp. 438–439 of transcript). It is quoted in Van Dyke, J. (1977). *Jury Selection Procedures*. Cambridge, Mass.: Ballinger.

[11] Davis, R. (1973). Black jurors. *Guild Practitioner, 30*, 112–113. Quoted in Van Dyke (1977).

[12] Gillespie, M. (1980, April). What the Miami race riots mean to all of us. *Ms.*, p. 87.

[13] Van Dyke (1977).

[14] Hans, V. P. (1982b). Gentlewomen of the jury. Paper presented at the meeting of the Law and Society Association, Toronto.

[15] Hans (1982a).

[16] *Hoyt v. Florida* 368 U.S. 57 (1961).

[17] *State v. Hall* 187 So. 2d 861 (Miss), appeal dismissed 385 U.S. 98 (1966).

[18] *Taylor v. Louisiana* (1975).

[19] *Glasser v. United States* 315 U.S. 60 (1942).

[20] *Jury Selection and Service Act of 1968*, 28 U.S.C. 1861–1869. Washington, D.C.: U.S. Government Printing Office.

[21] Kairys, D., Kadane, B., and Lehoczky, P. (1977). Jury representativeness: A mandate for multiple source lists. *California Law Review, 65*, 776–827.

[22] Ginger, A. F. (Ed.) (1975). *Jury Selection in Criminal Trials*. Tiburon, Calif.: Law Press.

[23] *Thiel v. Southern Pacific Company* (1946).

[24] Ibid., p. 224.

[25] *New York v. Attica Brothers*, Erie County Superior Court, June 27, 1974.

[26] *State of New Jersey v. Long*, decided January 7, 1985. See also Report on the Atlantic County Jury Selection System, submitted to Judge Raul R. Porreca, October 30, 1984, by David Kairys, Robert Moran, and Barry Cooper.

[27] We based our account on the Joan Little trial and related research on an excellent discussion of the role social scientists played in that trial: McConahay, J., Mullin, C., and Frederick, J. (1977). The uses of social science in trials with political and racial overtones: The trial of Joan Little. *Law and Contemporary Problems, 41*, 205–229.

[28] Vidmar, N., and Judson, J. (1981). The use of social science in a change of venue application. *Canadian Bar Review, 59*, 76–102.

Chapter 5

[1] *United States v. Wade*. (1936). *United States Reports, 299*, 123–151.

[2] See Vidmar, N., and Melnitzer, J. (1984). Juror prejudice: An empirical study of a challenge for cause. *Osgoode Hall Law Journal, 22*, 487–511.

[3] Brodie, I. (1982, March 1). Putting the brake on wheels of justice. *Daily Telegraph*, p. 15.

[4] Bailey, F. L., and Rothblatt, H. B. (1971). *Successful Techniques for Criminal Trials*. New York: Lawyers Cooperative, p. 83.

[5] Cavoukian, A. (1980, September). Eyewitness testimony: The ineffectiveness of discrediting information. Paper presented at the meeting of the American Psychological Association, Montreal Kassin, S. M., and Wrightsman, L. S. (1979). On the requirements of proof: The timing of judicial instruction and mock juror verdicts. *Journal of Personality and Social Psychology, 37*, 1877–1887.

[6] Broeder, D. (1965). *Voir dire* examinations: An empirical study. *Southern California Law Review, 38*, 503–528.

[7] Cited in Ginger, A. F. (Ed.) (1975). *Jury Selection in Criminal Trials*. Tiburon, Calif.: Law Press.

[8] Bailey and Rothblatt (1971), pp. 84–85.

[9] Quoted in Ginger (1975), p. 653.

[10] As quoted in Blauner, R. (1972). The Huey Newton jury *voir dire*. In R. Blauner (Ed.) *Racial Oppression in America*. New York: Harper.

[11] Van Dyke, J. (1977). *Jury Selection Procedures*. Cambridge, Mass.: Ballinger.

[12] Kairys, D., Schulman, J., and Harring, S. (Eds.) (1975). *The Jury System: New Methods for Reducing Prejudice*. Cambridge, Mass.: National Jury Project and National Lawyers Guild.

[13] Ginger (1975).

[14] Nietzel, M. T., and Dillehay, R. C. (1982). The effects of variations in *voir dire* procedures in capital murder trials. *Law and Human Behavior, 6,* 1–13.

[15] Darrow, C. (1936, May). Attorney for the defense. *Esquire*, pp. 36–37, 211–213.

[16] Bailey and Rothblatt (1971).

[17] *The Texas Observer*. (1973, May 11). Jury selection in a criminal case. *The Texas Observer*, p. 9.

[18] Van Dyke (1977), pp. 41–42, 153.

[19] Mossman, K. (1973). Jury selection: An expert's view. *Psychology Today, 6*(12), 78–79.

[20] Fahringer, H.P. (1980). "In the valley of the blind"—jury selection, in a criminal case. *Trial Diplomacy Journal, 3,* 34–39, 48–54. Quote from p. 34.

[21] Hawrish, E., and Tate, E. (1974–75). Determinants of jury selection. *Saskatchewan Law Review, 30,* 285–292. Penrod, S. (1979). Study of attorney and "scientific" jury selection models. Doctoral dissertation, Harvard University.

[22] Van Dyke (1977); *Center for Jury Studies Newsletter*. (1979). Issue No. 4, p. 5; Hans, unpublished data.

[23] *Swain v. Alabama* 380 U.S. 202 (1965).

[24] Gordon, C. (1985). Justice ignored: The discriminatory use of peremptory challenges. *University of Missouri, Kansas City Law Review, 53,* 446–467.

[25] *People v. Wheeler*, 22 Cal. 3d 258, 583 P. 2d 748, 148 Cal. Rptr. 890 (1978).

[26] Hunt, M. (1982, November 28). Putting jurors on the couch. *The New York Times Magazine*, pp. 70–72, 78, 82, 85–86, 88.

[27] Davis, J. H., Bray, R. M., and Holt, R. W. (1977). The empirical study of decision processes in juries: A critical review. In J. L. Tapp and F. J. Levine (Eds.) *Law, Justice, and the Individual in Society: Psychological and Legal Issues*. New York: Holt. Nemeth, C. (1981). Jury trials: Psychology and law. In L. Berkowitz (Ed.) *Advances in Experimental Social Psychology*, Vol. 13. New York: Academic Press.

[28] Hans, V. P. (1982). Gentlewomen of the jury. Paper presented at the meeting of the Law and Society Association, Toronto.

[29] Penrod (1979).

[30] Hepburn, J. R. (1980). The objective reality of evidence and the utility of systematic jury selection. *Law and Human Behavior, 4,* 89–102. Feild, H. S. (1978). Juror background characteristics and attitudes toward rape: Correlates of jurors' decisions in rape trials. *Law and Human Behavior, 2,* 73–93.

[31] Baldwin, J., and McConville, M. (1979). *Jury Trials*. London: Oxford University Press. Baldwin, J., and McConville, M. (1980). Does the composition of an English jury affect its verdict? *Judicature, 64,* 133–139.

[32] Feild (1978); Penrod (1979).

[33] Zeisel, H., and Diamond, S. (1978). The effect of peremptory challenges on jury and verdict: An experiment in a federal district court. *Stanford Law Review, 30,* 491–531.

Chapter 6

1 Our account is based on Hunt, M. (1982, November 28). Putting juries on the couch. *The New York Times Magazine*, pp. 70–72, 78, 82, 85–86, 88. Andersen, P. (1985, May 29). AT&T is ordered to pay MCI $37.8 million in antitrust case. *The Morning News*, p. A1.

2 Bryan, W. (1971). *The Chosen Ones: The Psychology of Jury Selection*. New York: Vantage.

3 *United States v. Ahmad* (Cr. No. 14950, Middle District of Pennsylvania, Harrisburg Division). The trial is sometimes referred to as the Harrisburg 7 trial.

4 Quoted in Hunt (1982), p. 78.

5 Schulman, J., Shaver, P., Colman, R., Emrick, B., and Christie, R. (1973, May). Recipe for a jury. *Psychology Today*, pp. 37–44, 77, 79–84.

6 See Berk, R. (1976). Social science and jury selection: A case study of a civil suit. In G. Bermant, C. Nemeth, and N. Vidmar (Eds.) *Psychology and the Law*. Lexington, Mass.: Lexington Books. Christie, R. (1976). Probability v. precedence: The social psychology of jury selection. In G. Bermant, C. Nemeth, and N. Vidmar (Eds.) *Psychology and the Law*. Lexington, Mass.: Lexington Books. Kairys, D., Schulman, J., and Harring, S. (Eds.) (1975). *The Jury System: New Methods for Reducing Prejudice*. Cambridge, Mass.: National Jury Project and National Lawyers Guild. McConahay, J., Mullin, C., and Frederick, J. (1977). The uses of social science in trials with political and racial overtones: The trial of Joan Little. *Law and Contemporary Problems, 41*, 205–229. Saks, M. (1976a). The limits of scientific jury selection: Ethical and empirical. *Jurimetrics Journal, 17*, 3–22. Tapp, J. L., Gunnar, M., and Keating, D. (1983). Socialization: Three ages, three rule systems. In D. Perlman and P. C. Cozby (Eds.) *Social Psychology*. New York: Holt. Zeisel, H., and Diamond, S. S. (1976). The jury selection in the Mitchell–Stans conspiracy trial. *American Bar Foundation Research Journal, 1*, 151–174.

7 Christie (1976).

8 *United States v. Briggs* (ND Fla 1973) 366 F Supp 1356. The trial is also referred to as the Gainesville 8 trial.

9 Hans, V. P., and Vidmar, N. (1982). Jury selection. In N. L. Kerr and R. M. Bray (Eds.) *The Psychology of the Courtroom*. New York: Academic Press.

10 McConahay *et al.* (1977).

11 Okun, J. (1968). Investigation of jurors by counsel: Its impact on the decisional process. *Georgetown Law Journal, 56*, 839–879. For the British experience, see Harman, H., and Griffith, J. (1979). *Justice Deserted*. London: National Council for Civil Liberties.

12 Bailey, F. L., and Rothblatt, H. B. (1971). *Successful Techniques for Criminal Trials*. New York: Lawyers Cooperative. Quote is from p. 85.

13 See Adorno, T., Frenkel-Brunswik, E., Levinson, D., and Sanford, R. (1950). *The Authoritarian Personality*. New York: Harper. See also Christie (1976).

14 Kassin, S. M. (1984). Mock jury trials. *Trial Diplomacy Journal, 7*, 26–30.

15 Vinson, D. E. (1982). The shadow jury: An experiment in litigation science. *American Bar Association Journal, 68*, 1242–1246.

16 See Bermant, G. and Shapard, J. (1981). The *voir dire* examination, juror challenges, and adversary advocacy. In B. D. Sales (Ed.), *The Trial Process*. New York: Plenum Press; King, W. (1975, October 20). Joan Little's lawyer scorns legal system and says he "bought" her acquittal. *The New York Times*, p. 23.

17 See: Berman, J., and Sales, B. D. (1977). A critical evaluation of the systematic approach to jury selection. *Criminal Justice and Behavior, 4*, 219–240; Hans and Vidmar (1982); Saks

(1976a); Saks, M. J. (1976b, January). Scientific jury selection. *Psychology Today*, pp. 48–57; Saks, M., and Hastie, R. (1978). *Social Psychology in Court*. Princeton, N.J.: Van Nostrand–Reinhold; Suggs, D., and Sales, B. D. (1978). The art and science of conducting the voir dire. *Professional Psychology, 9*, 367–388; Vidmar, N. (1976). Social science and jury selection. In Law Society of Upper Canada (Ed.) *Psychology and the Litigation Process.* Toronto: Law Society of Upper Canada; Zeisel and Diamond (1976).

[18] Bermant, G. (1975, May). Juries and justice: The notion of conspiracy is not tasty to Americans. *Psychology Today*, pp. 13–15.

[19] Zeisel and Diamond (1976).

[20] Monahan, J. (1981). *The Clinical Prediction of Violent Behavior.* Rockville, Md.: U.S. Department of Health and Human Services. Ennis, B. J., and Litwack, T. R. (1974). Psychiatry and the presumption of expertise: Flipping coins in the courtroom. *California Law Review, 62*, 693–752. The classic work on the difficulty of predicting human behavior is Mischel, W. (1968). *Personality and Assessment.* New York: Wiley.

[21] Vidmar (1976).

[22] Christie (1976); McConahay *et al.* (1977).

[23] Horowitz, I. A. (1980). Juror selection: A comparison of two methods in several criminal cases. *Journal of Applied Social Psychology, 10*, 86–99.

[24] See: Bermant and Shapard (1980); Berk, R. A., Hennessy, M., and Swan, J. (1977). The vagaries and vulgarities of "scientific" jury selection. *Evaluation Quarterly, 1*, 143–158; Berman and Sales (1977); Christie (1976); Etzioni, A. (1974, November/December). Creating an imbalance. *Trial, 10*, 28–30; Hunt (1982); McConahay *et al.* (1977).

[25] Etzioni (1974).

Chapter 7

[1] Information on the Harris trial was taken from *Mrs. Harris*, by D. Trilling. (1981). New York: Harcourt, Brace, Jovanovich.

[2] Feron, J. (1981, February 26). Jurors in Harris trial re-enacted night of murder in deliberations. *The New York Times*, pp. A1, B2.

[3] For example, Mary Timothy's book, *Jury Woman*. (1974). San Francisco, Calif.: Volcano Press. See also Melvyn B. Zerman's book: *Call the Final Witness: The People vs Darrell R. Mathes As Seen by the Eleventh Juror.* (1977). New York: Harper & Row.

[4] Kalven, H., and Zeisel, H. (1966). *The American Jury.* Boston: Little, Brown. The account is given on pp. vi–vii.

[5] Vinson, D. E. (1982). The shadow jury: An experiment in litigation science. *American Bar Association Journal, 68*, 1243–1246.

[6] Stasser, G., Kerr, N. L., and Bray, R. M. (1982). The social psychology of jury deliberations. In N. L. Kerr and R. M. Bray (Eds.) *The Psychology of the Courtroom.* New York: Academic Press.

[7] Timothy (1974) pp. 237–238.

[8] Our account of the Juan Corona case is from Villesenor, V. (1977). *Jury: The People vs. Juan Corona.* Boston: Little, Brown. Quote is from pp. 12–13.

[9] Ibid., p. 13.

[10] Ibid., pp. 13–14.

[11] Ibid., p. 15.

[12] Ibid., p. 22.

[13] Hawkins, C. (1960). Interaction and coalition realignments in consensus seeking groups: A study of experimental jury deliberations. Doctoral dissertation, University of Chicago.

[14] Hastie, R., Penrod, S., and Pennington, N. (1983). *Inside the Jury*. Cambridge, Mass.: Harvard University Press.

[15] Kalven and Zeisel (1966), p. 486.

[16] Hans, V. P. (1978). Unpublished transcript. University of Toronto. Subjects in the experiment were visitors to the Ontario Science Centre in Toronto. The initials used in the text are not those of the actual subjects. The transcript was edited to improve readability.

[17] Hans, V. P., and Doob, A. N. (1976). Section 12 of the Canada Evidence Act and the deliberations of simulated juries. *Criminal Law Quarterly, 18,* 235–253.

[18] Wright, W. (1983). *The Von Bulow Affair*. New York: Delacorte Press.

[19] Zerman (1977), p. 137.

[20] Goldberg, B. W. (1981, April). The trials of a juror. *The Pennsylvania Gazette*, pp. 19–25, 44–45. Quote is from p. 19.

[21] *McCloskey v. Delaware;* decided by Delaware Supreme Court on February 10, 1983. Forewoman's quote is from p. 4 of the opinion. See also: Friend, C. (1983, February 16). Murder conviction tossed out. *The Morning News*, p. B1.

[22] *McCloskey v. Delaware*, p. 14.

[23] See Davis, J. H., Bray, R. M., and Holt, R. W. (1977). The empirical study of decision processes in juries: A critical review. In J. L. Tapp and F. J. Levine (Eds.) *Law, Justice, and the Individual in Society: Psychological and Legal Issues*. New York: Holt; Kalven and Zeisel (1966); Hastie *et al.* (1983), pp. 63–76.

[24] Heuer, L., and Penrod, S. (1985). A field experiment on improving jury communication. Draft final report to the Wisconsin Judicial Council's Committee on Improving Jury Instructions.

[25] Timothy (1974).

[26] Ibid., p. 280.

[27] Zeisel, H. (1971). . . . And then there were none: The diminution of the federal jury. *University of Chicago Law Review, 38,* 710–724.

[28] Kennebeck, E. (1971). *Juror Number Four*. New York: W. W. Norton. Quote is from p. 231.

[29] Kalven and Zeisel (1966), p. 489.

[30] Bennett, W., and Feldman, M. (1981). *Reconstructing Reality in the Courtroom*. New Brunswick, New Jersey: Rutgers University Press. Holstein, J. A. (1985). Jurors' interpretations and jury decision making. *Law and Human Behavior, 9,* 83–100. McCabe, S., and Purves, R. (1974). *The Shadow Jury at Work*. Oxford: Basil Blackwell.

Chapter 8

[1] See Anderson, D. (1982, December 26). Jurors broke rules in Dalkon lawyer's trial. *Minneapolis Tribune*, p. 1A, 6A, 7A

[2] Griswold, E. N. (1962–1963). *Harvard Law School Dean's Report*, pp. 5–6, as cited in Kalven, H., and Zeisel, H. (1966). *The American Jury*. Boston: Little, Brown.

[3] Williams, G. (1963). *The Proof of Guilt* (3rd ed.). London: Stevens, pp. 271–272.

[4] See Lempert, R. (1981). Civil juries and complex cases: Let's not rush to judgment. *Michigan Law Review, 80,* 68–132; Sperlich, P. (1982). The case for preserving trial by jury in complex litigation. *Judicature, 65,* 395–419.

[5] See Langbein, J. II. (1981). Mixed court and jury court: Could the continental alternative fill the American need? *American Bar Foundation Research Journal, 1981*, 195–219.

[6] 167 F.2d 54 (2d Cir. 1948). Judge Frank, accepting the fact that the U.S. Constitution insisted on the right to a jury trial, was actually arguing for having the jury render only special verdicts on the facts in civil cases. However, his arguments apply generally against the jury.

[7] Nizer, L. (1978). *My Life in Court.* New York: Jove. Quote is from p. 359.

[8] Kadish, M., and Kadish, S. (1973). *Discretion to Disobey: A Study of Lawful Departure from Legal Rules.* Stanford, Calif.: Stanford University Press; Brooks, W. N., and Doob, A. N. (1975). Justice and the jury. *Journal of Social Issues, 31,* 171–182.

[9] Kalven and Zeisel (1966).

[10] Kalven, H. (1964). The dignity of the civil jury. *Virginia Law Review, 50,* 1055–1075; and Kalven and Zeisel (1966).

[11] Baldwin, J., and McConville, M. (1979a). Trial by jury: Some empirical evidence on contested criminal cases in England. *Law and Society Review, 13,* 861–890; Baldwin, J., and McConville, M. (1979b). *Jury Trials.* London: Oxford University Press.

[12] Myers, M. (1979). Rule departures and making law: Juries and their verdicts. *Law and Society Review, 13,* 781–798.

[13] For references to additional research examining jury competence, see Baldwin and McConville (1979b); Erlanger, H. (1970). Jury research in America. *Law and Society Review, 4,* 345–370; and Kerr, N. L., and Bray, R. M. (Eds.) (1982). *The Psychology of the Courtroom.* New York: Academic Press; McCabe, S., and Purves, R. (1974). *The Shadow Jury at Work.* Oxford: Basil Blackwell. Also, see the fascinating discussion of juries in fraud trials by Levi, M. (1983). Blaming the jury: Frauds on trial. *Journal of Law and Society, 10,* 257–269.

[14] Hastie, R., Penrod, S., and Pennington, N. (1983). *Inside the Jury.* Cambridge, Mass.: Harvard University Press.

[15] *Skidmore v. Baltimore and Ohio R.R.,* at 64.

[16] Charrow, R., and Charrow, V. (1979). Making legal language understandable: A psycholinguistic study of jury instructions. *Columbia Law Review, 79,* 1306–1374; Elwork, A., Sales, B. D., and Alfini, J. (1977). Juridic decisions: In ignorance of the law or in light of it? *Law and Human Behavior, 1,* 163–190; Elwork, A., Sales, B. D., and Alfini, J. (1982). *Making Jury Instructions Understandable.* Indianapolis: Michie/Bobbs–Merrill; Severance, L., and Loftus, E. F. (1982). Improving the ability of jurors to comprehend and apply criminal jury instructions. *Law and Society Review, 17,* 153–198. For other perspectives on juries and legal instructions, see McCabe and Purves (1974); Greene, E. (in press). A jury researcher on the jury. *Case and Comment.*

[17] See Charrow and Charrow (1979).

[18] See Elwork *et al.* (1977).

[19] See Severance and Loftus (1982).

[20] Other studies also support the argument that testimony or instructions given earlier in a trial affect the jury: e.g., Brekke, N., Borgida, E., and Mensing, D. (1983, May). Expert scientific testimony in rape trials. Paper presented at Midwestern Psychological Association, Chicago.

[21] Heuer, L., and Penrod, S. (1985). A field experiment on improving jury communication. Draft final report to the Wisconsin Judicial Council's Committee on Improving Jury Instructions.

[22] Broeder, D. W. (1958). The University of Chicago jury project. *Nebraska Law Review, 38,* 744–761.

[23] Hans, V. P. and Doob, A. N. (1976). Section 12 of the Canada Evidence Act and the deliberations of simulated juries. *Criminal Law Quarterly, 18,* 235–253; see also Doob, A. N., and Kirshenbaum, H. (1972). Some empirical evidence on the effect of s.12 of the Canada Evidence Act upon the accused. *Criminal Law Quarterly, 15,* 88–96; Sealey, A. P., and

Cornish, W. R. (1973). Juries and the rules of evidence. *Criminal Law Review, 16*, 208–223; Wissler, R., and Saks, M. J. (1985). On the inefficacy of limiting instruction: When jurors use prior conviction evidence to decide guilt. *Law and Human Behavior, 9*, 37–48.

[24] For a review of some of this research, see Vidmar, N. (1984). Social psychology and the legal process. In A. Kahn, E. Donnerstein, and M. Donnerstein (Eds.) *Social Psychology*. Dubuque, Iowa: W. C. Brown & Co.

[25] Molgrew, I. (1984, October 19). Pardoned man blames police, courts for error. *Toronto Globe and Mail*, p. N1. See also Wall, P. (1965). *Eyewitness Identification in Criminal Cases*. Springfield, Ill.: Charles C. Thomas; *Social Action and the Law:* Vol. 2, No. 2, April 1975; Vol. 2, No. 3, May 1975; Vol. 6, No. 5, 1980.

[26] See, e.g., Clifford, B., and Bull, R. (1978). *The Psychology of Person Identification*. London: Routledge & Kegan Paul; Lloyd-Bostock, S., and Clifford, B. (Eds.) (1983). *Evaluating Witness Evidence*. New York: Wiley; Loftus, E. F. (1979). *Eyewitness Testimony*. Cambridge, Mass.: Harvard University Press; Yarmey, D. (1979). *The Psychology of Eyewitness Testimony*. New York: Free Press.

[27] The question . . . [is] whether the alleged percentages of testimonial error . . . do really, in trials, produce misleading results in verdicts: Wigmore, J. H. (1909). Professor Munsterburg and the psychology of evidence. *Illinois Law Review, 3*, 399–455.

[28] Loftus, E. F. (1974). The incredible eyewitness. *Psychology Today, 8*, 116–119. See also Cavoukian, A. (1980). The influence of eyewitness identification evidence. Doctoral dissertation, University of Toronto.

[29] See, e.g., Wells, G., Lindsay, R., and Ferguson, T. (1979). Accuracy, confidence, and juror perception in eyewitness identification. *Journal of Applied Psychology, 64*, 440–448.

[30] Deffenbacher, K., and Loftus, E. F. (1982). Do jurors share a common understanding concerning eyewitness behavior? *Law and Human Behavior, 6*, 15–30; Yarmey, A., and Jones, H. (1983). Is the psychology of eyewitness identification a matter of common sense? In S. Lloyd-Bostock and B. Clifford (Eds.) *Evaluating Witness Evidence*. New York: Wiley.

[31] See Loftus, E. F. (1983). Silence is not golden. *American Psychologist, 38*, 564–575 in response to a contrary position taken by psychologists McCloskey, M., and Egeth, H. (1983). Eyewitness identification: What can a psychologist tell a jury? *American Psychologist, 38*, 550–563.

[32] See Wells, G., Lindsay, R., and Tousignant, J. (1980). Effects of expert psychological advice on human performance in judging the validity of eyewitness testimony. *Law and Human Behavior, 4*, 275–285; Loftus, E. F. (1980). Impact of expert psychological testimony on the unreliability of eyewitness identifications. *Journal of Applied Psychology, 65*, 9–15; Saunders, D., Vidmar, N., and Hewitt, E. (1983). Eyewitness testimony and the discrediting effect. In S. Lloyd-Bostock and B. Clifford (Eds.) *Evaluating Witness Evidence*. New York: Wiley. Saunders *et al.* have argued that these experiments lacked an appropriate control condition where there is a judicial admonition to treat the evidence with skepticism. It is also not clear from the experiments whether the expert testimony causes the jurors to be too skeptical and assign the eyewitness evidence no credibility when in fact it may be valid.

[33] Saunders *et al.* (1983).

Chapter 9

[1] Frank, J. (1945). *Courts on Trial*. Princeton, N.J.: Princeton University Press.

[2] Quoted in Sutherland, E. H., and Cressey, D. R. (1966). *Principles of Criminology*. New York: Lippincott.

[3] Smith, M. (1966). Percy Foreman: Top trial lawyer. *Life Magazine, 60,* 92–101.

[4] See Frank (1945).

[5] Kalven, H., and Zeisel, H. (1966). *The American Jury.* Boston: Little, Brown, p. 201.

[6] Baldwin, J., and McConville, M. (1979). *Jury Trials.* London: Oxford University Press.

[7] Dane, F., and Wrightsman, L. (1982). Effects of defendants' and victims' characteristics on jurors' verdicts. In N.L. Kerr and R.M. Bray (Eds.) *The Psychology of the Courtroom.* New York: Academic Press; Vidmar, N. (1979). The other issues in jury simulation research: A commentary with particular reference to defendant character studies. *Law and Human Behavior, 3,* 95–106.

[8] Dane and Wrightsman (1982), p. 109.

[9] Kalven and Zeisel (1966), pp. 193–220.

[10] Block, M. (Ed.) (1964). *The Art of Summation.* New York: New York State Association of Trial Lawyers, p. 41.

[11] Broeder, D. (1965). The Negro in court. *Duke Law Journal, 1965,* 19–31.

[12] Kalven and Zeisel (1966), p. 398.

[13] Ugwuegbu, D. (1979). Racial and evidential factors in juror attributions of legal responsibility. *Journal of Experimental Social Psychology, 15,* 133–146.

[14] Feild, H. (1979). Rape trials and jurors' decisions: A psychological analysis of the effects of victim, defendant, and case characteristics. *Law and Human Behavior, 3,* 261–284.

[15] Swett, D. (1969). Cultural bias in the American legal system. *Law and Society Review, 4,* 79–110.

[16] Gumperz, J. (1982). Fact and inference in courtroom testimony. In J. Gumperz (Ed.) *Language and Social Identity.* London: Cambridge University Press.

[17] Conley, J., O'Barr, W., and Lind, A. (1978). The power of language: Presentation style in the courtroom. *Duke Law Journal, 1978,* 1375–1399; Lind, A., Eriksen, B., and O'Barr, W. (1978). Social attribution and conversation style in trial testimony. *Journal of Personality and Social Psychology, 36,* 1558–1567.

[18] Rokeach, M., and Vidmar, N. (1973). Testimony concerning possible jury bias in a Black Panther murder trial. *Journal of Applied Social Psychology, 3,* 19–29.

[19] Kalven and Zeisel (1966), pp. 381–394.

[20] Dane and Wrightsman (1982), pp. 95–104.

[21] Kalven and Zeisel (1966), p. 385.

[22] Ibid., p. 165.

[23] Myers, M. (1979). Rule departures and making law: Juries and their verdicts. *Law and Society Review, 13,* 781–797.

[24] Dane and Wrightsman (1982), pp. 95–100.

[25] Kalven and Zeisel (1966), pp. 384–388.

[26] Belli, M. (1954). *Modern Trials,* Vol. 1. Indianapolis: Bobbs–Merrill; Bailey, F. L., and Rothblatt, H. B. (1974). *Fundamentals of Criminal Advocacy.* Rochester, N.Y.: The Lawyers Cooperative Publishing Co.; Rothblatt, H. (1961). *Successful Techniques in the Trial of Criminal Cases.* Englewood Cliffs, N.J.: Prentice–Hall.

[27] Broeder, D. (1965, March). Previous jury trial service affecting jury behavior. *Insurance Law Journal,* pp. 138–143.

[28] Kerr, N. (1981). Effects of prior jury experience on juror behavior. *Basic and Applied Social Psychology, 2,* 175–193.

[29] Dillehay, R. C., and Nietzel, M. T. (1985). Juror experience and jury verdicts. *Law and Human Behavior, 9,* 179–191.

[30] Tapp, J., Gunnar, M., and Keating, D. (1983). Socialization: Three ages, three rule systems. In D. Perlman and P. Crosby (Eds.) *Social Psychology.* New York: Holt, Rinehart & Winston.

[31] Kalven and Zeisel (1966), pp. 351–372, 392–394.

[32] Kerr, N. (1982). Trial participants' behavior and jury verdicts: An exploratory field study. In V. Konecni and E. Ebbesen (Eds.) *The Criminal Justice System: A Social-Psychological Analysis*. San Francisco: W. H. Freeman & Co.

Chapter 10

[1] "Eight in South Africa protest are acquitted of trespassing." (1985, May 19). *The New York Times*, p. 40.

[2] Quinn, H. (1984, November 19). Abortion wins another round. *Maclean's*, pp. 46–49.

[3] Steed, J. (1983, February 4). Will battered wife face a new murder trial? *Toronto Globe & Mail*, p. A1.

[4] Kalven, H., and Zeisel, H. (1966). *The American Jury*. Boston: Little, Brown. See Chapters 16 through 27.

[5] Beach, B. (1982, April 26). Is the party finally over? *Time*, pp. 59–60; Goodspeed, P. (1985, January 27). New prohibition sweeps U.S. *The Toronto Star*, p. H1.

[6] McCabe, S., and Purves, R. (1972). *The Jury at Work*. Oxford: Basil Blackwell; McCabe, S., and Purves, R. (1974). *The Shadow Jury at Work*. Oxford: Basil Blackwell; also see Zander, M. (1975). Juries' decisions and acquittal rates. In N. Walker (Ed.). *The British Jury System*. University of Cambridge: Institute of Criminology.

[7] Myers, M. (1979). Rule departures and making law: Juries and their verdicts. *Law and Society Review, 13*, 781–798.

[8] *Sparf v. United States* 156 U.S. 51 (1896). Quote is from p. 62 n. 1.

[9] Mitford, J. (1969). *The Trial of Dr. Spock*. New York: Alfred A. Knopf. Quote is from pp. 234–235.

[10] Ibid., pp. 227–228.

[11] Ibid., p. 232.

[12] *Duncan v. Louisiana* 391 U.S. 145 (1968) at 155.

[13] *Taylor v. Louisiana* 419 U.S. 522 (1975) at 530.

[14] Scheflin, A., and Van Dyke, J. (1980). Jury nullification: The contours of a controversy. *Law and Contemporary Problems, 43*, 51–115.

[15] Doob, A. N. (1979). Public's view of criminal jury trial. In *Studies on the Jury*. Ottawa: Law Reform Commission of Canada. Doob, A. N. (1979). Canadian trial judges' view of the criminal trial jury. In *Studies on the Jury*. Ottawa: Law Reform Commission of Canada.

[16] *United States v. Dougherty* 472 F.2d 1113 (D.C. Cir. 1972).

[17] Jacobsohn, G. J. (1976). The right to disagree: Judges, juries, and the administration of criminal justice in Maryland. *Washington University Law Quarterly, 1976*, 571–607.

[18] Horowitz, I. A. (1985). The effect of jury nullification instruction on verdicts and jury functioning in criminal trials. *Law and Human Behavior, 9*, 25–36.

[19] Judge Ulman, as quoted in Frank, J. (1945). *Courts on Trial*. Princeton, N.J.: Princeton University Press, p. 120.

[20] California Citizen's Commission on Tort Reform. (1977). *Righting the Liability Balance*, p. 9.

[21] Watkins, F. (1976). Social inflation: Our next trial. *Insurance Magazine, 77*, 42.

[22] Psychology factors affecting verdicts. (1984). *Personal Injury Valuation Handbooks, 4*, 687–751.

[23] Kalven, H. (1964). The dignity of the civil jury. *Virginia Law Review, 50*, 1055–1075; Kalven and Zeisel (1966).

[24] Peterson, M., and Priest, G. (1982). *Trends in Trials and Verdicts, Cook County, Illinois 1960–1979*. Santa Monica, Calif.: The Rand Corporation. Peterson, M. (1984). *Compensation of Injuries: Civil Jury Verdicts in Cook County*. Santa Monica, Calif.: The Rand Corporation. Chin, A., and Peterson, M. (1985). *Deep Pockets, Empty Pockets: Who Wins in Cook Countty Jury Trials*. Santa Monica, Calif.: The Rand Corporation.

Chapter 11

[1] *Williams v. Florida* 399 U.S. 78 (1970) at 89–90.

[2] Ibid. at 100.

[3] See Zeisel, H. (1971). . . . And then there were none: The diminution of the federal jury. *University of Chicago Law Review, 38*, 710–724.

[4] See Lempert, R. O. (1975). Uncovering "nondiscernible" differences: Empirical research and the jury-size cases. *Michigan Law Review, 73*, 643–708, for another analysis.

[5] Zeisel (1971), p. 720.

[6] *Colgrove v. Battin* 413 U.S. 149 (1973).

[7] Ibid., p. 159 n. 15.

[8] Ibid., pp. 166–167. Footnotes omitted.

[9] Saks, M. J. (1982). Innovation and change in the courtroom. In N. L. Kerr and R. M. Bray (Eds.) *The Psychology of the Courtoom*. New York: Academic Press.

[10] We only touch on some of the major criticisms here. For fuller discussion see: Saks, M. J. (1977). *Jury Verdicts*. Lexington, Mass.: Lexington Books. Zeisel, H., and Diamond, S. S. (1974). "Convincing empirical evidence" on the six-member jury. *University of Chicago Law Review, 41*, 281–295.

[11] *Ballew v. Georgia* 435 U.S. 223 (1978) at 239.

[12] Saks (1982), Tanke, E. T., and Tanke, T. J. (1979). Getting off a slippery slope: Social science in the judicial process. American Psychologist, *34*, 1130–1138.

[13] DiPerna, P. (1984). *Juries on Trial: Faces of American Justice*. New York: Dembner Books.

[14] For discussion of the origins of the unanimity requirement, see *Apodaca v. Oregon* 406 U.S. 404 (1972).

[15] Quoted in Brooks, N. (1978). The unanimity requirement: Essential or anarchronistic feature of the jury? Draft, Law Reform Commission of Canada.

[16] *Johnson v. Louisiana* 406 U.S. 356 (1972); *Apodaca v. Oregon* (1972). The decisions involved questions of federal jurisdiction over the states as well as issues relating to jury behavior.

[17] Hans, V. P. (1978). The effects of the unanimity requirement on group decision processes in simulated juries. Doctoral dissertation, University of Toronto.

[18] Hastie, R., Penrod, S. D., and Pennington, N. (1983). *Inside the Jury*. Cambridge, Mass.: Harvard University Press.

[19] See Saks (1977); Nemeth, C. (1977). Interactions between jurors as a function of majority vs. unanimity decision rules. *Journal of Applied Social Psychology, 7*, 38–56; Kerr, N. L., Atkin, R. S., Stasser, G., Meek, D., Holt, R. W., and Davis, J. (1976). Guilt beyond a reasonable doubt: Effects of concept definition and assigned decision rule on the judgments of mock jurors. *Journal of Personality and Social Psychology, 34*, 282–294.

Chapter 12

[1] Our account of the Hinckley trial is based on several sources, including: Kiernan, L. A. (1982, June 22). Hinckley not guilty, legally insane. *The Washington Post*, pp. A1, A12. Taylor,

S., Jr. (1982, June 22). Jury finds Hinckley not guilty, accepting his defense of insanity. *The New York Times*, pp. 1, D27. ABC News (1982a, June 21). Hinckley—Insane. *Nightline*. The insanity plea on trial. (1982, May 24). *Newsweek*, pp. 56–61. Judge Parker's account of the announcement of the verdict was given in: Margasak, L. (1982, September 9). Judge kept eye on Hinckley in fear of outburst at trial. *The News-Journal Papers*, p. A10.

[2] ABC News. (1982b, June 22). Insanity plea on trial. *Nightline*.

[3] Hans, V. P., and Slater, D. (1983). John Hinckley, Jr. and the insanity defense: The public's verdict. *Public Opinion Quarterly, 47*, 202–212.

[4] *The New York Times*. (1982, September 12). Letters to Hinckley judge criticize acquittal. *The New York Times*, p. 37.

[5] *Newsletter of the American Academy of Psychiatry and the Law*. (1982). How others see us. *Newsletter of the American Academy of Psychiatry and the Law, 7*, 24–27.

[6] Gerand, J. B. (1983). The insane Hinckley verdict. *Policy Review, 23*, 79–88.

[7] *Philadelphia Inquirer*. (1982, September 13). Smith asks revision on proof rules. *Philadelphia Inquirer*, p. 5A. Also: Putzel, M. (1982, September 13). Reagan: Tighten insanity, other legal loopholes. *Wilmington News Journal*, p. A3.

[8] Caplan, L. (1984, July 2). Annals of law: The insanity defense. *The New Yorker*, pp. 45–46, 48–52, 54–78.

[9] United States Congress. (1982). Limiting the insanity defense. Hearing before the Subcommittee on Criminal Law of the Committee on the Judiciary. United States Senate, 97th Congress, 2nd Session. (Testimony by the Hinckley jurors: June 24, pp. 155–201.)

[10] Quoted by Brenner, B. (1982, September). The insanity defense: Guilty by reason of Hinckley? *The Cresset*, p. 7.

[11] United States Congress, pp. 166–167.

[12] Ibid., p. 166.

[13] Quoted in *Social Action and the Law*. (1982). Vol. 8, No. 2, p. 38.

[14] United States Congress, p. 164.

[15] Ibid., p. 168.

[16] Ibid., p. 165.

[17] Ibid., p. 200.

[18] Taylor, S., Jr. (1982, June 25). *The New York Times*. Reprinted in the *Minneapolis Star-Tribune*, June 25, 1982, p. A3.

[19] See, e.g., Morris, N. (1982). *Madness and the Criminal Law*. Chicago: University of Chicago Press.

[20] Kaufman, I. K. (1982, August 8). The insanity plea on trial. *The New York Times Magazine*, pp. 16–20.

[21] Pasewark, R. A. (1981). Insanity plea: A review of the research literature. *The Journal of Psychiatry and Law, 9*, 357–401. Hans, V. P. (1984). The insanity plea: Public opinion and public policy. Paper presented at the meeting of the American Psychological Association, Toronto.

[22] Hans, V. P. (1985). An analysis of public attitudes toward the insanity defense. Unpublished manuscript.

[23] Cited in Quen, J. M. (1978). A history of the Anglo-American legal psychiatry of violence and responsibility. In R. L. Sadoff (Ed.) *Violence and Responsibility: The Individual, the Family, and Society*. New York: S P Medical and Scientific Books (Spectrum).

[24] Cited in Quen (1978), p. 21.

[25] Considerable debate has occurred over the spelling of McNaughtan's name. Over ten different versions have been used. We are convinced by the evidence reported by Richard Moran in his book, *Knowing Right from Wrong: The Insanity Defense of Daniel McNaughtan* (New

York: Free Press, 1981), that "McNaughtan" is the correct spelling and we have adopted it here.

[26] Moran (1981).

[27] Quoted in Moran (1981).

[28] Quoted in Moran (1981), p. 21. In 1840, eighteen-year-old Edward Oxford attempted to assassinate Queen Victoria. He was subsequently found not guilty by reason of insanity.

[29] Rosenberg, C. E. (1968). *The Trial of Assassin Guiteau*. Chicago: University of Chicago Press.

[30] Bartol, C. R. (1983). *Psychology and American Law*. Belmont, Calif.: Wadsworth.

[31] Freedman, L. Z. (Ed.) (1983). *By Reason of Insanity*. Wilmington, Del.: Scholarly Resources, Inc. Quote is from p. 85.

[32] Beram, N. J., and Tooney, B. G. (1979). The mentally disordered offender: A historical perspective. In N. J. Beram and B. G. Tooney (Eds.) *Mentally Ill Offenders and the Criminal Justice System*. New York: Praeger.

[33] See Bartol (1983) for his discussion of how the broad scope of the Durham Rule was its downfall.

[34] Simon, R. J. (1967). *Juries and the Defense of Insanity*. Boston: Little, Brown. See also: Simon, R. J. (1980). *The Jury: Its Role in American Society*. Lexington, Mass.: Lexington Books. Kalven and Zeisel also looked at the jury's reaction to the insanity defense in *The American Jury*. However, they noted that on this topic the jury seemed curiously disengaged. They could not detect any regular pattern in the jury's reaction to insanity cases. Perhaps this was due to the fact that there were very few cases in their sample (about 2%) where the defendant pleaded insanity. See discussion in: Kalven, H., and Zeisel, H. (1966). *The American Jury*. Boston: Little, Brown, Chapter 25.

[35] The different patterns in the incest and housebreaking cases could have been due to several factors. For instance, the psychiatric testimony was very different in the two cases. In the incest case, the psychiatrist concluded that the father's incestuous behavior was a product of his mental illness, but that he could still tell right from wrong. Thus, it makes sense that juries in the incest case were more likely to find the father not guilty by reason of insanity with the Durham Rule than the McNaughtan Rule. The former required only that the criminal behavior be a product of mental illness, while the latter required that the defendant be unable to tell right from wrong. In the housebreaking case, the psychiatrist did not state whether the defendant could tell right from wrong. Instead, he said that it had no bearing on the case, and the defendant's criminal behavior was clearly a product of his mental illness. Perhaps the equivocal testimony of the psychiatrist about the right versus wrong issue was the reason that juries found the housebreaking defendant not guilty by reason of insanity at the same rate for both legal instructions. Also, just ten groups per condition were run in the housebreaking case; with a larger number of juries, perhaps differences would have emerged.

[36] Finkel, N. J. (1982). Insanity defenses: Jurors' assessments of mental disease, responsibility, and culpability. Paper presented at the meeting of the American Psychological Association, Washington, D.C. Students evaluating the paranoid schizophrenic were more likely to find the defendant guilty in the DOM condition than in all other instructional conditions. The DOM doctrine was suggested by H. Finagrette, in a book entitled *The Meaning of Criminal Insanity*, published in 1972 by the University of California Press. The DOM doctrine focuses on culpability for allowing one's mental condition to deteriorate prior to the act in question rather than focusing on criminal responsibility at the moment of the act, as is the case for all other legal definitions of insanity. Other than this single difference in evaluating the paranoid schizophrenic with a DOM test, there were no differences as a function of legal instructions.

[37] Hans, V. P., and Slater, D. (1984). "Plain crazy": Lay definitions of legal insanity. *International Journal of Law and Psychiatry, 7,* 105–114.

[38] Ellsworth, P. C., Bukaty, R. M., Cowan, C. L., and Thompson, W. C. (1984). The death-qualified jury and the defense of insanity. *Law and Human Behavior, 8,* 81–93.

[39] Simon (1967), p. 164.

[40] Ibid., p. 165.

[41] Simon, R. J., and Shackelford, W. (1965). The defense of insanity: A survey of legal and psychiatric opinion. *Public Opinion Quarterly, 29,* 411–424.

Chapter 13

[1] Our account of the Big Dan rape trial is based on the excellent coverage of the trial by the *Boston Globe* over the time period February 5, 1984 to April 8, 1984. See especially notes 2–10 and stories by J. Kaufman: Men outnumbering women two-to-one as potential jurors in Big Dan rape case (February 15, pp. 23, 27); Big Dan trial on hold (February 23, p. 18); Big Dan's bartender on witness stand (March 1, pp. 17, 23); Silva takes stand in Big Dan's trial (March 15, pp. 19, 24).

[2] Goodman, E. (1984, March 8). Crimes of uninvolvement. *Boston Globe,* p. 19.

[3] Kaufman, J. (1984, February 29). Woman sticks to story in Big Dan's rape trial. *Boston Globe,* pp. 17, 20.

[4] Kaufman, J. (1984, March 11). Chilling effect of Big Dan's trial cited. *Boston Globe,* p. 33.

[5] Kaufman, J. (1984, March 18). Two convicted in Big Dan's rape. *Boston Globe,* pp. 1, 26. See also: Minsky, T. (1984, March 18). Shouts, pushing after verdict. *Boston Globe,* pp. 1, 26.

[6] Kaufman, J. (1984, March 19). Big Dan's security problem. *Boston Globe,* p. 17.

[7] Minsky, T. (1984, March 20). "Don't speak out" warning at Big Dan's trial. *Boston Globe,* p. 20.

[8] Kaufman, J. (1984, March 20). Cordeiro gives his version. *Boston Globe,* pp. 17, 20. Quote is from p. 20.

[9] Minsky, T. (1984, March 24). Thousands protest guilty verdicts. *Boston Globe,* pp. 1, 18. Quotes are from p. 18.

[10] Kaufman, J. (1984, March 23). Two more guilty, two acquitted in 2nd Big Dan's trial. *Boston Globe,* pp. 1, 10.

[11] Lipsey, D. (1982). Send rapists to jail—The public's verdict. *The Sunday Times.*

[12] Blumstein, A., and Cohen, J. (1980). Sentencing of convicted offenders: An analysis of the public's view. *Law and Society Review, 14,* 223–261. Burt, M. R. (1980). Cultural myths and support for rape. *Journal of Personality and Social Psychology, 38,* 217–230.

[13] Burt (1980).

[14] LaFree, G. D., Reskin, B. F., and Visher, C. A. (1985). Jurors' responses to victims' behavior and legal issues in sexual assault trials. *Social Problems, 32,* 389–404.

[15] Hans, V. P., and Brooks, N (1977). Effects of corroboration instructions in a rape case on experimental juries. *Osgoode Hall Law Journal, 15,* 701–716.

[16] Lear, M. W. (1972, January 30). Q: If you rape a woman and steal her TV, what can they get you for in New York? A: Stealing the TV. *The New York Times Magazine.*

[17] Starr, M., with King, P. (1985, May 20). Who is the real victim? *Newsweek,* pp. 69–70, 73.

[18] Press, A., with others. (1985, May 20). Rape and the law. *Newsweek,* pp. 60–64. Estrich's quote is from pp. 60–61.

[19] *Camp v. State* (1847) 3 Ga. (3 Kelly) 417, 422.

[20] *State v. Wood* 59 Ariz. 48, 49–50, 122 P. 2d 416, 418.

[21] The account is from Strick, A. (1977). *Injustice for All.* New York: Penguin. Quote is from p. 48.

[22] Borgida, E. (1981). Legal reform of rape laws. In L. Bickman (Ed.) *Applied Social Psychology Annual,* Vol. 2 (pp. 211–241). Beverly Hills: Sage.

[23] Kalven, H., and Zeisel, H. (1966). *The American Jury.* Boston: Little, Brown, p. 250.

[24] Ibid., p. 251.

[25] Levine, J. P. (1983a). Using jury verdict forecasts in criminal defense strategy. *Judicature, 66,* 448–461. See also Levine, J. P. (1983b). Jury toughness: The impact of conservatism on criminal court verdicts. *Crime and Delinquency, 29,* 71–87.

[26] Deitz, S. R., Blackwell, K. T., Daley, P. C., and Bentley, B. J. (1982). Measurement of empathy toward rape victims and rapists. *Journal of Personality and Social Psychology, 43,* 372–384.

[27] Hans, V. P. (1982, June). Gentlewomen of the jury. Paper presented at the annual meeting of the Law and Society Association, Toronto.

[28] Hagan, J. (1974). Extra-legal attributes and criminal sentencing: An assessment of a sociological viewpoint. *Law and Society Review, 7,* 357–383. For a compelling account of the public climate surrounding interracial rape, see Carter, D. T. (1979). *Scottsboro: A Tragedy of the American South* (rev. ed.). Baton Rouge, La.: Louisiana State University Press.

[29] *Criminal Victimization in the United States.* (1977). Law Enforcement Assistance Administration, Department of Justice. Washington, D.C.: U.S. Government Printing Office.

[30] Feild's work is described in: Feild, H. S. (1979). Rape trials and jurors' decisions: A psycholegal analysis of the effects of victim, defendant, and case characteristics. *Law and Human Behavior, 3,* 261–284. Feild, H. S., and Bienen, L. B. (1980). *Jurors and Rape.* Lexington, Mass.: Lexington Books.

[31] Feild, H. S. (1978). Juror background characteristics and attitudes toward rape: Correlates of jurors' decisions in rape trials. *Law and Human Behavior, 2,* 73–93.

[32] McCahill, T. W., Meyer, L. C., and Fischman, A. M. (1979). *The Aftermath of Rape.* Lexington, Mass.: Lexington Books.

[33] LaFree *et al.* (1983).

[34] Loh, W. (1981). Q: What has reform of rape legislation wrought? A: Truth in criminal labelling. *Journal of Social Issues, 37,* 28–52. Loh's data included both judge and jury verdicts. For other accounts of rape law reform projects, see Sallmann, P. A., and Chappell, D. (1982). *Rape law reform in South Australia. A study of the background to the Reforms of 1975 and 1976 and of their subsequent impact.* Adelaide Law Review Research Paper No. 3. Adelaide: University of Adelaide. Chappell, D. (1982, November). The impact of rape reform legislation: Some comparative trends. Paper presented at the meeting of the American Society of Criminology, Toronto.

[35] Marsh, J. C., Geist, A., and Caplan, N. (1982). *Rape and the Limits of Law Reform.* Boston: Auburn House Publishing Co.

[36] Ibid., p. 56.

[37] Ibid., pp. 56–57.

Chapter 14

[1] Sources: Clark, R. (1979, October 27). Spinkellink's last appeal. *The Nation,* p. 385. See also *Toronto Globe and Mail,* (1979, May 26). Murderer dies in Florida's electric chair, p. 12.

[2] Amnesty International. (1982, May 5). *Amnesty International and the Death Penalty*. Unpublished pamphlet.

[3] Haney, C. (Ed.) (1984a). Introduction: *Law and Human Behavior, 8*, 1–6.

[4] Vidmar, N., and Ellsworth, P. C. (1976). Public opinion and the death penalty. *Stanford Law Review, 26*, 1245–1270; Sarat, A., and Vidmar, N. (1976). Public opinion, the death penalty and the Eighth Amendment. *Wisconsin Law Review, 1976*, 171–206.

[5] See the following sources for more extensive discussion of the death penalty: Bedau, H. (Ed.) (1982). *The Death Penalty in America* (3rd ed.). London: Oxford University Press; Bedau, H., and Pierce, C. (Eds.) (1976). *Capital Punishment in the United States*. New York: AMS Press; van den Haag, E., and Conrad, H. (1983). *The Death Penalty: A Debate*. New York: Plenum Press. Most of our prologue is taken from these sources.

[6] Meltsner, M. (1973). *Cruel and Unusual: The Supreme Court and Capital Punishment*. New York: Random House.

[7] *Furman v. Georgia*, 408 U.S. 238 (1972).

[8] See note 5 for general sources.

[9] The abolition of capital punishment. (1954). *The Canadian Bar Review, 32*, 484–519.

[10] An eye for an eye. (1983, January 24). *Time*, pp. 22–31; A "more palatable way of killing." (1982, December 20). *Time*, pp. 16–17. To die or not to die. (1983, October 17). *Newsweek*, pp. 43–73.

[11] Bedau, H. (1982). Miscarriages of justice and the death penalty. In H. Bedau (Ed.) *The Death Penalty in America* (3rd ed.). London: Oxford University Press.

[12] Prosecutor opposed Texas execution. (1982, December 8). *Toronto Globe and Mail*, p. 12.

[13] Acquitted in Spinkellink's case, man says execution isn't fair. (1982, December 8). *Toronto Globe and Mail*, p. 12.

[14] Wolfgang, M., and Reidel, M. (1975). Race, rape and the death penalty in Georgia. *American Journal of Orthopsychiatry, 45*, 658–668.

[15] See *Gregg v. Georgia*, 428 U.S. 153 (1976).

[16] Bowers, W., and Pierce, G. (1980). Arbitrariness and discrimination under post-*Furman* capital statutes. *Crime and Delinquency, 26*, 563–635.

[17] Baldus, D., Pulaske, C., and Woodsworth, G. (1983). Judicial review of death sentences. *Journal of Criminal Law and Criminology, 74*, 661–753.

[18] *Witherspoon v. Illinois*, 391 U.S. 510 (1968).

[19] See Haney, C. (Ed.) (1984b). Special issue: Death qualification. *Law and Human Behavior, 8* (1/2). All of the Ellsworth studies are reported in this issue. They include: Fitzgerald, R., and Ellsworth, P. C. (1984). Due process vs. crime control: Death qualification and jury attitudes. *Law and Human Behavior, 8*, 31–51; Cowan, C. L., Thompson, W. C., and Ellsworth, P. C. (1984). The effects of death qualification on jurors' predisposition to convict and on the quality of deliberation. *Law and Human Behavior, 8*, 53–79; and Thompson, W. C., Cowan, C. L., Ellsworth, P. C., and Harrington, J. C. (1984). Death penalty attitudes and conviction proneness: The translation of attitudes into verdicts. *Law and Human Behavior, 8*, 95–113.

[20] Zeisel, H. (1968). *Some Data on Juror Attitudes toward Capital Punishment*. Center for Studies in Criminal Justice, University of Chicago.

[21] The Haney research is also reported in the special issue of *Law and Human Behavior*. Haney, C. (1984c). On the selection of capital juries: The biasing effects of the death-qualification process. *Law and Human Behavior, 8*, 121–132; Haney, C. (1984d). Examining death qualification: Further analysis of the process effect. *Law and Human Behavior, 8*, 133–151.

[22] Haney (1984d), p. 137.

[23] *Hovey v. Superior Court*, 28 Cal.3d 1 (1980).

[24] Nietzel, M., and Dillehay, R. (1982). The effects of variations in voir dire procedures in capital murder trials. *Law and Human Behavior, 6,* 1–13.

[25] *Grigsby v. Mabry,* 569 F. Supp. 1273 (E.D. Ark. 1983, aff'd ____) (1985).

[26] *Keeten v. Garrison,* 742 F.2d 129 (4th Cir. 1984).

[27] *Wainwright v. Witt,* 105 S. Ct. 844 (1985).

[28] *Barefoot v. Estelle,* 103 S.Ct. 3418 (1983).

[29] Simon, R. J. (1967). *The Jury and the Defense of Insanity.* Boston: Little, Brown.

[30] Weisberg, R. (1983). Deregulating death. In P. Kurland, G. Casper, and D. Hutchinson (Eds.) *The Supreme Court Review.* Chicago: University of Chicago Press.

Chapter 15

[1] Nizer, L. (1978). *My Life in Court.* New York: Jove. See also Sperlich, P. W. (1982). The case for preserving trial by jury in complex civil litigation. *Judicature, 65,* 395–419.

[2] de Tocqueville, A. (1835). *Democracy in America.* From the edited version entitled *American Institutions* (1851). New York: A. S. Barnes & Co.

[3] Devlin, P. (1956). *Trial by Jury.* London: Stevens.

[4] de Tocqueville (1835).

[5] See, e.g., Timothy, M. (1974). *Jury Woman.* San Francisco, Calif.: Volcano Press; Kennebeck, E. (1971). *Juror Number Four.* New York: W. W. Norton; Brill, S. (1984, December). Inside the DeLorean jury room. *American Lawyer,* pp. 1, 94–105.

[6] Some scholars take the view that in fact the jury is nothing more than a tool of the elite and powerful classes in our society, that juries, along with other institutions, are simply tools in a class struggle, and that their legitimating functions help to perpetuate basic inequities in social structure. This is a complex argument that goes beyond the scope of this book but it is important to observe that such a perspective does not deny the legitimating function, only its meaning. Readers unfamiliar with the "critical perspective" in law should read Kidder, R. (1983). *Connecting Law and Society.* Englewood Cliffs, N.J.: Prentice–Hall, for a general overview, and Chambliss, W. J., and Seidman, R. B. (1971). *Law, Order, and Power.* Reading, Mass.: Addison-Wesley, for a particular discussion of the jury.

[7] See, e.g., Burger, W. A. (1971). The state of the federal judiciary. *American Bar Association Journal, 57,* 855–861; Burger, W. A. (1981, February). Is our jury system working? *Readers Digest, 118,* 126–130.

[8] See Lempert, R. (1981). Civil juries and complex cases: Let's not rush to judgment. *Michigan Law Review, 80,* 68–132, and Sperlich (1982) for more detailed discussion of these issues.

[9] Lempert (1981); Austin, A. D. (1984). *Complex Litigation Confronts the Jury System.* Frederick, Md.: University Publications of America.

Name Index

Adams, J., 37
Adorno, T., 259
Aikens, E., 223
Alexander, J., 33, 255
Alfini, J., 122, 123, 193, 194, 262
Alfnoth, 23
Alligood, C., 58
Andersen, P., 259
Anderson, D., 113, 261
Apodaca, R., 174, 175
Arnold, E., 187
Atkin, R. S., 266
Austin, A. D., 272

Babcock, B. A., 72, 256
Bailey, F. L., 68, 69, 80, 84, 145, 257, 258, 259
Baldus, D., 230, 271
Baldwin, J., 77, 118, 119, 120, 129, 132, 258, 262, 264
Ballew, C. D., 165–166, 170, 171
Barefoot, T., 238, 239
Barland, T., 123
Bartol, C. R., 268
Beach, B., 265
Beartracks, Young, 138–139, 141, 142
Beccaria, C., 220
Bedau, H., 271
Belli, M., 47, 49, 57, 80, 145, 256, 264
Bennett, W., 261
Bentley, B. J., 270
Beram, N. J., 268
Berk, R., 259, 260
Berkowitz, L., 258
Berman, J., 259, 260
Bermant, G., 256, 259, 260
Berrigan, D., 81, 83
Berrigan, P., 81, 83

Bickman, L., 270
Bienen, L. B., 270
Black, C., 242
Blackmun, H. A., 170–171, 239
Blackstone, Sir W., 31
Blackwell, K. T., 270
Blauner, R., 258
Blazek, F., 102
Block, M., 264
Bloomstein, M. J., 254
Blumstein, A., 269
Bok, C., 121
Borgida, E., 209, 262, 270
Bowers, W., 229, 271
Bracton, H., 28
Brady, J., 179, 182
Branch, E., 223
Bray, R. M., 256, 258, 259, 260, 261, 262, 264, 266
Brekke, N., 262
Bremer, A. H., 190
Brennan, W. J., Jr., 168, 169, 170, 223
Brenner, B., 267
Brill, S., 13, 14, 17, 253, 254, 272
Brodie, I., 257
Broeder, D., 137, 142, 145, 146, 257, 262, 264
Brooks, C., 225–226
Brooks, W. N., 262, 266, 269
Broune, W., 113
Brown, N., 183
Brumm, F., 226
Brunner, R., 60–61
Bryan, W., 259
Bukaty, R., 194, 269
Bull, R., 263
Burger, W. A., 19, 209, 250, 254

273

Burt, M. R., 269
Bushell, E., 21, 22, 155

Callendar, J. T., 38
Campbell, T., 188
Caplan, L., 267
Caplan, M., 270
Carter, D. T., 270
Cartwright, R. E., 48, 256
Cavoukian, A., 257, 263
Chambers, J., 33
Chambliss, W. J., 272
Chappell, D., 270
Charrow, R., 121, 122, 262
Charrow, V., 121, 122, 262
Chase, S., 38
Chin, A., 266
Christie, R., 72, 81, 83, 84, 85, 259, 260
Clark, R., 270
Clifford, B., 263
Cloward, R., 50, 256
Coffin, W. S., 42, 156
Cohen, J., 269
Coke, Sir E., 29
Colman, R., 259
Conley, J., 140, 141, 264
Conrad, H., 271
Cook, P., 35
Cooper, B., 56, 257
Copelin, M. T., 184, 185
Coppolino, C., 80
Cordeiro, J., 199, 200, 203
Cornish, W. R., 263
Corona, J., 102, 103, 104, 260
Cosby, W., 32–33
Costello, F., 83–84
Cowan, C. L., 194, 269, 271
Cozby, P. C., 259
Cressey, D. R., 263
Crosby, P., 264
Cummings, J., 253

Daley, P. C., 270
Dane, F., 134, 264
Darrow, C., 73, 131, 146, 258
Davis, A., 69–70, 101, 110, 111
Davis, J. H., 258, 261, 266

Davis, R., 50, 58, 257
Deffenbacher, K., 263
Deitz, S. R., 270
Delahanty, T. K., 179
DeLancey, J., 34
DeLorean, John, 13–18, 67, 153, 204,
    245, 248, 253
Denning, Lord, 172
Dershowitz, A., 76
de Tocqueville, A., 248, 249, 272
Devlin, P., Lord Justice, 248, 272
Diamond, S., 77, 78, 90, 258, 259, 260,
    266
Dillehay, R. C., 72, 236, 258, 264,
    272
DiPerna, P., 266
Donnerstein, E., 263
Donnerstein, M., 263
Doob, A., 126, 261, 262, 265
Dotson, G., 206, 207
Douglas, W. O., 174, 226, 228
Drummond, E., 188
Durham, M., 191, 192, 193

Ebbesen, E., 265
Eddie, Chicago, 138–139, 142
Egeth, H., 263
Eisele, G. T., 237
Ellsworth, P. C., 194, 195, 232, 269, 271
Elwork, A., 122, 123, 193, 194, 198, 262
Emrick, B., 259
Ennis, B. J., 260
Eriksen, B., 264
Erlanger, H., 262
Estrich, S., 207, 269
Ethelred (k. of England), 23–24
Etzioni, A., 93, 260

Fahringer, H. P., 258
Feild, H., 138, 211–212, 258, 264, 270
Feldman, M., 261
Ferguson, T., 263
Feron, J., 260
Fields, W. C., 152
Finagrette, H., 268
Finkel, N., 193, 268
Fischman, A. M., 270
Fiske, J., 34

Fitzgerald, R., 271
Flynt, L., 13, 14, 82
Fonda, H., 110
Foreman, P., 131–132, 146
Forsyth, W., 254
Foster, J., 179, 180
Fox, N., 127
Francis, W., 224
Frank, J., 19, 115, 120, 121, 131, 148, 247, 262, 263, 264, 265
Franklin, B., 220
Frederick, J., 257, 259
Freedman, L. Z., 268
Frenkel-Brunswik, E., 259
Friend, C., 261
Fries, J., 38
Furman, W. H., 222–223

Garfield, J. A., 190
Garry, C., 70–71
Geist, A., 270
Genovese, K., 199
George III (k. of England), 188
Gerand, J. B., 267
Gerry, E., 37
Gillespie, M., 257
Gilmore, G., 219, 225
Ginger, A. F., 257, 258
Godwin (earl of Kent), 24–25
Goetz, B., 153
Goldberg, B. W., 261
Goodman, E., 269
Goodspeed, P., 265
Gordon, C., 258
Green, M., 136
Green, T. A., 254
Greene, E., 262
Griffith, J., 259
Griswold, E. N., 114, 261
Guiteau, C. J., 190
Gumperz, J., 264
Gunnar, M., 259, 264
Gutman, S. M., 255

Hadfield, J., 187–188
Hagan, J., 270
Hale, M., 187
Hallam, 254

Hamilton, A., 33, 34, 35, 36
Hamo of More, 26, 27
Haney, C., 234–235, 236, 271
Hans, V. P., 254, 255, 256, 257, 258, 259, 261, 262, 266, 267, 269, 270
Harman, H., 259
Harring, S., 256, 258, 259
Harrington, J. C., 271
Harris, J., 97, 98, 99, 104, 260
Hastie, R., 104, 120, 174, 175, 260, 261, 262, 266
Hawkins, C., 261
Hawrish, E., 258
Hennessy, M., 260
Henry, P., 37, 40
Hepburn, J. R., 258
Heuer, L., 123, 261, 262
Hewitt, E., 263
Hinckley, J., Jr., 179–181, 182, 183, 184, 185, 186, 188, 189, 191, 192, 196, 197, 198, 204, 249, 266, 267
Hinckley, J., Sr., 180
Hobgood, H., 90
Hoffman, J., 13, 15
Holdsworth, W., 254
Holstein, J. A., 261
Holt, R. W., 258, 261, 266
Horowitz, I., 159, 160, 260, 265
Howe, M. D., 255
Huggins, E., 50
Hughes, C. E., 63
Hunt, M., 80, 258, 259, 260

Innocent III (pope), 26
Iutzi, A., 64
Iutzi, R., 66
Iutzi, V., 64, 66

Jackson, A., 180
Jackson, L., 223
Jacobsohn, G., 158, 265
Jacoby, J., 256
James II (k. of England), 35
Jay, J., 38
Jefferson, T., 36, 37
Jenkins, R., 172
Johnson, A., 219
Johnson, F., 173

Johnson, R., 175
Johnson, W., 184
Jones, H., 263
Judson, J., 254, 257

Kadane, J. B., 57, 257
Kadish, M. R., 256, 262
Kadish, S. H., 256, 262
Kagebein, J. N., 225
Kahn, A., 263
Kairys, D., 56, 71, 256, 257, 258, 259
Kalven, H., 116, 117, 118, 119, 129, 132,
    134, 135, 137, 141, 142, 143, 144, 146,
    147, 148, 151, 153, 154, 163, 210, 212,
    215, 216, 260, 261, 262, 264, 265, 268,
    270
Kassin, S., 88, 257, 259
Katz, S., 255
Kaufman, I. K., 186, 267
Kaufman, J., 269
Keating, D., 259, 264
Kennebeck, E., 261, 272
Kennedy, J. F., 47, 190
Kerr, N., 145–146, 148, 256, 259, 260,
    262, 264, 265, 266
Kidder, R., 272
Kiernan, L. A., 266
King, P., 269
King, W., 259
Kiralfy, A. K. R., 254
Kirshenbaum, H., 262
Kirst, R. W., 256
Kissinger, H., 81
Konecni, V., 265

LaFree, G., 213, 269, 270
Lahr, V., 16
Lambard, W., 187
Langbein, J. H., 262
Lassiter, G. T., 184
Lawrence, R., 180
Lear, M. W., 269
Lehoczky, P., 257
le King, P., 26
Lempert, R., 170, 255, 256, 261, 266,
    272
Levi, M., 262

Levine, F. J., 258, 261
Levine, J. P., 211, 270
Levinson, D., 259
Lind, A., 140, 141, 264
Lindsay, R., 263
Lindsey, R., 253
Lipsey, D., 269
Little, J., 58, 59, 60, 64, 82, 83, 84, 86,
    87, 90, 91, 93, 257, 259
Litwack, T. R., 260
Lloyd-Bostock, S., 263
Loftus, E., 122, 126, 128, 129, 262, 263
Loh, W., 270
Long, R., 56

MacDonald, K., 253
Machados, C., 201–202
Madison, J., 37
Margasak, L., 267
Margolick, D., 253
Mark, Sir R., 133
Marsh, J. C., 270
Marshall, T., 168–169, 176, 223, 224,
    226
Mathews, J., 253, 254
McCabe, S., 261, 262, 265
McCahill, R. W., 270
McCarthy, T., 179
McConahay, J., 257, 259, 260
McConville, M., 77, 118, 119, 120, 129,
    132, 258, 262, 264
McDonald, W., 256
McKinnon, Judge, 59, 60
McNaughtan, D., 188–189, 190, 191, 192,
    193, 267–268
Mead, W., 21–22
Medeiros, J., 200, 203
Medeiros, V., 200, 202, 203
Meek, D., 266
Melnitzer, J., 257
Meltsner, M., 221, 271
Mensing, D., 262
Meyer, L. C., 270
Minsky, T., 269
Mischel, W., 260
Mitchell, J., 82, 90
Mitford, J., 156, 265
Molgrew, I., 263

Monahan, J., 238, 260
Moore, L. E., 255
Moore, R. D., 255
Moran, Richard, 267, 268
Moran, Robert, 56, 257
Morgentaler, H., 150, 155, 248
Morris, L. W., 255
Morris, N., 267
Mossman, K., 258
Mullin, C., 257, 259
Myers, M., 120, 129, 137, 144, 154, 262, 264, 265

Nemeth, C., 258, 259, 266
Neubauer, D. W., 255
Newton, H., 70, 80, 140
Nietzel, M., 72, 236, 258, 264, 272
Nizer, L., 115–116, 262, 272

O'Barr, W., 140, 141, 264
Okun, J., 259
Onslow, Lord, 187
Oswald, L. H., 47, 190
Owen, J., 103
Oxford, E., 268

Parker, B., 180, 181, 182, 267
Pasewark, R. A., 267
Paul, J., 58, 90
Peel, Sir R., 188, 189
Penn, W., 21–22, 28, 29, 32, 149, 155
Pennington, N., 104, 120, 174, 261, 262, 266
Penrod, S., 76–77, 104, 120, 123, 174, 258, 261, 262, 266
Perl, N., 113, 114, 120, 129
Perlman, D., 259, 264
Peterson, M., 266
Phillips, E., 102
Pierce, C., 271
Pierce, G., 229, 271
Piggan, E., 26, 27
Pluncknett, R. F. T., 254
Ponting, C., 155
Porreca, R. R., 257
Press, A., 269
Priest, G., 266
Pulaske, C., 271

Purves, R., 261, 262, 265
Putzel, M., 267

Quen, J. M., 267
Quinn, H., 265

Rand, A., 85
Raposo, V., 200, 203
Re, D., 13, 18, 253
Reagan, R., 179
Reidel, M., 226, 271
Reskin, B., 213, 269
Rockefeller, N., 55
Rokeach, M., 264
Rooney, A., 182
Rosenberg, C. E., 268
Rothblatt, H., 68, 69, 84, 257, 258, 259, 264
Ruby, J., 47, 49, 57, 58, 190
Rush, B., 220

Sacco, N., 127
Sacramento, C., 202
Sadoff, R. L., 267
Saks, M., 169, 170, 259, 260, 263, 266
Sales, B. D., 122, 123, 193, 194, 256, 259, 260, 262
Sallmann, P. A., 270
Sanford, R., 259
Sarat, A., 271
Saunders, D., 263
Scheflin, A., 265
Schulman, J., 69, 81, 82, 256, 258, 259
Seale, B., 50
Sealey, A. P., 262
Seidman, R. B., 272
Severance, L., 122, 126, 262
Shackelford, W., 269
Shapard, J., 256, 259, 260
Shaver, P., 81, 259
Sheppard, S., 80
Silva, D., 200, 202
Simon, R. J., 192, 193, 196, 268, 269, 272
Simpson, E. M., 131–132
Slater, D., 267, 269
Smith, M., 264
Smith, W., 33

Sperlich, P., 261, 272
Spinkellink, J., 219, 224, 226, 270, 271
Spock, B., 41, 42, 156, 157, 256
Stafford, J., 150, 152, 158, 248
Stans, M., 82, 90
Starr, M., 269
Stasser, G., 260, 266
Steed, J., 265
Stewart, P., 226, 228
Strick, A., 270
Stubbs, R. S., II, 255
Suggs, D., 260
Sutherland, E. H., 263
Swain, R., 75
Swan, J., 260
Swett, D., 138, 139, 264

Takasugi, R., 14, 16, 17, 253
Tanke, E. T., 266
Tanke, T. J., 266
Tapp, J. L., 146, 249, 258, 259, 261, 264
Tarnower, H., 97, 98
Tate, E., 258
Taylor, B., 53
Taylor, S., Jr., 266–267
Thompson, J., 207
Thompson, W. C., 194, 269, 271
Throckmorten, Sir N., 22–23
Timothy, M., 101, 102, 110, 260, 261, 272
Tisa, B., 15
Tooney, B. G., 268
Tousignant, J., 263
Trilling, D., 260
Tryforos, L., 97

Ugwuegbu, D., 138, 264
Ulman, Judge, 265

van den Haag, E., 271
Van Dyke, J., 52, 75, 257, 258, 265
Vanzetti, B., 127
Victoria (q. of England), 189, 268
Vidmar, N., 254, 256, 257, 259, 260, 263, 264, 271

Vieira, J., 200, 202, 203
Villesenor, V., 260, 261
Vinson, D. E., 259, 260
Visher, C. A., 213, 269
von Bulow, C., 107
von Bulow, S., 107
von Glahn, R., 98
Vutao, S., 202

Walker, N., 265
Wall, P., 263
Wallace, G. C., 190
Walsh, J., Jr., 13, 14, 15
Watkins, F., 265
Webb, C. C., 206–207
Weisberg, R., 239, 240, 272
Weitzman, H., 13, 14, 15, 18
Wells, G., 263
White, B. R., 173, 226, 228
Wigmore, J., 128, 155, 263
Williams, G., 114, 261
William the Conqueror (k. of England), 23, 25
Wissler, R., 263
Witherspoon, W., 230–231, 232
Wolfgang, M., 226, 271
Woodsworth, G., 271
Wright, W., 261
Wrightsman, L., 134, 257, 264

Yarmey, A. D., 263
Young, W., 200, 202, 203

Zander, M., 265
Zeisel, H., 77, 78, 90, 111, 116, 117, 118, 119, 129, 132, 134, 135, 137, 141, 142, 143, 144, 146, 147, 148, 151, 153, 154, 163, 167, 168, 210, 212, 215, 216, 233, 256, 258, 259, 260, 261, 262, 264, 265, 266, 268, 270, 271
Zenger, J. P., 32, 33, 34, 35, 36, 149, 158, 248, 255
Zerman, M. B., 260, 261

Subject Index

Abortion, 150
Acquittal. *See* Sentences; Verdicts
Aetna Insurance Company, 113
Affirmative registration, 52–53
Age differences, 134
Agreement of judge and jury, 116–120
A. H. Robins Company, 113
American Law Institute, 191–192
American Medical Association, 197
American Revolution, 32–37, 40
American Telephone and Telegraph
    Company, 79–80
American Trial Lawyers Association, 48,
    49
Antitrust cases, 79–80
Assassination
  insanity defense and, 179–185
  Kennedy, 47
Attica Prison riot, 55–56
Attorney, impact of, 132, 146–148
Attractiveness. *See* Physical attractiveness
Australia, 30
Authoritarianism
  group dynamics and, 86
  scientific jury selection and, 84–85

Battle. *See* Trial by battle
Bias. *See* Prejudice
Blacks. *See* Prejudice; Race

Cal Comp, 100
Canada, 30
  change of venue in, 60–61
  impartiality rule in, 63
  jury nullification in, 150
  jury selection in, 31, 48
  race and, 140
Capital punishment. *See* Death penalty

Challenging jurors. *See* Jury selection; *Voir
    dire*
Change of venue, 47
  community rule and, 57–58
  evidence for, 59
  origins of, 29
  pretrial publicity and, 60–61
  reasons for, 58–59
Character
  of defendant, 143–144, 213–214
  of victim, 208–209, 213–214. *See also*
    Rape
Civil cases
  competency issue, 115, 251
  emotional factors, 136
  insurance coverage and, 124–125
  judge/jury agreement in, 117
  jury nullification, 160–162
  jury survival and, 250
Civil War (U.S.), 149
Cocaine, 13
Community rule (jury selection), 57–61
  See also Cross section requirement
Competency issue, 113–130
  assessment of, 245
  civil juries and, 251
  controversy over, 114–116
  empirical studies of, 116–120
  Robins case, 113–114
  specific instructions and, 120–127
Compurgators, 23, 24, 25
Computer-assisted jury selection, 56–57
Confidentiality, 99
Consensus. *See* Unanimity rule
Conspiracy, 90, 113
Constitution (U.S.), 35
  competency issue and, 114
  complex civil cases and, 251

Constitution (U.S.) (*cont.*)
  death penalty and, 220
  jury size and, 168–169, 170–171
  jury survival and, 250
  jury trial and, 31, 36–37, 43, 49
  unanimity and, 172–173
  women jurors and, 51–52
  See also Supreme Court (U.S.)
Contributory negligence, 152
Conviction. *See* Sentences; Verdicts
Corroboration, 205–207
Criminal law, 152
Criminal record
  competency issue and, 125–127
  prejudice and, 144
Cross-cultural comparison
  judge tribunals, 247
  juries, 29–30, 31
  jury selection, 48–49, 63
  (*See also entries under specific countries*)
Cross section requirement (jury
      composition), 49–57
  assessment of, 246
  death penalty and, 230–237
  jury size and, 165–166, 167
  prejudice and, 142
Culture
  prejudice and, 139–140
  See also Cross-cultural comparison

Dalkon Shield, 113
Damage awards, 124–125, 160–163
Deadlocked juries. *See* Hung juries
Death penalty, 219–242
  deterrence and, 224
  errors in, 225–226
  evidence and, 237–238
  Furman case, 222–223
  history and, 220–222
  jury discretion and, 31
  jury nullification and, 149
  jury responsibility and, 239–240
  jury selection and, 230–237
  jury survival and, 250
  law and, 240–241
  morality and, 219–220, 241–242
  psychiatry and, 238–239
  race and, 222, 226, 229–230

Death penalty (*cont.*)
  Supreme Court (U.S.) and, 42, 220,
      226–229
  See also Executions
Decision-making process
  competency issue and, 120
  DeLorean case and, 16
  See also Deliberation process
Decision rule. *See* Unanimity rule
Declaration of Independence, 35, 36
Deliberation process, 97–112
  confidentiality and, 99
  confusion in, 102–103
  foreperson selection, 100–102
  group dynamics and, 100, 108–109,
      111–112
  Harris case, 97–99
  mock juries, 105–107
  polling, 104
  rape, 210
  unanimity and, 110–111
  See also Decision-making process
DeLorean case, 13–18
De minimus principle, 152–153
Directed verdicts, 39
  See also Instructions
Disagreement of judge and jury. *See*
      Agreement of judge and jury
Discrimination
  jury composition and, 55, 56
  See also Prejudice; Race
Disqualifications, 54
Domestic violence, 150–153
Draft. *See* Military draft
Drunk driving, 152, 153
Due process
  complex civil cases, 251
  death penalty and, 228

Educational level
  emotional factors and, 134
  scientific jury selection and, 81
Emotional factors, 131–147
  assessment of, 245
  effects of, 131–132
  jury selection and, 132
  lawyers and, 146–148
  prejudice and, 136–146

Emotional factors (*cont.*)
 prior jury experience and, 145–146
 sympathy, 132–136
England. *See* United Kingdom and England
Entrapment
 DeLorean case, 15, 17
 jury nullification, 153
Ethics, 93–94
Ethnicity
 cross section requirement and, 51
 rape and, 199
 See also Prejudice; Race
Euthanasia, 158
Evidence
 change of venue, 59
 competency issue, 115, 118, 127–129
 death penalty and, 237–238
 insanity defense and, 195–197
 judges and, 39
 jury deliberations and, 98, 104, 105
 jury nullification and, 154–155
 jury origins and, 28
 rape and, 205
Exclusions, 52–53
Executions
 decline in, 222
 statistics of, 221
 torture and, 224–225
 See also Death penalty
Exemptions
 jury composition and, 54
 women jurors, 52–53
Experts, influence of, 195–197
Eyewitness evidence, 127–129

Federal Bureau of Investigation, 13, 15
Fifth Amendment. *See* Self-incrimination
Foreman. *See* Jury foreperson
France, 30
Fraud, 113–114
Freedom of the press, 32
Fugitive Slave Laws, 149

General Motors, 88–89
Gender differences. *See* Sex differences; Women
Great Britain. *See* United Kingdom and England

Group dynamics
 deliberation process and, 100, 108–109, 111–112
 scientific jury selection and, 85–86

Handicapped defendants, 135
Heroin, 13
History of jury, 21–29, 31–43
Hung juries, 167–168

IBM, 89, 100
Illicit drugs, 13
Impartiality rule, 63–78
 peremptory challenge and, 72–76
 prejudice and, 64–67
 scientific jury selection and, 93
 sociology and, 76–78
 "state of mind" definition, 63–64
 voir dire and, 67–72, 91
Incompetency issue. *See* Competency issue
Information networks, 83–84
Insanity defense, 179–198
 assassination and, 179–185
 history of, 187–192
 legal definitions and, 192–195
 psychiatric testimony and, 195–197
 public opinion and, 186–187
 rationale for, 185–186
Institutional racism, 138–139
 See also Discrimination; Prejudice; Race
Instructions
 competency issue, 120–127
 insanity defense, 193–194
 law and, 158–160
 rape, 206
 See also Law
Insurance coverage, 124–125
Internal Revenue Service, 84

Judges
 competency issue, 113–114
 competency of, 247
 evidence and, 39
 jury agreement studies, 117–118
 jury deliberations and, 103, 105, 109
 verdicts by, 115
 voir dire and, 40, 43

Judge tribunals (European), 247
Juries
    American Revolution and, 32–37
    cohesiveness of, 15–16
    Constitution (U.S.) and, 36–37
    controversy over, 18–19
    cross-cultural differences, 29–30, 31
    decision-making process in, 120
    law and, 38, 39–40, 42
    origins of, 23–24, 26–29
    restrictions on, 38–40
    Supreme Court (U.S.) and, 42–43
Jury competence. See Competency issue
Jury composition
    peremptory challenge and, 74–75
    race prejudice and, 142
Jury decision-making. See Decision-making
    process
Jury decision rule. See Unanimity rule
Jury deliberation. See Deliberation process
Jury foreperson
    deliberation process and, 100–102
    DeLorean case, 16
    group dynamics and, 86
Jury nullification, 149–157
    assessment of, 245–246
    civil cases, 160–162
    contributory negligence and, 152
    defined, 149
    de minimus principle, 152–153
    law and, 154–155
    mitigating circumstances and, 153
    morality and, 151
    politics and, 155–157
    property defense and, 152
    self-defense and, 151–152, 153
    special instructions and, 158–160
    See also Law
Jury questionnaires, 54
Jury selection
    community rule, 57–61
    cross section requirement, 49–57, 246
    death penalty and, 230–237
    DeLorean case, 14
    emotional factors and, 132
    historical practices of, 29
    impartiality and, 63–78
    importance of, 47, 48

Jury selection (cont.)
    politics and, 35–36
    procedures, 53–57, 67–76
    rape and, 200
    science of, 79–94
    voir dire and, 43
    See also Impartiality rule; Scientific jury
        selection
Jury Selection and Service Act of 1968, 53
Jury size, 165–171
    Constitution (U.S.) and, 170–171
    cross section requirement and, 165–166,
        167
    deadlocked juries and, 167–168
    empirical studies, 169–170
    Supreme Court (U.S.) and, 43
    unanimity and, 174
Jury unanimity. See Unanimity rule

Key man system, 53–54

Language
    emotional factors and, 139
    race and, 140–141
Law, 149–163
    competency issue, 113–114, 115,
        120–127
    death penalty and, 222, 227–228,
        240–241
    deliberation process and, 103, 105, 109
    insanity defense and, 192–195
    juries and, 38, 39–40, 42, 250
    rape and, 214–216
    specific instruction and, 158–160
Lawyers, 146–148
Leadership. See Jury foreperson
League of Women Voters, 52, 53
Legitimacy
    cross section requirement and, 51
    juries and, 19, 248–249
    scientific jury selection and, 93
Libel law, 32–35
Liberalism
    attitude and, 15, 16
    scientific jury selection and, 81
Liberation hypothesis, 144
Linguistics, 121–122
Litigation Sciences, 89, 90

Majority verdicts. *See* Unanimity rule
M.C.I. Communications Corporation,
    79–80, 87
Media
    DeLorean case and, 13–14
    insanity defense and, 181–182, 183
    jury deliberations and, 98, 99
    jury selection and, 67
    rape and, 201
    voir dire and, 69
Military draft, 41–42
Minorities. *See* Ethnicity; Prejudice; Race
Mitigating circumstances, 153
Mock juries
    deliberation process, 99, 105–107
    effectiveness of, 91–92
    prejudice and, 143
    sympathy factors and, 134
    use of, 87–89
Morality
    death penalty and, 219–220, 241–242
    jury nullification and, 151, 158
    prejudice and, 143–144

National Jury Project, 71
National Women's Rights Party, 52
Nonverbal communication
    interpretation of, 90
    scientific jury selection and, 84
"Not proven" verdicts, 30
Nullification. *See* Jury nullification; Law

Occupation, 73
Ordeal
    forms of, 24
    opposition to, 26
    religion and, 25

Peine forte et dure, 27–28
Peremptory challenge
    impartiality rule and, 72–76
    jury composition and, 74–75
    number of, 67
Perjury, 25–26
Physical attractiveness
    emotional factors and, 134
    prejudice and, 143
    race and, 139–140

Plea bargaining, 19
Police files, 84
Politics
    civil cases and, 251
    juries and, 32, 43–44, 248–249
    jury deliberations and, 100
    jury development and, 35
    jury nullification and, 149–150, 155–157
    jury selection and, 35–36
    scientific jury selection and, 92
    Vietnam War and, 41–42
Prejudice, 136–146
    change of venue and, 59–60
    impartiality rule and, 64–67
    rape and, 204–205
    voir dire and, 68–69, 70
    See also Emotional factors; Race
Pretrial publicity
    change of venue and, 60–61
    DeLorean case, 13–14
    rape and, 200
    scientific jury selection and, 81
Pretrial questioning
    criticism of, 48–49
    effects of, 14
    See also Voir dire
Procedural reform, 122–123
Procedures (rape), 205–206
Property
    forfeiture of, 27–28
    jury nullification and, 152
Prosecutors, 74–75
Psychiatry
    death penalty and, 238–239
    insanity defense and, 195–197
    See also Insanity defense
Publicity. *See* Pretrial publicity
Public opinion
    death penalty and, 221
    insanity defense and, 181–182, 186–187
    rape and, 204
    scientific jury selection and, 82–83
Punishment. *See* Death penalty;
    Sentencing; Verdicts

Quakers, 21
Questionnaires. *See* Jury questionnaires

Race
    change of venue and, 59–60
    cross section requirement and, 50–51
    death penalty and, 222, 226, 229–230
    emotional factors, 137–140
    judges and, 247–248
    jury composition and, 55–56
    peremptory challenge and, 75
    rape and, 212
    voir dire and, 70
    See also Ethnicity; Prejudice
Random sampling methods, 56–57
Rape, 199–217
    ambivalence about, 204
    conviction rates and, 211
    corroboration requirement, 205–207
    evidence and, 205
    Fall River case, 199–204, 216–217
    false charges of, 206–207
    jury deliberations and, 210
    jury nullification and, 152, 153
    law and, 214–215
    prejudice and, 204–205
    procedures and, 205–206
    race and, 212
    sexual behavior and, 208–209, 213–214
    special instructions and, 206
Religion, 24–25, 26
Religious nonconformity, 21
Russia, 30

Scientific jury selection, 79–94
    assessment of, 246–247
    effectiveness of, 89–92
    ethics and, 93–94
    group dynamics and, 85–86
    information networks in, 83–84
    intuition in, 86
    M.C.I. case and, 79–80
    mock juries, 87–89
    public opinion polling, 82–83
    voir dire and, 80–81
    See also Jury selection
Scotland, 29–30
Self-defense, 151–152, 153
Self-incrimination, 144
Sentencing
    competency issue, 113
    deterrence and, 224

Sentencing (*cont.*)
    jury discretion and, 31–32, 40–41
    See also Verdicts
Sex crimes, 137–138
    See also Rape
Sex differences
    emotional factors and, 134–135
    peremptory challenges and, 73
    rape and, 211
Simulated juries. *See* Mock juries
Size. *See* Jury size
Slavery, 149
Socioeconomic class
    emotional factors, 134
    foreperson selection, 100–101
    group dynamics, 85–86
    judges, 248
    jury composition and, 53
    jury deliberations and, 100
    prejudice and, 140–141
Special instructions. *See* Instructions
Special verdicts, 39
Speech. *See* Language
Statute of Westminster, 27
Sting operations, 13, 15
Supreme Court (Delaware), 109
Supreme Court (Mississippi), 52–53
Supreme Court (U.S.)
    affirmative registration and, 53
    death penalty and, 42, 220, 223,
        226–229, 250
    death qualified juries and, 237
    impartiality rule and, 63
    instructions on the law and, 40
    juries and, 43
    jury composition and, 51, 55
    jury nullification and, 155–156, 157
    jury selection and, 48, 49
    jury size and, 166–167, 168, 170, 171
    peremptory challenge and, 75–76
    unanimity and, 172–173, 174, 175
    women jurors and, 52
    See also Constitution (U.S.)
Sympathy
    effects of, 132–136
    See also Emotional factors; Prejudice

Trial by battle, 25
Trial by ordeal. *See* Ordeal

Unanimity rule, 171–175
  Constitution (U.S.) and, 172–173
  decision-making process and, 16
  deliberation process and, 104–105,
    110–111
  England, 172
  history and, 171–172
  Supreme Court (U.S.) and, 43
United Kingdom and England
  competency issue, 118–120
  emotional factors and, 133
  jury nullification, 149
  jury selection, 31, 48
  law and, 153–154
  libel law, 34
  rape, 204
  unanimity rule, 172
  women jurors, 51, 52

Verdicts
  competency issue and, 117, 119–120
  deliberation process and, 104, 112
  directed verdicts, 39
  instructions and, 159–160
  judge decided, 115
  jury nullification and, 150–151
  jury origins and, 27
  jury discretion and, 39
  law and, 154
  "not proven," 30
  prejudice and, 142
  prior jury experience and, 145
  rape and, 211

Verdicts (cont.)
  special verdicts, 39
  sympathy and, 133–136
  unanimity rule, 43
  wrongful verdicts, 22, 28
Vietnam Veterans Against the War
    (VVAW), 83, 85, 86
Vietnam War, 41–42
  jury nullification and, 156, 158
  scientific jury selection and, 81
Voir dire
  Constitution (U.S.) and, 37–38
  controversy about, 71–72
  cross-cultural perspective on, 31
  impartiality rule and, 67–72, 91
  judges and, 40, 43
  scientific jury selection and, 80–81, 83,
    84, 247
  uses of, 68
Voters' list system (jury selection), 53–54

Wager of law, 25–26
Witnesses
  competency issue and, 127–129
  credibility of, 15
  jury origins and, 23–24, 26, 27, 28–29
Women
  foreperson selection, 101
  history of participation on jury, 51–53
  See also Sex differences
Wrongful verdicts
  Bushell case, 22
  discontinuance of practice, 28